PLANNING AND CONTROL

USING

MICROSOFT® PROJECT

AND

PMBOK® GUIDE

THIRD EDITION

BY

PAUL EASTWOOD HARRIS

DISCLAIMER

PUBLISHER, AUTHOR AND DISTRIBUTOR

Paul E Harris
Eastwood Harris Pty Ltd
PO Box 4032
Doncaster Heights 3109
Victoria, Australia
Email: harrispe@eh.com.au
Website: http://www.eh.com.au
Tel: +61 (0)4 1118 7701
Fax: +61 (0)3 9846 7700

3 February 2006

ISBN 1-921059-07-9 - A4 Spiral
ISBN 1-921059-08-7 - B5 Perfect

SUMMARY

The book was written so it may be used as:

> ➢ A training manual for a two-day training course,
> ➢ A self teach book, or
> ➢ A reference manual.

The screen shots for the book are taken from Microsoft Project Standard 2003 however the book may be used to learn Microsoft Project Professional 2003 and all versions of Microsoft Project 2002 and 2000.

The book has been written to be used as the basis for a two-day training course and includes exercises for the students to complete at the end of each chapter. Unlike many training course publications this book may also be used by the students as a reference book after the course.

This publication is ideal for people who would like to quickly gain an understanding of how the software operates and explains how the software differs from Primavera P3 and SureTrak, thus making it ideal for people who wish to convert from these products.

SPELLING

This book is written in US English.

AUTHOR'S COMMENT

As a professional project planner and scheduler, a Certified Cost Engineer and an Approved PRINCE2 Trainer I have used a number of planning and scheduling software packages for the management of a range of project types and sizes. There appeared to be very little literature aimed at the professional who understands how to run projects but requires a practical guide on how to use Microsoft Project in project environment using the processes outlined in the *PMBOK® Guide*. The first books I published were user guides/training manuals for Primavera SureTrak and P3 users. These were well received by professional project managers and schedulers, so I decided to turn my attention to Microsoft Project 2000, 2002 and 2003. To produce this book I edited my Microsoft Project 2003 book to explain how Microsoft Project may be used with the *PMBOK® Guide*. I trust this book will assist you in understanding how to use Microsoft Project on your projects. Please contact me if you have any comments you may wish to make on this book.

BOOKS PUBLISHED BY EASTWOOD HARRIS

Planning Using Primavera Project Planner P3® Version 3.1
ISBN 0-9577783-7-6 A4 Paperback   ISBN 0-9577783-8-4 A4 Spiral Bound
First Published March 2000

Planning Using Primavera SureTrak Project Manager® Version 3.0
ISBN 0-9577783-9-2 A4 Paperback   ISBN 0-9751503-0-8 A4 Spiral Bound
First Published June 2000

Planning and Scheduling Using Microsoft® Project 2002
ISBN 0-9751503-1-6 B5 Paperback   ISBN 0-9751503-2-4 A4 Spiral Bound
First Published January 2002

Planning and Scheduling Using Microsoft® Project 2003
ISBN 0-9751503-3-2 B5 Paperback   ISBN 0-9751503-4-0 A4 Spiral Bound
First Published June 2004

Project Planning and Scheduling Using Primavera® Version 4.1
For Engineering & Construction and Maintenance & Turnaround
ISBN 1-921059-00-1 A4 Paperback   ISBN 1-921059-01-X A4 Spiral Bound
First Published January 05

Project Planning and Scheduling Using Primavera® Version 4.1
For IT Project Office and New Product Development
ISBN 1-921059-02-8 A4 Paperback   ISBN 1-921059-03-6 A4 Spiral Bound
First Published March 05

Project Planning and Scheduling Using Primavera ®Contractor Version 4.1
For the Construction Industry
ISBN 1-921059-04-4 A4 Paperback   ISBN 1-921059-05-2 A4 Spiral Bound
First Published January 05

PRINCE2 ™ Planning & Control Using Microsoft® Project
ISBN 1 921059 06 0 B5 Paperback   ISBN 1-921059-06-0 A4 Spiral Bound
First Published May 2005

Planning and Control Using Microsoft® Project and PMBOK® Guide Third Edition
ISBN 1-921059-08-7 B5 Paperback   ISBN 1-921059-07-9 A4 Spiral Bound
First Published June 2005

Planning and Scheduling Using Primavera® Version 5.0 For Engineering & Construction
ISBN 1-921059-09-5 A4 Paperback   ISBN 1-921059-10-9 A4 Spiral Bound
First Published December 05

Planning and Scheduling Using Primavera® Version 5.0 For IT Project Office
ISBN 1-921059-11-7 A4 Paperback   ISBN 1-921059-12-5 A4 Spiral Bound
First Published December 05

1 INTRODUCTION

1.1 *Purpose*

The purpose of this book is to provide you with methods of using Microsoft Project and the *PMBOK® Guide* processes in a single project environment. Not all the *PMBOK® Guide* processes are simply transposed to Microsoft Project and some may not be managed in Microsoft Project at all. This book makes some suggestions on how to best handle these areas of incompatibility and provide you with techniques to manage your projects with Microsoft Project and the *PMBOK® Guide* Processes.

The screen shots in this book were captured using Microsoft Project Standard 2003 and Windows XP. Readers using Microsoft Project Professional 2003 will have some additional menu options to those shown in this book, which will operate when their software is connected to Microsoft Project Server software. Users of Microsoft Project 2002 and 2000 will find some minor differences in how the software functions which are outlined in the relevant areas of this book and in **Chapter 23 WHAT IS NEW IN MICROSOFT PROJECT** at the end of this book.

When the term "Section" is used in this book it is referring to the appropriate section number in the *PMBOK® Guide Third Edition*. This book should be read in conjunction with the *PMBOK® Guide Third Edition*.

At the end of this book, you should be able to:

- Understand the steps required to create a project plan using the *PMBOK® Guide* Processes.

- Set up the software.

- Define calendars.

- Add tasks which will represent the *PMBOK® Guide* **Activities**.

- Organize tasks and format the display.

- Add logic and constraints outlined in the *PMBOK® Guide* process **6.2 Activity Sequencing**.

- Use Tables, Views and Filters which are used to create the printouts and reports to support the *PMBOK® Guide* **Project Communications Management** processes.

- Print the above reports.

- Record and track progress which support the *PMBOK® Guide* processes of **Schedule Control**, **Cost Control**, **Scope Control** and **Performance Reporting**.

- Customize the project options.

- Create and assign resources which would be used in the *PMBOK® Guide* process **6.3 Activity Resource Estimating**.

- Understand the impact of task types and effort driven tasks.

- Status projects that contain resources, which support the *PMBOK® Guide* processes of **Schedule Control**, **Cost Control**, **Scope Control** and **Performance Reporting**.

- Understand the different techniques for scheduling.

This book does not cover every aspect of Microsoft Project, however it does cover the main features required to create and status a project schedule. It should provide you with a solid grounding, which will enable you to go on and learn the other features of the software from experimenting with it, using the help files and reviewing other literature.

This book has been written to minimize superfluous text, allowing the user to locate and understand the information contained in the book as quickly as possible. It does NOT cover functions of little value to common project scheduling requirements. If at any time you are unable to understand a topic in this book, it is suggested that you use the Microsoft Project Help menu to gain a further understanding of the subject.

1.2 Required Background Knowledge

This book does not teach you how to use computers or to manage projects. This book is intended to teach you how to Plan and Control a project using Microsoft Project and the *PMBOK® Guide* processes. Therefore, to be able to follow this book you should have the following background knowledge:

- An understanding of how the *PMBOK® Guide* Knowledge Areas and Processes are used to plan and control a project.

- The ability to use a personal computer and understand the fundamentals of the operating system.

- Experience using application software such as Microsoft Office which would have given you exposure to Windows menu systems and typical Windows functions such as copy and paste.

1.3 Purpose of Planning

The ultimate purpose of planning is to build a model that allows you to predict which tasks and resources are critical to the timely completion of the project. Strategies may then be implemented to ensure that these tasks and resources are managed properly, thus ensuring that the project will be delivered **On Time** and **Within Budget**.

Planning aims to:
- Identify the Products required to deliver a project
- Evaluate different project delivery methods
- Identify and optimize the use of resources
- Optimize time and evaluate if target dates may be met
- Identify risks and set priorities
- Provide a baseline plan against which progress is measured
- Communicate to all Stakeholders the plan including what is to be done, when and by whom
- Provide early warning of potential problems and enable proactive and not reactive action to be taken
- Assist management to think ahead and make informed decisions

Planning helps to avoid:

- Increased project costs or reduction in scope and/or quality

- Additional change over and/or operation costs

- Extensions of time claims

- Loss of your client's revenue

- Contractual disputes and associated resolution costs

- The loss or reputation of those involved in a project

- Loss of a facility or asset in the event of a total project failure

1.4   Definition of a Planning & Control

PMBOK® Guide defines:

- The **Planning Process** as those processes performed to define and mature the project scope, develop the project management plan, and identify and schedule the project activities that occur within the project.

- The **Control Technique** as comparing actual performance with planned performance, analyzing variances, assessing trends to effect process improvements, evaluating possible alternatives, and recommending appropriate corrective action as needed.

A plan is therefore not just a Microsoft Gantt chart (bar chart), but a Gantt chart is an important output of the planning process.

Microsoft Project is also able to record timings, costs and targets and other basic information could be kept in the Notes or Custom (user defined) Fields. It is not designed as a quality assurance nor a document management software package and specialist packages should be considered for these processes.

1.5   PMBOK® Guide Process Groups and Knowledge Areas

Like other methodologies, such as PRINCE2 which has a time bound processes including a clearly defined Planning Process and Controlling Processes, the *PMBOK® Guide* has five Process Groups:

- Initiating Process Group

- Planning Process Group

- Executing Process Group

- Monitoring and Controlling Process Group

- Closing Process Group

The *PMBOK® Guide* summarizes project management processes under nine Knowledge Areas, each with three or more Processes in each Knowledge Area. These are similar to the PRINCE2 Components.

The table over the page maps Processes to Process Groups & Knowledge Areas using the chapter numbers from the *PMBOK® Guide*:

KNOWLEDGE AREAS	PROCESS GROUPS				
- Processes	Initiating	Planning	Executing	Monitoring & Controlling	Closing
PROJECT INTEGRATION MANAGEMENT					
- Develop Project Charter	4.1				
- Develop Preliminary Project Scope Statement	4.2				
- Develop Project Management Plan		4.3			
- Direct and Manage Project Execution			4.4		
- Monitor and Control Project Work				4.5	
- Integrated Change Control				4.6	
- Close Project					4.7
PROJECT SCOPE MANAGEMENT					
- Scope Planning		5.1			
- Scope Definition		5.2			
- Create WBS		5.3			
- Scope Verification				5.4	
- Scope Control				5.5	
PROJECT TIME MANAGEMENT					
- Activity Definition		6.1			
- Activity Sequencing		6.2			
- Activity Resource Estimating		6.3			
- Activity Duration Estimating		6.4			
- Schedule Development		6.5			
- Schedule Control				6.6	
PROJECT COST MANAGEMENT					
- Cost Estimating		7.1			
- Cost Budgeting		7.2			
- Cost Control				7.3	
PROJECT QUALITY MANAGEMENT					
- Quality Planning		8.1			
- Perform Quality Assurance			8.2		
- Perform Quality Control				8.3	
PROJECT HUMAN RESOURCE MANAGEMENT					
- Human Resource Planning		9.1			
- Acquire Project Team			9.2		
- Develop Project Team			9.3		
- Manage Project Team				9.4	
PROJECT COMMUNICATIONS MANAGEMENT					
- Communications Planning		10.1			
- Information Distribution			10.2		
- Performance Reporting				10.3	
- Manage Stakeholders				10.4	
PROJECT RISK MANAGEMENT					
- Risk Management Planning		11.1			
- Risk Identification		11.2			
- Qualitative Risk Analysis		11.3			
- Quantitative Risk Analysis		11.4			
- Risk Response Planning		11.5			
- Risk Monitoring and Control				11.5	
PROJECT PROCUREMENT MANAGEMENT					
- Plan Purchases and Acquisitions		12.1			
- Plan Contracting		12.2			
- Request Seller Responses			12.3		
- Select Sellers			12.4		
- Contract Administration				12.5	
- Contract Closure					12.6

1.6 Project Planning

It may be seen from the previous table the Planning Process Group has many more processes than other Process Groups, which is one indication of the importance of planning a project prior to execution.

The plans indicated in the Planning Processes above would often be written in a document using Microsoft Word. The activities required to create these plans and then execute them including their associated resources and costs, could be scheduled in Microsoft Project.

The following Processes in the Planning Group, indicated in the table above, may be managed in Microsoft Project:

- **5.3 Create WBS**

- **6.1 Activity Definition**

- **6.2 Activity Sequencing**

- **6.3 Activity Resource Estimating**

- **6.4 Activity Duration Estimating**

- **6.5 Schedule Development**

The following Processes in the Planning Group may be managed in simpler projects using Microsoft Project:

- **7.1 Cost Estimating**

- **7.2 Cost Budgeting**

The planning data may then be displayed using Microsoft Project as Gantt Charts, Tables or Histograms. As work is authorized and work progresses, then the progress is measured and recorded in Microsoft Project and the performance may be compared to the plan.

Thus many elements of the *PMBOK® Guide* Processes outlined above may be entered into Microsoft Project, this book will show which of these processes and process elements may be managed in Microsoft Project.

1.7 Levels of Planning

Projects are often planned at a summary level and then detailed out in the schedule before the work is commenced. Smaller projects may be detailed out during project planning but other large or complex may require several levels before the project is fully detailed out.

The main reason for not detailing out a project early is that there may not be enough information early in a project to detail out activities in the future and time would be wasted in preparing detailed schedules that will be made redundant by change. The following techniques may be considered:

- The *PMBOK® Guide* discusses the **Rolling Wave** technique. This technique involves adding more detail to the schedule as the work approaches and which is often possible as more is known about the scope as the project is executed. The initial planning could be completed at a high level in the **Work Breakdown Structure** (**WBS**). As the work approaches the planning may be completed at a WBS Component and then to **Work Package** level planning.

- The *PMBOK® Guide* also discusses the use of **Subprojects**. These are useful in larger projects where more than one person is working on the project schedule. This situation may exist when portions of projects are contracted out. A subproject may be detailed out when the work is awarded to a contractor.

- The *PMBOK® Guide* also discusses the use of **Phases**. A Phase is different to a PRINCE2 Stage as Phases may overlap in time. Phases may be defined for example as Design, Procure & Install. These Phases may overlap as Procurement may commence before Design is complete. The Phase development of a schedule is the detailing out of all WBS elements prior to the commencement of that Phase.

- Projects which are subject to many changes may require the work to be granulated out immediately prior to the work starting. For example, at the end of every week the next two weeks work (that will have had been planned at a summary level) would be planned out in detail. This is a type of **Rolling Wave** development of the project. This is often found in a software testing phase, where the next portion of work is dependent on what has passed and what has failed testing.

The *PMBOK® Guide* does not have strict definitions for levels of plans but assumes that this process is planned when decomposing the **Work Breakdown Structure (WBS)**. There are some other models below that may be used as guidelines such as the PMI "Practice Standard for Work Breakdown Structures".

PRINCE2 Level of Plans
Stages in PRINCE2 are defined as time bound periods of a project, which do not overlap and are referred to as Management Stages. Under PRINCE2 a Project Plan in divided into Stages and a Stage plan is detailed out prior to the commencement of a Stage.
PRINCE2 defines the following levels of plans:

- **Programme Plan** – which may include Project Plans or one or more portfolios of multiple projects,

- **Project Plan** – this is mandatory and is updated through the duration of a project,

- **Stage Plan** – there are a minimum of two Stage Plans, an **Initiation Stage Plan** and **First Stage Plan**. There would be usually one Stage Plan for each Stage.

- **Exception Plan** – which is at the same level and detail as a Stage Plan and replaces a Stage Plan at the request of a Project Board when a Stage is forecast to exceed tolerances, and

- **Team Plan** – which is optional and would be used on larger projects where Teams are used for delivering Products which require detailed planning. A typical example is a contractor's plan which would be submitted during the bid process.

Jelen's Cost and Optimization Engineering
This book defines the following levels of plans:

- Level 0: This is the total project and is, in effect, a single bar spanning the time from start to finish.

- Level 1: This schedules the project by its major components. For example, a level 1 schedule for a process plant may be broken in process area, storage and handling area, site and services, and utilities. It is shown in bar chart format.

- Level 2: Each of the level 1 components is further subdivided. For example, utility systems are broken into water, electrical, gas, sanitary, etc. In most cases this schedule level can only be shown in bar chart format although a bar chart with key constraints may be possible.

- Level 3: The subdivision continues. This is probably the first level that a meaningful critical path network can be drawn. It is also a good level for the project's overall control schedule since it is neither too summarized nor too detailed.

- Levels 4-?: The subdivision continues to whatever level of detail is needed by the user. When operating at these more detailed levels, the planners generally work with less than the total schedule. In most cases these 'look-ahead' schedules span periods of 30-180 days. The user may utilize either bar chart or CPM format for these schedules."

This paragraph was reproduced from "Jelen's Cost and Optimization Engineering", author F. Jelen, copyright date 1983, ISBN 0-07-053646-5 with the written permission from the publisher McGraw-Hill.

1.8 Monitoring and Controlling a Project

After a plan has been produced, it should be followed and the work authorized in accordance with the plan. If there is to be a change in the plan, then the plan should be formally changed. If necessary, the client should be informed and if required by the contract, approval should be sought. If this process is not followed then it may be difficult to obtain approval for extension of time claims and will make litigation more difficult.

Monitoring a project ensures:

- The required products are being produced

- The required quality is being met

- The products are being produced on time, with the planned resources and to budget

- The project products will achieve the Business Case

Controlling a project provides the next level of management with information allowing them to:

- Monitor the progress of products

- Compare the progress with the plan

- Review options

- Forecast problems as early as possible enabling corrective action to be taken as early as possible

- Record historical data for use in assisting in planning future projects

- Providing data required for preparing extension of time claims and for litigation

A number of *PMBOK® Guide* Executing and Monitoring & Controlling processes may be managed partially or completely with Microsoft Project and the extent that Microsoft Project may be used will be outlined towards the end of this chapter.

1.9 Project Planning Metrics

There are three components that are usually measured and controlled using planning and scheduling software:

- Time

- Effort (resources)

- Cost

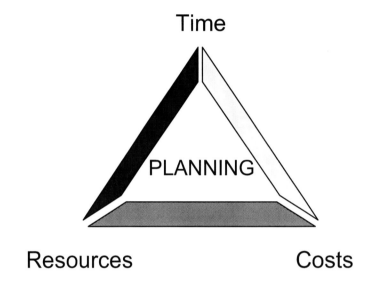

A change in any one of these components normally results in a change in one or both of the other two.

There are other project management functions that were not traditionally managed with planning and scheduling software. The development of Enterprise Project Management systems has brought about more of these functions being included in project planning and scheduling software, including:

- Timesheets and effort recording

- Document management and control

- Issue Management

- Risk Management and

- Collaboration tools.

PLANNING AND CONTROL

USING

MICROSOFT® PROJECT

AND

PMBOK® GUIDE

THIRD EDITION

BY

PAUL EASTWOOD HARRIS

Windows, Microsoft Project, Microsoft Project Standard, Microsoft Project Professional, and Excel are registered trademarks of Microsoft Corporation.

Primavera Project Planner, P3, SureTrak Project Manager, SureTrak, Primavera Enterprise, TeamPlay, P3e and P3e/c are registered trademarks of Primavera Systems, Incorporated.

Adobe® and Acrobat® are registered trademarks of Adobe Systems Incorporated.

"PMBOK" and "PMI" are registered trademarks of the Project Management Institute, Inc.

All other company or product names may be trademarks of their respective owners.

Screen captures were reprinted with authorization from Microsoft Corporation.

This publication was created by Eastwood Harris Pty Ltd (ABN 18 133 912 173) and is not a product of Microsoft Corporation.

The Project Management Institute did not participate in the development of this material, and has not reviewed its contents for accuracy. PMI does not endorse or otherwise sponsor this material, and makes no warranty, guarantee, or representation, expressed or implied, as to the accuracy of it's content.

DISCLAIMER
The information contained in this book is to the best of the author's knowledge true and correct. The author has made every effort to ensure accuracy of this publication, but cannot be held responsible for any loss or damage arising from any information in this book.

PUBLISHER, AUTHOR AND DISTRIBUTOR
Paul E Harris
Eastwood Harris Pty Ltd
PO Box 4032
Doncaster Heights 3109
Victoria, Australia
Email: harrispe@eh.com.au
Website: http://www.eh.com.au
Tel: +61 (0)4 1118 7701
Fax: +61 (0)3 9846 7700

3 February 2006

ISBN 1-921059-07-9 - A4 Spiral
ISBN 1-921059-08-7 - B5 Perfect

SUMMARY
The book was written so it may be used as:
> A training manual for a two-day training course,
> A self teach book, or
> A reference manual.

The screen shots for the book are taken from Microsoft Project Standard 2003 however the book may be used to learn Microsoft Project Professional 2003 and all versions of Microsoft Project 2002 and 2000.

The book has been written to be used as the basis for a two-day training course and includes exercises for the students to complete at the end of each chapter. Unlike many training course publications this book may also be used by the students as a reference book after the course.

This publication is ideal for people who would like to quickly gain an understanding of how the software operates and explains how the software differs from Primavera P3 and SureTrak, thus making it ideal for people who wish to convert from these products.

SPELLING
This book is written in US English.

AUTHOR'S COMMENT
As a professional project planner and scheduler, a Certified Cost Engineer and an Approved PRINCE2 Trainer I have used a number of planning and scheduling software packages for the management of a range of project types and sizes. There appeared to be very little literature aimed at the professional who understands how to run projects but requires a practical guide on how to use Microsoft Project in project environment using the processes outlined in the *PMBOK® Guide*. The first books I published were user guides/training manuals for Primavera SureTrak and P3 users. These were well received by professional project managers and schedulers, so I decided to turn my attention to Microsoft Project 2000, 2002 and 2003. To produce this book I edited my Microsoft Project 2003 book to explain how Microsoft Project may be used with the *PMBOK® Guide*. I trust this book will assist you in understanding how to use Microsoft Project on your projects. Please contact me if you have any comments you may wish to make on this book.

BOOKS PUBLISHED BY EASTWOOD HARRIS

Planning Using Primavera Project Planner P3® Version 3.1
ISBN 0-9577783-7-6 A4 Paperback   ISBN 0-9577783-8-4 A4 Spiral Bound
First Published March 2000

Planning Using Primavera SureTrak Project Manager® Version 3.0
ISBN 0-9577783-9-2 A4 Paperback   ISBN 0-9751503-0-8 A4 Spiral Bound
First Published June 2000

Planning and Scheduling Using Microsoft® Project 2002
ISBN 0-9751503-1-6 B5 Paperback   ISBN 0-9751503-2-4 A4 Spiral Bound
First Published January 2002

Planning and Scheduling Using Microsoft® Project 2003
ISBN 0-9751503-3-2 B5 Paperback   ISBN 0-9751503-4-0 A4 Spiral Bound
First Published June 2004

Project Planning and Scheduling Using Primavera® Version 4.1
For Engineering & Construction and Maintenance & Turnaround
ISBN 1-921059-00-1 A4 Paperback   ISBN 1-921059-01-X A4 Spiral Bound
First Published January 05

Project Planning and Scheduling Using Primavera® Version 4.1
For IT Project Office and New Product Development
ISBN 1-921059-02-8 A4 Paperback   ISBN 1-921059-03-6 A4 Spiral Bound
First Published March 05

Project Planning and Scheduling Using Primavera ®Contractor Version 4.1
For the Construction Industry
ISBN 1-921059-04-4 A4 Paperback   ISBN 1-921059-05-2 A4 Spiral Bound
First Published January 05

PRINCE2 ™ Planning & Control Using Microsoft® Project
ISBN 1 921059 06 0 B5 Paperback   ISBN 1-921059-06-0 A4 Spiral Bound
First Published May 2005

Planning and Control Using Microsoft® Project and PMBOK® Guide Third Edition
ISBN 1-921059-08-7 B5 Paperback   ISBN 1-921059-07-9 A4 Spiral Bound
First Published June 2005

Planning and Scheduling Using Primavera® Version 5.0 For Engineering & Construction
ISBN 1-921059-09-5 A4 Paperback   ISBN 1-921059-10-9 A4 Spiral Bound
First Published December 05

Planning and Scheduling Using Primavera® Version 5.0 For IT Project Office
ISBN 1-921059-11-7 A4 Paperback   ISBN 1-921059-12-5 A4 Spiral Bound
First Published December 05

1 INTRODUCTION

1.1 *Purpose*

The purpose of this book is to provide you with methods of using Microsoft Project and the *PMBOK® Guide* processes in a single project environment. Not all the *PMBOK® Guide* processes are simply transposed to Microsoft Project and some may not be managed in Microsoft Project at all. This book makes some suggestions on how to best handle these areas of incompatibility and provide you with techniques to manage your projects with Microsoft Project and the *PMBOK® Guide* Processes.

The screen shots in this book were captured using Microsoft Project Standard 2003 and Windows XP. Readers using Microsoft Project Professional 2003 will have some additional menu options to those shown in this book, which will operate when their software is connected to Microsoft Project Server software. Users of Microsoft Project 2002 and 2000 will find some minor differences in how the software functions which are outlined in the relevant areas of this book and in **Chapter 23 WHAT IS NEW IN MICROSOFT PROJECT** at the end of this book.

When the term "Section" is used in this book it is referring to the appropriate section number in the *PMBOK® Guide Third Edition*. This book should be read in conjunction with the *PMBOK® Guide Third Edition*.

At the end of this book, you should be able to:

- Understand the steps required to create a project plan using the *PMBOK® Guide* Processes.

- Set up the software.

- Define calendars.

- Add tasks which will represent the *PMBOK® Guide* **Activities**.

- Organize tasks and format the display.

- Add logic and constraints outlined in the *PMBOK® Guide* process **6.2 Activity Sequencing**.

- Use Tables, Views and Filters which are used to create the printouts and reports to support the *PMBOK® Guide* **Project Communications Management** processes.

- Print the above reports.

- Record and track progress which support the *PMBOK® Guide* processes of **Schedule Control**, **Cost Control**, **Scope Control** and **Performance Reporting**.

- Customize the project options.

- Create and assign resources which would be used in the *PMBOK® Guide* process **6.3 Activity Resource Estimating**.

- Understand the impact of task types and effort driven tasks.

- Status projects that contain resources, which support the *PMBOK® Guide* processes of **Schedule Control**, **Cost Control**, **Scope Control** and **Performance Reporting**.

- Understand the different techniques for scheduling.

This book does not cover every aspect of Microsoft Project, however it does cover the main features required to create and status a project schedule. It should provide you with a solid grounding, which will enable you to go on and learn the other features of the software from experimenting with it, using the help files and reviewing other literature.

This book has been written to minimize superfluous text, allowing the user to locate and understand the information contained in the book as quickly as possible. It does NOT cover functions of little value to common project scheduling requirements. If at any time you are unable to understand a topic in this book, it is suggested that you use the Microsoft Project Help menu to gain a further understanding of the subject.

1.2   *Required Background Knowledge*

This book does not teach you how to use computers or to manage projects. This book is intended to teach you how to Plan and Control a project using Microsoft Project and the *PMBOK® Guide* processes. Therefore, to be able to follow this book you should have the following background knowledge:

- An understanding of how the *PMBOK® Guide* Knowledge Areas and Processes are used to plan and control a project.

- The ability to use a personal computer and understand the fundamentals of the operating system.

- Experience using application software such as Microsoft Office which would have given you exposure to Windows menu systems and typical Windows functions such as copy and paste.

1.3   *Purpose of Planning*

The ultimate purpose of planning is to build a model that allows you to predict which tasks and resources are critical to the timely completion of the project. Strategies may then be implemented to ensure that these tasks and resources are managed properly, thus ensuring that the project will be delivered **On Time** and **Within Budget**.

Planning aims to:

- Identify the Products required to deliver a project

- Evaluate different project delivery methods

- Identify and optimize the use of resources

- Optimize time and evaluate if target dates may be met

- Identify risks and set priorities

- Provide a baseline plan against which progress is measured

- Communicate to all Stakeholders the plan including what is to be done, when and by whom

- Provide early warning of potential problems and enable proactive and not reactive action to be taken

- Assist management to think ahead and make informed decisions

Planning helps to avoid:

- Increased project costs or reduction in scope and/or quality

- Additional change over and/or operation costs

- Extensions of time claims

- Loss of your client's revenue

- Contractual disputes and associated resolution costs

- The loss or reputation of those involved in a project

- Loss of a facility or asset in the event of a total project failure

1.4 Definition of a Planning & Control

PMBOK® Guide defines:

- The **Planning Process** as those processes performed to define and mature the project scope, develop the project management plan, and identify and schedule the project activities that occur within the project.

- The **Control Technique** as comparing actual performance with planned performance, analyzing variances, assessing trends to effect process improvements, evaluating possible alternatives, and recommending appropriate corrective action as needed.

A plan is therefore not just a Microsoft Gantt chart (bar chart), but a Gantt chart is an important output of the planning process.

Microsoft Project is also able to record timings, costs and targets and other basic information could be kept in the Notes or Custom (user defined) Fields. It is not designed as a quality assurance nor a document management software package and specialist packages should be considered for these processes.

1.5 PMBOK® Guide Process Groups and Knowledge Areas

Like other methodologies, such as PRINCE2 which has a time bound processes including a clearly defined Planning Process and Controlling Processes, the *PMBOK® Guide* has five Process Groups:

- Initiating Process Group

- Planning Process Group

- Executing Process Group

- Monitoring and Controlling Process Group

- Closing Process Group

The *PMBOK® Guide* summarizes project management processes under nine Knowledge Areas, each with three or more Processes in each Knowledge Area. These are similar to the PRINCE2 Components.

The table over the page maps Processes to Process Groups & Knowledge Areas using the chapter numbers from the *PMBOK® Guide*:

| KNOWLEDGE AREAS | PROCESS GROUPS | | | | |
	Initiating	Planning	Executing	Monitoring & Controlling	Closing
- Processes					
PROJECT INTEGRATION MANAGEMENT					
- Develop Project Charter	4.1				
- Develop Preliminary Project Scope Statement	4.2				
- Develop Project Management Plan		4.3			
- Direct and Manage Project Execution			4.4		
- Monitor and Control Project Work				4.5	
- Integrated Change Control				4.6	
- Close Project					4.7
PROJECT SCOPE MANAGEMENT					
- Scope Planning		5.1			
- Scope Definition		5.2			
- Create WBS		5.3			
- Scope Verification				5.4	
- Scope Control				5.5	
PROJECT TIME MANAGEMENT					
- Activity Definition		6.1			
- Activity Sequencing		6.2			
- Activity Resource Estimating		6.3			
- Activity Duration Estimating		6.4			
- Schedule Development		6.5			
- Schedule Control				6.6	
PROJECT COST MANAGEMENT					
- Cost Estimating		7.1			
- Cost Budgeting		7.2			
- Cost Control				7.3	
PROJECT QUALITY MANAGEMENT					
- Quality Planning		8.1			
- Perform Quality Assurance			8.2		
- Perform Quality Control				8.3	
PROJECT HUMAN RESOURCE MANAGEMENT					
- Human Resource Planning		9.1			
- Acquire Project Team			9.2		
- Develop Project Team			9.3		
- Manage Project Team				9.4	
PROJECT COMMUNICATIONS MANAGEMENT					
- Communications Planning		10.1			
- Information Distribution			10.2		
- Performance Reporting				10.3	
- Manage Stakeholders				10.4	
PROJECT RISK MANAGEMENT					
- Risk Management Planning		11.1			
- Risk Identification		11.2			
- Qualitative Risk Analysis		11.3			
- Quantitative Risk Analysis		11.4			
- Risk Response Planning		11.5			
- Risk Monitoring and Control				11.5	
PROJECT PROCUREMENT MANAGEMENT					
- Plan Purchases and Acquisitions		12.1			
- Plan Contracting		12.2			
- Request Seller Responses			12.3		
- Select Sellers			12.4		
- Contract Administration				12.5	
- Contract Closure					12.6

1.6 Project Planning

It may be seen from the previous table the Planning Process Group has many more processes than other Process Groups, which is one indication of the importance of planning a project prior to execution.

The plans indicated in the Planning Processes above would often be written in a document using Microsoft Word. The activities required to create these plans and then execute them including their associated resources and costs, could be scheduled in Microsoft Project.

The following Processes in the Planning Group, indicated in the table above, may be managed in Microsoft Project:

- **5.3 Create WBS**

- **6.1 Activity Definition**

- **6.2 Activity Sequencing**

- **6.3 Activity Resource Estimating**

- **6.4 Activity Duration Estimating**

- **6.5 Schedule Development**

The following Processes in the Planning Group may be managed in simpler projects using Microsoft Project:

- **7.1 Cost Estimating**

- **7.2 Cost Budgeting**

The planning data may then be displayed using Microsoft Project as Gantt Charts, Tables or Histograms. As work is authorized and work progresses, then the progress is measured and recorded in Microsoft Project and the performance may be compared to the plan.

Thus many elements of the *PMBOK® Guide* Processes outlined above may be entered into Microsoft Project, this book will show which of these processes and process elements may be managed in Microsoft Project.

1.7 Levels of Planning

Projects are often planned at a summary level and then detailed out in the schedule before the work is commenced. Smaller projects may be detailed out during project planning but other large or complex may require several levels before the project is fully detailed out.

The main reason for not detailing out a project early is that there may not be enough information early in a project to detail out activities in the future and time would be wasted in preparing detailed schedules that will be made redundant by change. The following techniques may be considered:

- The *PMBOK® Guide* discusses the **Rolling Wave** technique. This technique involves adding more detail to the schedule as the work approaches and which is often possible as more is known about the scope as the project is executed. The initial planning could be completed at a high level in the **Work Breakdown Structure** (WBS). As the work approaches the planning may be completed at a WBS Component and then to **Work Package** level planning.

- The *PMBOK® Guide* also discusses the use of **Subprojects**. These are useful in larger projects where more than one person is working on the project schedule. This situation may exist when portions of projects are contracted out. A subproject may be detailed out when the work is awarded to a contractor.

- The *PMBOK® Guide* also discusses the use of **Phases**. A Phase is different to a PRINCE2 Stage as Phases may overlap in time. Phases may be defined for example as Design, Procure & Install. These Phases may overlap as Procurement may commence before Design is complete. The Phase development of a schedule is the detailing out of all WBS elements prior to the commencement of that Phase.

- Projects which are subject to many changes may require the work to be granulated out immediately prior to the work starting. For example, at the end of every week the next two weeks work (that will have had been planned at a summary level) would be planned out in detail. This is a type of **Rolling Wave** development of the project. This is often found in a software testing phase, where the next portion of work is dependent on what has passed and what has failed testing.

The *PMBOK® Guide* does not have strict definitions for levels of plans but assumes that this process is planned when decomposing the **Work Breakdown Structure (WBS)**. There are some other models below that may be used as guidelines such as the PMI "Practice Standard for Work Breakdown Structures".

PRINCE2 Level of Plans
Stages in PRINCE2 are defined as time bound periods of a project, which do not overlap and are referred to as Management Stages. Under PRINCE2 a Project Plan in divided into Stages and a Stage plan is detailed out prior to the commencement of a Stage.
PRINCE2 defines the following levels of plans:

- **Programme Plan** – which may include Project Plans or one or more portfolios of multiple projects,

- **Project Plan** – this is mandatory and is updated through the duration of a project,

- **Stage Plan** – there are a minimum of two Stage Plans, an **Initiation Stage Plan** and **First Stage Plan**. There would be usually one Stage Plan for each Stage.

- **Exception Plan** – which is at the same level and detail as a Stage Plan and replaces a Stage Plan at the request of a Project Board when a Stage is forecast to exceed tolerances, and

- **Team Plan** – which is optional and would be used on larger projects where Teams are used for delivering Products which require detailed planning. A typical example is a contractor's plan which would be submitted during the bid process.

Jelen's Cost and Optimization Engineering
This book defines the following levels of plans:

- Level 0: This is the total project and is, in effect, a single bar spanning the time from start to finish.

- Level 1: This schedules the project by its major components. For example, a level 1 schedule for a process plant may be broken in process area, storage and handling area, site and services, and utilities. It is shown in bar chart format.

- Level 2: Each of the level 1 components is further subdivided. For example, utility systems are broken into water, electrical, gas, sanitary, etc. In most cases this schedule level can only be shown in bar chart format although a bar chart with key constraints may be possible.

- Level 3: The subdivision continues. This is probably the first level that a meaningful critical path network can be drawn. It is also a good level for the project's overall control schedule since it is neither too summarized nor too detailed.

- Levels 4-?: The subdivision continues to whatever level of detail is needed by the user. When operating at these more detailed levels, the planners generally work with less than the total schedule. In most cases these 'look-ahead' schedules span periods of 30-180 days. The user may utilize either bar chart or CPM format for these schedules."

This paragraph was reproduced from "Jelen's Cost and Optimization Engineering", author F. Jelen, copyright date 1983, ISBN 0-07-053646-5 with the written permission from the publisher McGraw-Hill.

1.8 Monitoring and Controlling a Project

After a plan has been produced, it should be followed and the work authorized in accordance with the plan. If there is to be a change in the plan, then the plan should be formally changed. If necessary, the client should be informed and if required by the contract, approval should be sought. If this process is not followed then it may be difficult to obtain approval for extension of time claims and will make litigation more difficult.

Monitoring a project ensures:

- The required products are being produced

- The required quality is being met

- The products are being produced on time, with the planned resources and to budget

- The project products will achieve the Business Case

Controlling a project provides the next level of management with information allowing them to:

- Monitor the progress of products

- Compare the progress with the plan

- Review options

- Forecast problems as early as possible enabling corrective action to be taken as early as possible

- Record historical data for use in assisting in planning future projects

- Providing data required for preparing extension of time claims and for litigation

A number of *PMBOK® Guide* Executing and Monitoring & Controlling processes may be managed partially or completely with Microsoft Project and the extent that Microsoft Project may be used will be outlined towards the end of this chapter.

1.9 Project Planning Metrics

There are three components that are usually measured and controlled using planning and scheduling software:

- Time

- Effort (resources)

- Cost

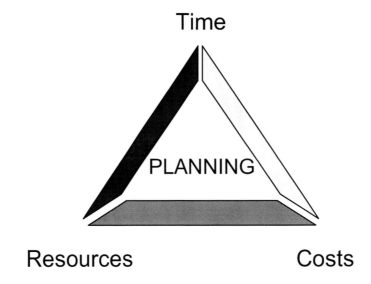

A change in any one of these components normally results in a change in one or both of the other two.

There are other project management functions that were not traditionally managed with planning and scheduling software. The development of Enterprise Project Management systems has brought about more of these functions being included in project planning and scheduling software, including:

- Timesheets and effort recording

- Document management and control

- Issue Management

- Risk Management and

- Collaboration tools.

1.10 Planning Cycle

The planning cycle is an integral part of managing a project. A software package such as Microsoft Project makes this task much easier for larger and more complex projects.

When the original plan is agreed to, either Project or at a more detailed level such as Phase or Stage and the **Baseline** is set. The **Baseline** is a record of the original plan. The **Baseline** dates may be recorded in Microsoft Project in data fields titled **Baseline Start** and **Baseline Finish**.

Work should then be authorized and executed in accordance with the plan. When a plan may not be achieved then it should be revised and the revised plan approved, re-baselined and executed.

The actual progress is monitored, recorded in **Schedule Control** and **Cost Control** and the progress is compared to the **Baseline**.

The plan and progress should be evaluated, variances analyzed, understood and reported.

The plan may be amended by adding or deleting tasks and adjusting Remaining Durations or Resources. Should the current forecast timings be unacceptable, then options should be considered to bring the project back on track.

The achieved progress and the revised plan is then published as progress continues using processes defined in **10.1 Communication Planning**, **10.2 Information Distribution** and **10.3 Performance Reporting**.

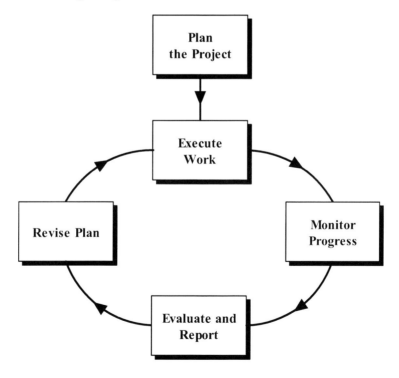

1.11 PMBOK® Guide Processes and Microsoft Project

It would be possible to use Microsoft Project in almost all the *PMBOK® Guide* Processes, even if it is just to schedule when the work is planned to be executed and by whom. The table below explains some practical ways of using Microsoft Project in many of the processes outside just scheduling the work and assigning resources to the work:

Initiating		
4.1	Develop Project Charter	This is where the planning tool such as Microsoft Project may be selected.
4.2	Develop Preliminary Scope Statement	Typically this document would be developed in a word processor.
		The scope may be entered into Microsoft Project as **Tasks** and notes about the scope content recorded in the **Notes** facilities.
		The disadvantage of using Microsoft Project for developing the Preliminary Scope Statement is that people without access to Microsoft Project, or do not know how to use it may not be able to review the data and the use of a word processor or a spreadsheet should be considered. This information may be cut and pasted from another application into Microsoft Project to develop the schedule.
Planning		
4.3	Develop Project Management Plan	Typically a word processor such as Microsoft Word would be used to create this document.
		Microsoft Project may be nominated in this process as a planning tool but it would not be used to define the Project Management Plan.
5.1	Scope Planning	Typically the Scope Management Plan would not be developed using Microsoft Project, however may be used to plan the development of the **Scope Management Plan** showing the activities and people required.
5.2	Scope Definition	The scope could be developed as **Tasks** in Microsoft Project. The **Task Notes** and user definable fields could be used to record additional information.
5.3	Create WBS	The **Outlining** feature of Microsoft Project or a **Custom Outline Code** may be used to define the Work Breakdown Structure (WBS) of a project. The Project Management Institute Practice Standard for Work Breakdown Structures provides guidance for the development of a project WBS.
		The Microsoft Project outlining feature is useful for granulating a WBS into more detail, but may not be printed as a hierarchical tree diagram for review.

6.1	Activity Definition	Microsoft Project is designed to be used for the purposes of listing Activities, Milestones and additional activities may be added for Requested changes.
		A **Customized Field** may be used to record **Requested Changes** against tasks.
		Additional information about an activity may be recorded on the **Task Notes** field.
		Some people like to keep tasks in a schedule at a summary level and then included activities as notes in the **Task Notes** form.
6.2	Activity Sequencing	Microsoft Project will handle this process as this is one of the primary purpose of the product. Outputs may be presented in **Gantt Chart** or as a **Network Diagram** and there are other reporting facilities available.
6.3	Activity Resource Estimating	Resources may be assigned to tasks and the resource requirement viewed as tables using either the **Resource Usage** table, or **Resource Graphs** (histograms) and using the **Resource Graph** function, or exported to Excel for further analysis using the **Analysis toolbar**.
6.4	Activity Duration Estimating	Microsoft Project is designed to handle this function by assigning resources, the number of resources and the quantity of work to tasks.
		It also has the ability to assign calendars to both tasks and resources to further refine the task Finish Date.
6.5	Schedule Development	This is one of the primary purposes of Microsoft Project and various execution options may be considered and planned in Microsoft Project to optimize a project timing.
7.1	Cost Estimating	Microsoft Project may be used for estimating and there are a number of functions that would assist including Labor Resources, Material Resources and Costs.
		A user must be aware that a detailed schedule with many resources and costs is very difficult to update and maintain as the project progresses. The use of an external estimating system or a spreadsheet may be considered and then the summary costs transferred to Microsoft Project for analysis.
7.2	Cost Budgeting	Cost from a project plan may be rolled up in a number of ways using **Outlining** or the **Grouping** feature which will operate on a number of user definable fields. This will provide the costs elements of work as well as the total project cost.
		A cash flow may also be produced, this is normally best achieved by exporting to Excel for presentation using the **Analysis toolbar**.

8.1	Quality Planning	The relevant standards for each task could be recorded in the **Task Notes** or a user definable field. Activities should be included in the schedule for checking quality.
9.1	Human Resource Planning	All people involved on a project may be entered into the **Resource Sheet**. Information about resources may be entered into either existing fields or user definable fields which may be used to identify their roles, responsibilities and the project organizational structure. Resources may be grouped using the **Grouping** function and an organizational structure may be created in a table format.
10.1	Communications Planning	Once the reporting requirements have been defined then the Microsoft Project **Filters**, **Table** and **Layouts** or **Reports** may be used to create reports for project stakeholders.
11.1	Risk Management Planning	Microsoft Project is not a Risk Analysis tool and this function should be undertaken outside of Microsoft Project. A **Risk Log** item number and or description may be assigned to a task using a user definable field.
11.2	Risk Management Planning	This typically would not involve the use of Microsoft Project.
11.3	Risk Identification	This typically this would not involve the use of Microsoft Project but the process of planning may assist in the identification of risks and additional activities added as part of a risk mitigation strategy.
11.4	Qualitative Risk Analysis	This typically would not involve the use of Microsoft Project but it may be used to model the effect of a realized risk on a project.
11.5	Risk Response Planning	It may be used to evaluate options and include risk countermeasure activities but it is recommended that a risk analysis is conducted outside of Microsoft Project.
12.1	Plan Purchases and Acquisitions	Planning of purchases may involve grouping several tasks together under a single order. These activities may be tagged using a user defined field and grouped together using the **Grouping** function, or selected and displayed together using a filter, which limits the number of tasks that are being displayed.
12.2	Plan Contracting	Planning of contracts may involve grouping several tasks together under a single contract. These activities may be tagged using a user defined field and grouped together using the **Grouping** function, or selected and displayed together using a filter, which limits the number of tasks that are being displayed.

Executing		
4.4	Direct and Manage Project Execution	Work should be authorized and executed in accordance with the plan.
		If the plan is no longer valid then it should be changed, approved and then the revised plan followed. The process of claiming an extension of time is normally simpler when an approved plan is followed.
8.2	Perform Quality Assurance	Activities should be included in the plan to represent the Quality Assurance processes.
		When products fail Quality Tests then new activities may be added to the schedule to represent the retesting of these products.
9.2	Acquire Project Team	The requirements for resources, including people and equipment may be calculated by Microsoft Project.
		Team Members may be added to the Resource Dictionary as they join the team.
9.3	Develop Project Team	As the project team is developed they may be recorded in Microsoft Project.
		People who are expected to use products like Microsoft Project should be trained in the use of the product and it is generally better to train a small number of specialized people to a high level than many people to a low level.
		There are many people who will never be able to master the use of any scheduling tool to a high level of competence and the training of these people is often a waste of time and money. It may be better to support these people with specialists people from a project or programme office.
10.2	Information Distribution	Reports designed in **Communications Planning** may be run from Microsoft Project and distributed.
12.3	Request Seller Responses	Sellers may be requested to submit a schedule with their response.
		If it is intended to included a sellers schedule into the project schedule then it is advised that a template schedule is supplied to the seller for them to work with that includes the summary tasks they should schedule under, calendars, resources and any tailored Customized Fields.
12.4	Select Sellers	It is important that reporting requirements are carefully spelt out at this point in time so data that is used to update the project schedule is made available as and when required and in the correct format so it is useful to update the schedule.
12.5	Contract Administration	During Contract administration the data required to update the schedule, including changes, should be supplied in accordance with the Contract and activities added to the schedule to reflect the changes.

Monitoring & Controlling		
4.5	Monitor and Control Project Work	Progress should be recorded in Microsoft Project on a regular basis. The actual performance should be compared with the planned and where there are unacceptable deviations from the plan then action should be take to rectify the issues.
4.6	Integrated Change Control	The effects of potential changes in both cost and time may be entered into Microsoft Project and supply management with the appropriate data to make decisions on potential changes.
5.4	Scope Verification	Scope Verification and acceptance of the scope by all the Stakeholders may be assisted by the presentation of a well constructed and clear schedule.
5.5	Scope Control	Scope changes should be represented as Tasks in Microsoft Project by adding additional tasks to the schedule.
6.6	Schedule Control	As work progresses the task status should be recorded with **Actual Start Dates, Percent Completes** and **Actual Finish Dates** depending on the status of the tasks. The tasks in Microsoft Project should be updated on a regular basis.
7.3	Cost Control	As work progresses the **Actual Hours, Actual Costs, Hours to Complete** and **Cost to Compete** may be entered into Microsoft Project and a **Cost at Completion** calculated.
8.3	Perform Quality Control	Quality Control is performed throughout the delivery of products and the project plan should be updated as products are Quality Approved and accepted into the project. The plan should be changed to reflect any changes due to the running of the Change Control Process which may add or remove task from the plan.
9.4	Manage Project Team	Microsoft Project may be used to assist in the management of the team mainly by the ability to assign resources to tasks, which is in effect assigning the work to people. The responsibility for the management of tasks may be achieved by creating a user defined field for responsibility.
10.3	Performance Reporting	Microsoft Project may produce some basic Earned Value data and date variance data for Performance Reporting.
10.4	Manage Stakeholders	Updated schedule reports may be run and distributed to Stakeholders in accordance with the **Communications Plan**.
1.5	Risk Response Planning	Risk responses once planned could be scheduled in Microsoft Project.
12.6	Contract Closure	At closure the schedule should be checked to ensure all tasks are complete and all products delivered to the project.
Closing		
4.7	Close Project	The schedule should be updated to reflect the actual finish of the project and a record of the final duration of project made available in the Lessons Learned Report and saved.

2   CREATING A PROJECT SCHEDULE

The aim of this chapter is to give you an understanding of what a schedule is and some practical guidance on how your schedule may be created and statused during the life of a project. Schedule development is covered in section **6.5 Schedule Development** of the *PMBOK® Guide*.

2.1   *Understanding Planning and Scheduling Software*

A project is essentially a set of unique operations or tasks to be completed in a logical order to achieve a defined outcome by a definitive end time. A schedule is an attempt to model these tasks, their durations and their relationships to other tasks. These tasks take time to accomplish and may employ resources such as people, materials, equipment, and money that may have a limited availability.

Planning and scheduling software allows the user to:

- Break a project down into a WBS and activities that may be entered into the software as tasks,

- Assign tasks with their durations, predecessors, successors and constraints and then calculate the start and finish dates of all the tasks,

- Assign resources to the tasks and calculate the planned project resource requirements,

- Monitor the actual progress of tasks against the original plan and revise the plan when required,

- Monitor the consumption of resources and re-estimate the resources required to finish the project.

There are four modes or levels in which planning and scheduling software may be used.

	Planning	Tracking
Without Resources	**LEVEL 1** Planning without resources	**LEVEL 2** Tracking progress without Resources
With Resources	**LEVEL 3** Planning with resources	**LEVEL 4** Tracking progress with Resources

As the level increases, the amount of information required to maintain the schedule will increase. More importantly, your skill and knowledge in using the software will also need to increase. This book is designed to take you from Level 1 through to Level 4.

2.2 Understanding Your Project

Before you start the process of creating a project plan, it is important to have an understanding of the project and how it will be executed. On large, complex projects, this information is usually available from the following types of documents:

- Project Charter

- Project Scope Statement

- Functional specification

- Requirements baseline

- Contract documentation

- Plans and drawings

- Project execution plan

- Contracting and purchasing plan

- Equipment lists

- Installation plan

- Testing plan

It is important to gain a good understanding of the project process before starting to plan your project. A project scope should be defined during the process **4.2 Develop Preliminary Project Scope Statement** and further refined during **5.2 Scope Definition**.

The **Project Management Plan** should be developed before opening up Microsoft Project. This is covered in section **4.3 Develop Project Management Plan** and would include the **Schedule Management Plan** which should outline the tools to be used, level of detail required in the schedule and define other scheduling parameters such as the calendars, coding structures and resources required.

The WBS is defined in section **5.3 Create WBS** and the scope verified in section **5.4 Scope Verification**. At this point the project should be planned and this normally involves understanding the relationship between project deliverables and planning the order that the project deliverables (as defined in the WBS) are created. This document is often called the **Project Execution Plan** and would be the basis for creating a schedule in Microsoft Project.

It is also necessary to understand what level of reporting is required. Providing too little or too much detail will often lead to the schedule being discarded and not being used. These requirements should be outlined in detail in the **Project Management Plan,** detailed out in **10.1 Communications Planning** and considered in the construction of the schedule.

There are three processes required to create or maintain a plan at each of the four levels:

- Collecting the relevant project data

- Entering and manipulating the data in the software

- Distributing, reviewing and revising the plan

The ability of the scheduler to collect the data is as important as the ability to enter and manipulate the information using the software. On larger projects, it may be necessary to write policies and procedures to ensure accurate collection of data from the various people, departments, stakeholders/companies, and sites.

2.3   Level 1 – Planning Without Resources

This is the simplest mode of planning.

2.3.1   Creating Projects

To create the project, you will require the following information:

- Project Name

- The Project Start Date (and perhaps the Finish Date)

Other important information may be recorded in the software such as:

- Client name

- Location

- Project number

- Type of project

2.3.2   Defining the Calendars

Before you start entering tasks into your schedule it is advisable to set up the calendars. These are used to model the working time for each task in the project. For example, a six-day calendar is created for those tasks that will be worked for six days a week. The calendar should include any public holidays and any other exceptions to available working days such as planned days off.

The finish date and time of a task (when there are no resources assigned to a task) is calculated from the start date and time plus the task duration over the calendar assigned to the task.

The picture below shows the effect of non-work days (the shaded days) on the finish date of a 7 day duration task. The elapsed duration is 13 days due to a long weekend holiday and a two day weekend.

The *PMBOK® Guide* discusses project calendars in section **6.4 Activity Duration Estimating**, however it does not cover the use of Task Calendars which may be assigned to individual activities on un-resourced schedules to represent the times and dates that the task may be worked. For example; a task may either have a 5 day or a 6 day per week calendar.

2.3.3   Defining the Work Breakdown Structure - WBS

A WBS may be defined as a deliverable based hierarchical breakdown of all the project deliverables or products. The sum of all the WBS Components (Nodes) should encompass the total project scope. Each WBS Component would normally granulated (broken down) into the activities required to deliver the deliverables defined by the WBS Component.

Section **5.3 Create WBS** gives advice on how to create a Work Breakdown Structure and has some practical examples. These structures may be represented in Microsoft Project. Section **5.3.2 Create WBS: Tools and Techniques** discusses the decomposition of a project schedule and gives practical advice on how to granulate a schedule.

Before creating a project and adding tasks to the schedule, you should design your Work Breakdown Structure by asking the following questions:

- What are the most suitable Work Breakdown Structures?

- Which phases are involved in the project? (E.g. Design, Procure, Install and Test)

- Which disciplines are participating? (E.g. Civil, Mechanical and Electrical)

- Which departments are involved in the project? (E.g. Sales, Procurement and Installation)

- What work is expected to be contracted out and which contractors are to be used?

- How many sites or areas are there in the project?

Use the responses to these and other similar questions to create the Work Breakdown Structure.

A project schedule may be completed at:

- Any level in the WBS or

- At activity level where detailed scheduling is undertaken.

Planning at a high level of a WBS is often completed during the feasibility stage of a project. More detailed planning is undertaken as the Scope of Work is developed and the level of detail is increased before the work is executed. Levels of plans were discussed in Chapter 1, paragraph 1.7 Levels of Planning of this book.

Section **6.1.2.5 Activity Definition: Tools and Techniques** discusses the **Rolling Wave Planning** technique. This technique involves granulating or detailing out the work as it appears on the horizon. For example in the software testing phase of a project it is often difficult to plan very far in advance. This is normally because the work to be completed in the near future often depend on which tests were a success and which were not and have to be repeated. In this situation a detailed 2 week look ahead could be planned every week.

There are other methods of granulating a project schedule. The PRINCE2 methodology advocates the **Stage** approach to planning a project. A Stage is a time bound period of a project where all the Products or Deliverables to be produced in a Stage are planned in detail and the plan approved before the work on the Stage is commenced.

Section **6.1.2.5 Activity Definition: Tools and Techniques** discusses the use of **Control Accounts** and **Planning Packages**. Both of these may be accommodated by using Outlining, Custom Fields or Custom Outline Codes.

Section **5.3.2 Create WBS: Tools and Techniques** outlines the use of **Work Packages**. A Work Package is defined as the lowest level of each branch of a WBS and may be identified as an Outlined task in Microsoft Project.

The development of a **Project Scope Statement** precedes the development of the WBS and the schedule. The scope may be recorded in Microsoft Project in a number of methods including Notes or Custom Fields. Usually this is not the primary location of this information as the accessibility to this data is then restricted to people with access to Microsoft Project and is not often used.

2.3.4   Defining Other Project Breakdown Structures

A project breakdown structure is a way of categorizing the activities of a project into numerous codes that relate to the project. The codes act as tags or attributes for each activity and is used to Sort, Group or Filter tasks providing different perspectives of the project or programme schedule.

The *PMBOK® Guide* advocates the use of a Work Breakdown Structure as the primary Project Breakdown Structure, but recognizes that there are other structures that may need to be identified in a project schedule such as the following listed in Section **5.3.3 Create WBS: Outputs**:

- **Organizational Breakdown Structure** (OBS)

- **Bill of Materials** (BOM)

- **Risk Breakdown Structure** (RBS)

- **Resource Breakdown Structure** (RBS)

2.3.5   Project Breakdown Structure Functions in Microsoft Project

The principal method of assigning a Project Breakdown Structure to your project with Microsoft Project is using a function entitled **Outlining**. The Outlining function may be used to define only one Project Breakdown Structure. The *PMBOK® Guide* advocates the use of a hierarchical WBS and the Outlining feature is usually used to represent the WBS.

Defining the **Work Breakdown Structure** using a hierarchical tree structure indicated diagrammatically in the section **5.3 Create WBS** may not be duplicated graphically in Microsoft Project. Graphical flow charting tools or specialist planning tools, like Project Consort, may be used to create the tree structure and duplicate this process exactly.

The WBS structure may be represented using Outlining or a Custom Outline Codes, both of which lend themselves to the Decomposition Process of breaking down the WBS to greater detail at each level.

The picture on the right is created using outlining and is the same WBS as the *PMBOK® Guide* Figure 5-7.

	Task Name	Outline Level	Summary Task
1	⊟ **Software Product Release**	1	Yes
2	⊟ **Project Management**	2	Yes
3	Planning	3	No
4	Meetings	3	No
5	Administrationm	3	No
6	⊟ **Product Requirements**	2	Yes
7	Software	3	No
8	User Documentation	3	No
9	Training Program Materials	3	No
10	⊟ **Detail Design**	2	Yes
11	Software	3	No
12	User Documentation	3	No
13	Training Program Materials	3	No
14	⊟ **Construct**	2	Yes
15	Software	3	No
16	User Documentation	3	No
17	Training Program Materials	3	No
18	⊟ **Integration and Test**	2	Yes
19	Software	3	No
20	User Documentation	3	No
21	Training Program Materials	3	No

The Outline Level represents the level in the WBS structure. Tasks tagged YES under the "Summary Task" column are Summary Tasks and are often referred to as **Parent Tasks**, those tagged NO are not Summary tasks and often refereed to as **Detailed Tasks** or **Child Tasks**.

When Outlining is NOT used to represent the Work Breakdown Structure and is used to represent another Project Breakdown Structure, then a **Custom Outline Codes** may be used to represent the Work Breakdown Structure and provides another view of the project activities. The task below are grouped by a Custom Outline Code renamed WBS Code:

2.3.6 Defining Activities

The *PMBOK® Guide* outlines the process **6.1 Activity Definition** where work to be performed is identified and documented. It suggests that **Activity Lists**, **Activity Attributes** and **Milestone Lists** should be created and the data associated with all these may be recorded in Microsoft project using Notes or Custom Fields. This section provides some valuable advice on how to define your activities which would be entered into Microsoft Project as detailed tasks. The Activity definition process could be performed either outside Microsoft Project in a Word Processor, a Spreadsheet, a customized database or a specialized product like Project Consort.

Project Activities are normally entered into Microsoft Project as Detailed Tasks under a Summary Task. These Activities must be clearly defined before they are entered into the schedule. It is important that you consider the following factors carefully:

- What is the scope of the task? (What is included and excluded?)

- How long the task is going to take?

- Who is going to perform it?

Activities may have variable durations depending on the number of resources assigned. You may find that one activity that takes 4 days using 4 workers may take 2 days using 8 workers or 8 days using 2 workers. Section **6.4 Activity Duration Estimating** gives some valuable advice on estimating the duration of activities.

Usually Progress Reports are issued on a regular basis such as every week or every month. It is recommended that, if possible, a task should not span more than two reporting periods. That way the tasks should only be **In-Progress** for one report. Of course, it is not practical to do this on long duration activities such as procurement and delivery tasks that may span many reporting periods.

It is also recommended that you have a measurable finish point for each group of tasks such as a Stage. These may be identified in the schedule by **Milestones** and are designated with zero duration. Documentation may be used to officially highlight the end point of one task and the start point of another, thereby adding clarity to the schedule. Examples of typical documents that may be issued for clarity are:

- Issue of a drawing package

- Completion of a specification

- Placing of an order

- Receipt of materials (Delivery logs, tickets or Dockets)

- Competed testing certificates for equipment

2.3.7   Adding Tasks to the Schedule

Tasks in Microsoft Project may be used to represent either:

- A WBS Component, where the Task would typically be a Parent or Summary task created using Outlining,

- **Planning Packages**,

- **Work Packages**, or

- An **Activity** under a WBS Component and would be part or all of the work required to deliver the deliverable defined by the WBS Component.

These may be represented as Summary or Detailed tasks. The lowest level task in Outlining is always a Detailed task and the duration of a Summary task is determined by its detailed or lower level summary tasks and may not be entered directly, see the picture below:

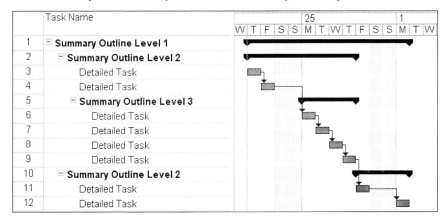

If **Control Accounts** are used and defined in a way that they span multiple WBS branches then these should be identified using either Custom Outline Codes or Custom Fields and displayed using Grouping and/or Filters. If each Control Account is defined uniquely within a WBS Branch then a Task could be used to represent a Control Account.

2.3.8   Adding the Logic Links

The logic is added to the schedule to provide the order in which the tasks must be undertaken. The logic is designated by indicating the predecessors to or the successors from each activity.

The *PMBOK® Guide* discusses the process **6.2.2 Activity Sequencing: Tools and Techniques** in detail and identifies two methods used to sequence activities:

- Precedence Diagramming Method (PDM) and

- Arrow Diagramming (ADM)

Most current project planning and scheduling software is PDM including Microsoft Project. A PDM diagram may be created using the Microsoft Project 2003 Network Diagramming Method.

The *PMBOK® Guide* section **6.2.2.4 Dependency Determination** discusses **Mandatory dependencies**, **Discretionary dependencies** and **External dependencies**.

Mandatory dependencies are also known as **Hard Logic** and are relationships between activities that may be not be broken. For example a hole has to be dug before it is filled with concrete or a computer delivered before software is loaded onto it.

Discretionary dependencies also know as Sequencing Logic are used to order activities but these relationships may be changed when the plan is changed. For example if there are five holes to be excavated and only one machine available, or 5 computers to be assembled and one person available to work on them, then the order of these tasks could be set with sequencing logic but changed at a later date.

Both **Mandatory dependencies** and **Discretionary dependencies** may be entered into Microsoft Project 2003 as task relationships or logic links. The software does not provide a method of identifying the type of relationship as notes or codes may not be attached to relationships. A **Task Note** may be added to either the predecessor or successor task to explain the relationship.

External dependencies are usually events outside the control of the project team that impact on the schedule. An example would be the availability of a site to start work. These are usually represented in Microsoft Project by a Milestone which has a constraint applied to it. This topic will be discussed in more detail in the next paragraph.

The software will calculate the start and finish dates for each task and the end date of the project based on the start date of the project, the logic amongst the tasks, any **Leads** or **Lags** applied to the logic and durations of the tasks. The picture below shows the effect of a lead and lag on the start of a successor task:

	Task Name		25		1	
		W T F S S	M T W T F S S	M T W		
1	Predessor Task					
2	Successor Task With a 3 Day Lag					
3						
4	Predessor Task					
5	Successor Task With a 3 Day Lead					

It is good practice to create a **Closed Network** with the logic. All tasks have one or more predecessors and one or more successors in a **Closed Network** except:

- One or more project start milestones or first task which has no predecessors, and

- One or more finish milestones or finish tasks which has no successors.

The project's logic must not loop back on itself. Looping would occur if the logic were stated that A preceded B, B preceded C, and C preceded A. That's not a logical project situation and will cause an error comment to be generated by the software during network calculations.

Thus, when the logic is correctly applied, a delay to a task will delay all its successor tasks and delay the project end date when there is insufficient spare slippage time to accommodate the delay. This spare time is normally called **Float** but Microsoft Project uses the term **Slack**. The picture below shows Product 4 has **2 days Float**

2.3.9   Constraints

External dependencies are applied to a schedule using **Constraints** and these may be model the impact of events outside the logical sequence of tasks. A constraint would be imposed to specific dates such as the availability of a facility to start work or the required completion date of a project. Constraints should be cross-referenced to the supporting documentation such as Milestone Dates from contract documentation. Typical examples of constraints would be:

- **Start No Earlier Than** for the availability of a site or building, and

- **Finish No Later Than** for the date that a product must be delivered by.

2.3.10 Scheduling the Project

The software calculates the shortest time in which the project may be completed. Unstatused tasks without logic or a constraint will be scheduled to start at the Project Start Date.

Scheduling the project will also identify the **Critical Path(s)**. The Critical Path(s) is the chain(s) of tasks that takes the longest time to accomplish. This chain defines the Earliest Finish date of the project. The calculated completion date depends on the critical tasks starting and finishing on time. If any of them are delayed, the whole project will be delayed.

Tasks that may be delayed without affecting the project end date have **Float**.

Total Float is the amount of time a task may be delayed without delaying the project end date. The delay of a task with a positive Total Float value may delay other tasks with positive Total Float but will not delay the end date of the project unless the delay is greater than the Total Float. The delay of any task with a zero Total Float value (and is, therefore, on the **Critical Path)** will delay other subsequent tasks with zero Total Float and extend the end date of the project.

Free Float is the amount of time a task may be delayed without delaying the start date of any of its immediate successor tasks.

Product 2 may be delayed 4 days before it will delay Product 5 (work will not take place over the weekend) therefore has 4 days Total Float. Product 2 may be delayed 6 days before it will delay the end of the project and therefore has 6 days Total Float.

2.3.11 Formatting the Display – Views, Tables and Filters

There are tools to manipulate and display the tasks to suit the project reporting requirements to create Programme, Portfolio, Project, Work Package, Control Account and any other type of report defined in the Communications Plan. These functions are covered in the **Chapter 12 FILTERS** and **Chapter 13 VIEWS, TABLES AND DETAILS.**

2.3.12 Printing and Reports

There are software features that allow you to present the information in a clear and concise manner to communicate the requirements to all project members. These functions are covered in **Chapter 14 PRINTING AND REPORTS.**

Section **6.5.3 Schedule Development: Outputs** explains different outputs that should be considered and Microsoft Project will manage all the types listed.

2.3.13 Issuing and Optimizing the Schedule

All members of the project team should review the project plan in an attempt to:
- Optimize the process and methods employed, and
- Gain consensus among team members as to the project's logic, task durations, and if required the Work Breakdown Structure.

Correspondence should be used to communicate expectations of team members while providing each with the opportunity to contribute to the schedule and further improve the outcome.

Techniques for schedule optimization will be discussed later in this chapter.

2.4   Level 2 – Monitoring Progress Without Resources

Many projects are managed utilizing un-resourced schedules which are updated on a regular basis to manage the only timing elements of a project. The resource and cost aspects of the project are managed outside the scheduling software. Resource loading a schedule should be considered when there are a limited number of resources available and the schedule is complex.

The *PMBOK® Guide* discusses updating the schedule and managing changes in the section **6.6 Schedule Control**.

Typically a schedule should be updated or statused between 10 and 20 times in its life. When the timing aspects of a schedule are important then the schedule should be statused more frequently and the final forecast completion date reviewed more regularly.

Time lost at the start of a project is often harder to catch up than later on in the project life. For example if a Board of Management meets once a month and a project submission misses this approval date then a month will be lost and may not be easily recovered. Where as during the construction of a project it is often possible to work longer hours or employ more people to speed up the progress of a project. It is therefore recommended that more detail is entered in a schedule for the first few periods and the schedule should be reviewed more often at the start of a project than during the progress of a project.

Some people just enter a percent complete against tasks as the wok progresses. They do not adjust the actual start and actual finish dates of complete tasks or the actual start and finish dates of in-progress tasks. This process may result in completed activities being scheduled in the future or incomplete task in the past which is not logical. As a result of using this process the project progress may be identified, however the following important information is NOT calculated or recorded:

- The revised end date of the project, which calculates how far ahead or behind the project is from the plan.

- The difference in the planned duration, as recorded in the Baseline, and the Actual Duration of completed tasks. This gives an objective measurement of the productivity and may be used to forecast the revised duration of similar unstarted tasks.

- The progress of an in-progress task may be very slow and the percent complete may be used to recalculate the finish date based on progress to date.

- The recording of delays resulting of other organizations actions or in-actions that may support an extension of time claim.

2.4.1   Setting the Baseline

A Baseline is a copy of an optimized and agreed-to plan and is used for measuring progress and monitoring change. The software can record the baseline dates of each activity and these dates are used to compare actual progress against the plan during the life of the project. These planned dates are stored in the **Baseline Date** fields.

Microsoft Project will store multiple baselines which allows for a schedule to be re-baselined after a major change.

2.4.2   Tracking Progress

The schedule should be **Statused** (updated or progressed) on a regular basis and progress is recorded at a point in time.

Whatever the frequency chosen for statusing, you will have to collect the following task information in order to status a schedule:

- Actual Start Dates of tasks that have begun, whether they were planned to start or not,

- Percentage Complete and Remaining Duration or Expected Finish date for started, but incomplete tasks,

- Actual Finish Dates for completed tasks and

- Any revisions to tasks that have not started.

The schedule may be statused after this information has been collected, and then the recorded progress is compared to the **Baseline Dates**.

At this point, it may be necessary to further optimize the schedule to meet the required end date by discussing the schedule with the appropriate project team members. The date as of when progress is reported is commonly known as the **Data Date** or **Status Date** or **Update Date** or **Time Now**. The **Data Date** is **NOT** the date that the report is printed out but rather the date that reflects when the status information was gathered.

2.4.3   Managing Changes

Managing changes in a schedule is often difficult and the processes proposed for a project should be documented in the Project Management Plan.

Changes that affect a project schedule need to be recorded in the schedule and their affects on the project finish date quantified and if required appropriate changes made to the schedule to bring the project back on track. Here are some techniques that may be applied.

- Any new work should be inserted into the schedule as new task(s).

- The increase in the scope of an existing task that results in an increase in the duration of that task is often better represented as a new task underneath the old task with a description indicating that it is increased scope.

- A Text column may be used to tag tasks, for example recording the Change Number from the Change Log, and then all changes may be filtered out or multiple tasks associated with one change grouped together under one heading.

- All client inputs, such as the availability of equipment or sites, should be included in the schedule as milestones. When these are delayed then the schedule should be adjusted.

- All client tasks, such as approval of drawings and specifications, should be included in the schedule as tasks. When these are delayed then the schedule should be adjusted.

A new contract finish date resulting from client scope changes and claimable project delays may be calculated by taking an unprogressed schedule and using the following techniques:

- Adding new tasks to the schedule to represent new scope,

- Making the appropriate calendar with a non-work periods where work could not be undertaken due to weather and/or industrial actions in the calendar. Some times more than one calendar may be required. For example:

> ➢ Crane work may be assigned a wind calendar and when the weather does not permit lifting by crane this calendar is edited.
> ➢ Earthworks may be assigned a wet condition calendar and when the ground is too wet to operate this calendar is edited.
> ➢ General construction work may have an inclement weather calendar so when it is too hot, cold or it is raining or snowing then this calendar is edited.
> ➢ Software testing could have its own calendar and when there is not software available to test the calendar is edited.
>
> Microsoft Project does not allow notes to be made against calendar days so this information needs to be documented elsewhere.

- Deleting task that are removed from the scope.

- Delaying Client deliverable Milestones to reflect when they actually happened.

The final calculated end date of the unprogressed schedule with the changes added is then:

- Compared to the current progressed schedule and the end dates to calculate how late or early the project is and

- Compared to the original baseline to calculate an Extension of Time Claim or value of liquidated damages.

2.4.4 Performance Measurement and Reporting

There are less parameters that may be measured in an un-resourced schedule than a resourced schedule. Typically the following comparisons may be made with an un-resourced schedule:

- The Variance between the Baseline dates and the Current Schedule dates may be compared which gives an indication of how far behind or ahead of planned progress the schedule is.

- The Actual Duration of in-progress and completed tasks may be compared to the Baseline Duration which gives an indication of actual productivity against planned. This productivity may be applied to future unstarted or in-progress tasks to reforecast the finish date of the schedule.

- Buffer of Contingent Time tasks may be adjusted in duration to bring the project back on schedule and the consumption of Buffer time may be monitored.

2.4.5 Corrective Action

At this point in time it may be necessary to take corrective action to bring the schedule back on time. There are some suggestions for corrective actions at the end of **Chapter 15 – TRACKING PROGRESS**.

2.5   Level 3 – Scheduling With Resources

When scheduling with resources there are several elements that may be planned:

- Resources requirements in terms of the total number of hours, days or quantity that people, equipment or material are required to complete a project.

- The time phased requirement of resources may then be developed from the above information.

- The cost of a project that may be generated from a rate applied to a resources or fixed costs assigned to tasks.

- The cash flow of a project may be created using resources with rates of assigning fixed costs to tasks.

The following philosophies may be considered for the use of resources with planning and scheduling software:

- Only key resources are entered into a schedule to forecast the projects future requirements. These may be entered at Skill or Trade level and not as individual people or even at Team or Crew level. This is common in construction and building project schedules, where only resources that are in short supply would be assigned to tasks.

- IT companies often assign an individual by name to each task for short to medium term planning to generate detailed assignments for each person.

- Many schedules do not have costs assigned to resources and the cost management is handled in another system.

- Some schedules have the costs assigned at summary level using the Fixed Costs function to calculate a cash flow.

The requirements for resource loading and/or costs in a schedule should be determined in the **Project Management Plan**.

2.5.1   Types of Resourced Schedule

A resourced schedule may be created for the following purposes:

- **Estimating Schedule**. This type of schedule is used for estimating the cost and duration of a project or part of a project. This type of schedule is often used for the detail costing of repeatable processes and the results of this small schedule may then be summarized to one activity in a Control Schedule. Statusing a schedule with a large number of resources may be very time consuming, however any number of resources may be assigned to each task in an estimating schedule because it is not intended to status it.

- **Control Schedule**. This type of schedule is used to control the progress of a project. In this situation the number of resources should be minimized as far as possible because when the schedule is statused each resource assignment will have to be reviewed and possibly updated. Therefore in a large schedule, with many tasks and many resources assigned to each task, the statusing of a schedule may become a very time consuming operation. In this situation the scheduler may loose sight of their primary aim, which is to forecast the project end date and possibly the Final Forecast Cost, and is in danger of becoming an expensive time recording system and thus unable to provide essential forecasts.

2.5.2   Creating and Using Resources

The *PMBOK® Guide* discusses resources in section **6.3 Activity Resource Estimating**.

First, establish a resource pool by entering all the project resources required on the project into a table in the software. You then assign the required quantity of each resource to the tasks.

A resource in planning and scheduling software may represent an individual person, a skill or trade, individual pieces of equipment, fleets of equipment, a team or crew, material, space or funds. Each resource may have a quantity and an associated cost.

Entering a cost rate for each resource enables you to conduct a resource cost analysis such as comparing the cost of supplementing overloaded resources against the cost of extending the project deadline.

Time-phased cash flows and budgets may be produced from this resource/cost data.

2.5.3   Task Types

Tasks may be assigned a **Type**, which affects how resources are calculated. There are additional software features that enable the user to more accurately model real-life situations. These features are covered in **Chapter 18 CREATING RESOURCES**.

2.5.4   Schedule Optimization

A resourced schedule may have to be optimized before the schedule is Baselined to:

- Minimize peaks in resource requirements, or

- Provide a more favorable cash flow.

Section **6.5.2 Schedule Development: Tools & Techniques** provides guidance in techniques that may be optimized a schedule. These tools are more effective with resourced schedules as the effects of optimizing on the requirements for resources may be seen. The following techniques are discussed:

- **Schedule Compression** by "**Crashing a Schedule**" which aims to shorten a schedule with a minimum increase in cost. This is often achieved by using Leads on relationships.

- **Schedule Compression** by "**Fast Tracking**" which involves undertaking work in parallel that is normally executed in series. This often results in a high amount of risk and rework.

- **Critical Chain Method** which is project scheduling and management methodology based on concepts from the **Theory of Constraints** developed by **Eliyahu Goldratt**. The principals of Critical Chain scheduling are:
  - Average task durations are used for all tasks,
  - Scheduling is calculated from the date the project is to be delivered backwards in time, thus all work is initially scheduled As Late As Possible, and the Earliest Project Start Date is calculated,
  - **Buffer** tasks (contingent time) are inserted into the plan at strategic points,
  - The schedule is resource optimized, and
  - The consumption of the Buffer time is managed and the duration of Buffer tasks adjusted (normally reduced) to keep the project delivery on time.

Some software packages have a Critical Chain scheduling mode. Microsoft Project 2003 does not but Critical Chain scheduling may be executed using it.

2.6   Level 4 – Monitoring Progress of a Resourced Schedule

The **Project Plan** should clearly document what resources are to be entered into the schedule and the output required from the schedule. The resources should be entered into the schedule in a way that will provide data or reports to satisfy the reporting requirements. The method that is used to enter resources should be aligned to the **Communication Plan** reporting requirements; thus for example if costs are not entered into a schedule then a cash flow may not be created. These reporting requirements will determine:

- What information will be required to be entered into the schedule

- How the calculation Options are set which in turn determines

- How the Actual and Remaining Work and Costs of in-progress tasks are calculated

2.6.1   Statusing Projects with Resources

There are several parameters to be considered when setting up the software options:

- Is the Actual Work to be entered into the software from a time recording system or is the Actual Work to be calculated from a % Complete entered against a task.

- Are the Actual Costs to be entered into the software from a cost recording system or is this to be calculated from the resource Unit rate and actual number of hours.

- Is the Work and Cost to complete to be calculated by the software from a % Complete of is it to be entered manually.

As more data is entered into a schedule then the longer it takes to update and check a statused schedule. Sometimes this additional effort is not justified and a simpler schedule would suffice.

Therefore when statusing a project with resources, some additional information may need to be collected:

- The quantities and/or costs spent to-date per task for each resource, and

- The quantities and/or costs required per resource to complete each task.

You may then status a resourced schedule with this data and this part of the book covers the scheduling option you will need to consider when statusing a resourced schedule.

2.7 Tools and Techniques for Scheduling

At this point, the book covers some additional software functions making creating and editing schedules simpler.

2.8 The Balance Between the Number of Activities and Resources

On large or complex schedules, you need to maintain a balance between the number of activities and the number of resources that are to be planned and tracked. As a general rule, the more activities a schedule has, the fewer resources should be created and assigned to tasks.

When you have a schedule with a large number of tasks and a large number of resources assigned to each task, you may end up in a situation where you and members of the project team are unable to understand the schedule and you are unable to maintain it. Instead of assigning individual resources such as people by name, consider using Skills or Trades, and on very large project use Crews or Teams.

This technique is not so important when you are using a schedule for estimating the direct cost of a project (by assigning costs to the resources) or if you will not be using the schedule to track a project's progress (such as a schedule that is used to support written proposals).

It is more important to minimize the number of resources in large schedules that will be updated regularly, since updating every resource assigned to each task at each schedule update is very time consuming. At this point in time you would be acting as a timekeeper updating resources and not a scheduler looking after the future of the project.

2.9 Managing Portfolios, Projects and Work Package Plans

Microsoft Project may be used for the management of Programmes, Portfolios, Projects, Phases and Work Packages. When using Microsoft Project there are several options for managing these plans and the same techniques may be applied to programmes and portfolios:

- The Project and Phase schedules could be managed as individual schedules (e.g. each has its own individual file) and the Project schedule is manually updated from the Phase schedules. This is technically the simplest to operate. The advantage of having two separate schedules is the ability of the Project Manager to provide a tight schedule, with a small Tolerances or Buffers, at Phase level, allowing the Project Manager to pressure contractors to supply Products earlier than indicated by the Project Plan. Also in this situation different people may manage each schedule.

- All Phases could all be entered into one schedule and managed as one schedule with each Phase identified say at Outline Level 1. Resourced schedules would share one resource pool. This situation is good when one person is updating all the levels of schedule.

- The Project and Phase schedules could be separate schedules and the Phase could be inserted into the Project schedule. In this Master Project and Subproject environment Resources may be shared from a Resource Pool. This process should be only attempted once a scheduler has some experience with Microsoft Project as this is not a simple process to administer and the skill level of personnel using Microsoft Project needs to be higher.

- **Microsoft Project Server** could be implemented when the project personnel are in different locations or access is required over the internet by subcontractors.

3   CREATING PROJECTS AND SETTING UP THE SOFTWARE

When using Microsoft Project 2003, ensure that you check the internet for the latest updates as some of the critical functions such as outlining did not function correctly in the original release.

There are three principal methods of creating a new project:

- Start with a blank project, or

- Use a template that contains default data and formats, or

- Open an old project and save it with a new file name.

3.1   File Types

Before creating a project file it is important that you understand the file types that Microsoft Project 2003 will open and save. Microsoft Project is compatible and will operate with the following file types:

- **Project (*.mpp)**. This is the default file format that Microsoft Project 2003, Microsoft Project 2002 and Microsoft Project 2000 uses to create and save files. This is a different format than the ***.mpp** file created by Microsoft Project 98.

- **Microsoft Project 98 (*.mpp)**. This is the format created by Microsoft Project 98.
  - ➢ Microsoft Project 98 will not open or save a **Project (*.mpp)** file, created by Microsoft Project 2000 and later.
  - ➢ Microsoft Project 2000/2/3 will open and save to a **Microsoft Project 98 (*.mpp)** file.

- **MPX (*.mpx)**. This is a text format data file created by Microsoft Project 98 and earlier versions of Microsoft Project.
  - ➢ This format may be opened by Microsoft Project 2003 but is not created by Microsoft Project 2003.
  - ➢ MPX is a format that may be imported and exported by many other project scheduling software packages.
  - ➢ Some third-party software will convert mpx files to and from Microsoft Project 2003 mpp format files. You may search the Internet for the latest available products.

- **Template (*.mpt)**. This format is used for creating project templates.

- **Project Database (*.mpd)**. This is a Microsoft Project database format that may be used for exporting data and is intended to replace the mpx format.

- **Microsoft Access Database (*.mdb)**. This is the Microsoft Access format.

- Data may be saved to (and imported from) files in the following additional formats using **File/Save**, **File/Save As** and **File/Open**:
  - ➢ Excel (*.xls)
  - ➢ Excel **Pivot Table** (save only)
  - ➢ Web page (save only) (*.html; *.htm)
  - ➢ Tab delimited text files (*.asc)
  - ➢ Comma delimited text files (*.txt)
  - ➢ Extensible Markup Language format (*.xml)

3.2   Starting Microsoft Project

When opening Microsoft Project 2003, you will be presented with a blank project that you may start working with immediately. The **Startup Task** pane shown in the picture below with a heading **Getting Started** may be displayed on the left-hand side of the screen; this may be closed by clicking on the icon ⊠ as shown below, and you may start work immediately.

Close the **Startup Task** pane by clicking here

Getting Started menu

Getting Started Pane

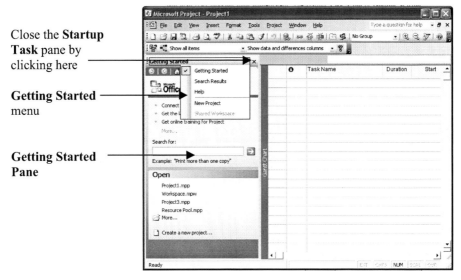

To prevent the pane titled **Getting Started** from being displayed every time Microsoft Project is opened select **Tools**, **Options…**, select the **General** tab and uncheck the **Show Startup Task pane** box.

After closing the **Getting Started** pane your screen may look like the picture below showing a pane on the left hand side titled **Tasks**, this is the called the **Project Guide**. This guide may be used to assist in the creation of project schedules.

Close the **Project Guide** by clicking here:

To prevent the **Project Guide** pane from being displayed every time Microsoft Project is opened select **Tools**, **Options…**, select the **Interface** tab and uncheck the **Display Project Guide** box.

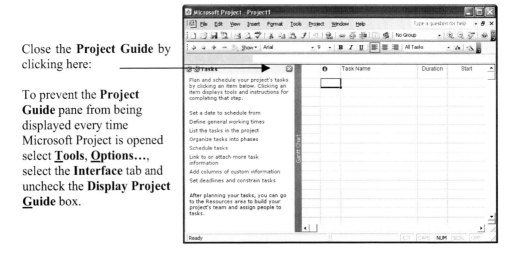

3.3   Creating a Blank Project

A blank project may be created from the **New Project** pane which is displayed by:

- Keying in **Ctrl+N**, or

- Clicking on the **New** tool bar icon, or

- You may also select **File**, **New**, or

- Selecting **New Project** from the **Startup Task** drop down menu, see picture on the previous page.

Select **Blank Project** and a new blank project will be created.

At this point the Project **Start date** is normally set in the **Project Information** form, select **Project**, **Project Information…** to open this form:

- When **Schedule from:** is set to the **Project Start Date**, which is the usual method of scheduling projects:
  - ➤ Enter the **Start date:** – This is the date before which no task will be scheduled to start.
  - ➤ The **Finish date:** – This is a calculated date and is the date of the completion of all tasks.

- When **Schedule from:** is set to the **Project Finish Date**:
  - ➤ All new tasks are set with a constraint of **As Late As Possible**, and
  - ➤ Therefore, all new tasks are scheduled before the **Project Finish Date** not after a start date.

- **Current Date:** – This field defaults to **today's date**; it represents the date today and may be changed at any time. This date has no effect on any calculations.

- **Status Date:** – This is an optional field used when statusing a project. This topic is covered in the **TRACKING PROGRESS** chapter.

- **Calendar:** – This is the project **Base** calendar that is used to calculate the durations of all tasks unless they have:
  - ➤ A resource with an edited resource calendar.
  - ➤ Assigned with a different task calendar.

- **Priority:** – This is the project priority when sharing resources over a number of projects. 1000 is highest priority and 0 the lowest.

- Click on the [Statistics...] button to open the **Project Statistics** form, which outlines statistical information about the project.

- The **Project Information** form may be set to be displayed when a new project is created by selecting **Tools**, **Options**, **General** tab and checking the **Prompt for project info for new projects** check box.

A new blank project copies default values such as the Standard Calendar from the **Global.mpt** file. The **Global.mpt** file may be edited using the **Tools**, **Organizer…** utility.

 The default Microsoft Project 2003 blank project has a Standard calendar based on 5 days per week without any holidays, which will not suit many projects. It is recommended that the **Global.mpt** Standard calendar be replaced with a project calendar that has been edited to represent your local public holidays using the **Tools**, **Organizer…** utility.

3.4 Opening an Existing Project

Another method of creating a new project is to open an existing project, saving with a new name and then modifying it. To open an existing project display the **Open** form by selecting:

- **File**, **Open**, or

- **Ctl+O**, or

- Click on the New toolbar icon

Then select the file you want to open.

The startup **Task Pane** may be used to open an existing project:

- Select **File**, **New** and this will always display the startup **Task Pane** menu,
  - Then select the **Choose project…** item under the **New from existing project** heading, or
  - Select **More projects…** item under the **Open a project** heading.

Then use **File**, **Save As** to save the file under a different name:
  - Enter a new Project Name,
  - Select in which **Current Folder** you want to save the project, and
  - Click on [Save] to save the new project.

You may now alter the contents of this existing plan to reflect the scope of your new project.

3.5 Creating a New Project from a Template

Project templates allow organizations to create project models containing default information applicable to the organization and, in particular, a calendar with the local public holidays. It is normal for organizations to create their own templates to save time when creating a new project.

An organization's **Project Management Methodology,** discussed in *PMBOK® Guide* section 4.1.2, may be built into project templates and assist in the compliance to the organization's methodology.

To create a new project from a template:
- Select **File**, **New** to open the startup **Task Pane**, there are three options for template locations:
  - ➢ **Templates on Office Online**, this will take you to a Microsoft web page through Microsoft Explorer.
  - ➢ **On my computer…**, this will allow you to open templates on your computer and is covered in the next paragraph.
  - ➢ **On my Web sites…**, this opens an Explorer style window where web site addresses may be recorded and templates from these sites used to create projects and templates saved to the sites.
- Click on the **On my computer…**, item under the **New from template** heading to open the **Templates** form to select a Microsoft template. After you have created your own template these will be available from the **General** tab.

- Select the required template from the form by double-clicking on the template icon or selecting the template by clicking on it and clicking on the ⟨ OK ⟩ button.

At this point you would normally set the Project **Start date** in the **Project Information** form, select **Project**, **Project Information…** to open this form.

3.6 Creating a Project Template

To save time when you create new projects, you should create your own templates to suit the different types of projects your organization undertakes. Create a template by saving a project, with or without tasks, in **Template, (*.mpt)** format. This template will be available when you select **File**, **New**.

This directory where user templates are saved may be changed by selecting **Tools**, **Options…**, **Save** tab.

Templates may be deleted by right-clicking to open a menu.

3.7 Saving Additional Project Information

Often additional information about a project is required to be saved with the project such as location, client and type of project. This data may be saved in the **File**, **Properties** form:

- **Hyperlink base:** This allows you to enter the path to a file or web page.

- **Save preview picture**. This saves a thumbnail sketch, which may be seen when viewing files in Windows Explorer.

3.8 File Naming Convention

It is important that a file naming convention is established in the **Project Management Plan**. This will ensure:

- That the correct schedule is being used at an point in time, and

- In the situation that litigation is a possibility then every issued copy of the schedule is preserved in electronic format and is clearly identified by an appropriate file name.

WORKSHOP 1

Creating our Project

Preamble

You are an employee of OzBuild Pty Ltd and are responsible for planning the Bid preparation required to ensure that a response to an RFQ (Request For Quote) from Wilson Bedding is submitted on time.

While short-listed, you have been advised that the RFQ will not be available prior to December 2006.

Note: The date format will be displayed according to a combination of your system default settings and the Microsoft Project Options settings. You may adjust your date format under the system Control Panel, Regional and Language Options and the Microsoft Project settings in the Options form, which is covered in the **OPTIONS** chapter.

Assignment

1. Create a new project and set the **Start date:** to **Mon 04 Dec 06** with the **Project**, **Project Information...** form but do not edit the **Current date**. Press the **OK** button to save the input data.

Note: Completed workshops may be downloaded from the Eastwood Harris web site at www.eh.com.au.

continued over...

---

2.   Add the following project information in the **File**, **Properties** form.

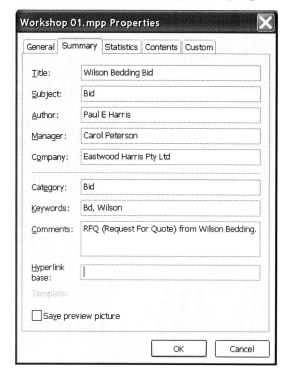

3.   **Save** your project as **OzBuild Bid**.

4 NAVIGATING AROUND THE SCREEN

4.1 *Identify the Parts of the Project Screen*

After a blank project has been created from a template, the default Microsoft Project 2003 screen will look like this:

Microsoft Project 2003 has a Windows-style menu system with a typical Windows look-and-feel.

- The project name is displayed after **Microsoft Project** at the top of the left-hand side of the screen.

- The drop-down menus are just below the project name.

- The toolbars are displayed below the menu.

- The left-hand side of the line underneath the toolbars is the **Entry Bar** and **Edit Box**. Any editable data may be edited in the **Edit Box** or directly in the field.

The ▨ and ▨ icons are displayed on the left of the **Edit Box** only when performing editing, and may used for accepting and not accepting data changes that are made from within the edit box.

- The main display has the **Bar Chart** on the right-hand side, with the **Timescale** above, and the **Data Columns** on the left-hand side with their column titles above them. The divider between the two areas may be dragged from side to side by holding down the left mouse button.

- The **View Bar** is designed for the users to select the various chart views and is located on the far left of the screen, this may be hidden or displayed by:
  - ➢ Selecting **View**, **View Bar**, or
  - ➢ Holding the mouse pointer over the **View Bar**, right-clicking to display a menu, and selecting **View Bar**.

- The horizontal **Scroll Bars** are at the bottom of the screen and the **Status Bar** is below the **Scroll Bars**. The vertical **Scroll Bar** is at the right-hand side of the screen.

4.2   Customizing the Screen

The screen may be customized in a number of ways to suit your preferences. The toolbars and menu bar may be moved around the screen by holding down the right mouse button and dragging them to a new position on the screen.

4.2.1   Toolbars

Toolbars will not be covered in detail but significant productivity improvements may be made by ensuring that functions of frequent use are available on a toolbar.

- There are many built-in toolbars in Microsoft Project 2003. These may be displayed or hidden by:
  - ➢ Using the command **View**, **Toolbar** or **Tools**, **Customize**, **Toolbars…** and selecting the **Toolbar** tab, then checking or un-checking the required boxes to display or hide the toolbars.
  - ➢ Right-clicking the mouse in the toolbar area to display a Toolbar menu.

- Icons may be added to a bar by selecting **Tools**, **Customize**, **Toolbars…**, **Commands** tab. **Toolbar Icons** may be selected from the dialog box and dragged onto any toolbar.

- Icons may be removed from the toolbars when the **Customize** (Toolbar) form is open by holding down the left mouse button on the icon and dragging them off the toolbar.

- Icons may be reset to default by selecting **Tools**, **Customize**, **Toolbars…**, selecting the **Toolbar** tab and clicking on ⬚ Reset… ⬚.

- Other toolbar display options are found under **Tools**, **Customize**, **Toolbars…** and then selecting the **Options** tab.

4.2.2   Menu Bar

The **Menu Bar** display options are found under **Tools**, **Customize**, **Toolbars…** and then selecting the **Options** tab.

4.3 Setting up the Options

The basic parameters of the software must be configured so it will operate the way you desire. In order for the software to operate and/or calculate the way you want, some of the defaults must be turned on, or off, or changed. These configuration items may be found under **Tools**, **Options…**.

We will discuss some of the more important options now. All the Options are discussed in the **OPTIONS** chapter. Select **Tools**, **Options…** to display the **Options** form.

Select the **View** tab:

- **Date format:** This is used to select the display style of the dates for all projects. The date format will be displayed according to a combination of your system default settings and the Microsoft Project 2003 Options settings. You may adjust your date format under the system Control Panel, Regional and Language Options and the Microsoft Project 2003 settings in the Options form, which are covered in the **OPTIONS** chapter.

 On international projects, to avoid the confusion between the numerical US date style, (mmddyy) and the numerical European date style, (ddmmyy) you should consider adopting the ddmmmyy style, **28 Jan '02** or mmddyy style, **Jan 30 '00**. For example in the United States 020703 is read as 07 Feb 03 and in many other countries as 02 Jul 03.

- Select the Schedule tab:

- **Duration is entered in:** – This option specifies the format in which durations are entered via the keyboard. If **Day** is selected as the default, then duration of 2 days is entered as 2 (without the d) and a 2-hour duration should be entered as 2h, and vice versa if **Hours** are selected as **Default type**.

The settings above are the setting normally used by the author as a default and are changed as required.

4.4   Splitting the Screen Views and Details Forms

The screen may be split horizontally into two panes. A different **View** may be displayed in each pane. This is termed **Dual-Pane view**. To open or close the dual-pane view:

- Select <u>W</u>indow, <u>S</u>plit or <u>W</u>indow, Remove <u>S</u>plit, or

- Grab the horizontal dividing bar at the bottom of the screen (see the picture in paragraph 4.1) by holding down the left mouse button and drag the line to resize the panes.

- Right-click in the right-hand side of the top pane and you will, in most views, be able to display a menu to open or remove the split.

- Double-click the dividing line or dragging it also removes or opens the split window.

Active
pane has
dark blue
band

Grab this
line with
the mouse
to split the
screen

A pane needs to be **Active** before menu items pertaining to that pane become available. A dark blue band (with the standard Windows color scheme) on the left-hand side is displayed in the **Active Pane**.

The menu options will often change when different **Views** are selected in a pane.

A **Pane** is made **Active** just by:

- Clicking anywhere in the pane, or

- Pressing **F6** to swap active panes.

Some **Views** displayed in **Panes** have further options for displaying data. These are titled **Details** forms. The **Details** forms may be selected, when available, by:

- Making the pane active, then

- Selecting:
  - ➢ **Format**, **Details**, or
  - ➢ Right-clicking in the right-hand side of the screen and clicking the required form.

4.5 *Right-clicking with the Mouse*

It is very important that you become used to using the right-click function of the mouse as this is often a quicker way of operating the software than using the menus. The right-click will normally display a menu, which is often different depending on the displayed View and which pane is the Active Pane. It is advised that you experiment with each view to become familiar with the menus.

WORKSHOP 2

Setting your Project Options

Preamble

For control purposes it is expected that all tasks will be entered in days.

Assignment

1. Open the **Project Options** form and click on each tab and familiarize yourself with the forms. Select **Tools**, **Options...** and set your options as follows:

   ➤ Select **View** tab, set the **Date format** to:
   1. "**ddmmmyy**" i.e. 31 Jan '00, or
   2. "**mmmddyy**" i.e. Jan 31 '00.

   The available date format will depend on your system settings.

   ➤ Select the **Schedule** tab and set your options as per below:

   ➤ Press **OK** to commit the changes.

2. Hide and display the **Standard** and **Formatting** toolbars using the **View**, **Toolbars** menu.

3. Experiment by dragging the toolbars around the screen with your mouse.

4. Hide and display the **View** bar.

5. Split the the screen into two panes by right-clicking with the mouse in the right-hand side of the screen, and selecting **Split** from the menu.

6. Activate the lower pane by clicking in it; note the highlighted bar on the left-hand side of the screen has moved from the top pane to the bottom pane.

7. Activate the upper pane, by clicking in it.

8. Resize the panes by dragging the Split screen bar.

9. Close the split screen using the **Window** menu command.

10. Split the screen by right-clicking.

11. Save your **OzBuild Bid** Project.

5   DEFINING CALENDARS

The finish date (and time) of a task is calculated from the start date (and time) plus the duration over the calendar associated with the task. Therefore, a five-day duration task that starts at the start of the workday on a Wednesday, and is associated with a five-day workweek calendar (with Saturday and Sunday as non-work days) will finish at the end of the workday on the following Tuesday.

Duration	17 Oct '05							24 Oct '05					
	S	M	T	W	T	F	S	S	M	T	W	T	F	S
5 days														

Microsoft Project 2003 is supplied with three calendars, which are termed **Base Calendar**s:

- **Standard** – This calendar is 5 days per week, 8 hours per day.

- **24 Hour** – This calendar is 7 days per week and 24 hours per day.

- **Night shift** – This calendar is 7 days per week and 8 hours per day during the night.

You may create new or edit existing Base Calendars to reflect your project requirements, such as adding holidays or additional workdays or adjusting work times. For example, some tasks may have a 5-day per week calendar and some may have a 7-day per week calendar.

A **Base Calendar** is assigned to each project. Microsoft Project 2003 also uses the term **Project Calendar** to describe this calendar. By default all un-resourced tasks use the **Project Calendar** to calculate the end date of the task.

A **Task Calendar** is a calendar assigned to one or more tasks to reflect the unique timing requirements of these tasks, such as a 4 days working week or a 10-hour day.

A **Resource Calendar** reflects the availability of individual resources and would reflect when a person is unavailable such as holidays.

This chapter will cover the following topics:

Topic	Menu Command
• Assigning a base calendar to a project	**Project, Project Information...**
• Editing a calendar's working days	**Tools, Change Working Time...**
• Creating a new calendar	**Tools, Change Working Time..., New...**
• Renaming an existing calendar	**Tools, Organizer...**, **Calendars** tab, **Rename...**
• Deleting a calendar	**Tools, Organizer...**, **Calendars** tab, **Delete**
• Copying a calendar to Global.mpt for use in future projects	**Tools, Organizer...**, **Calendars** tab, **Copy >>**
• Copying calendars between projects	**Tools, Organizer...**, **Calendars** tab, **Copy >>**

5.1 Calendars & the PMBOK® Guide

The *PMBOK® Guide* discusses calendars in section **6.4 Activity Duration Estimating**. It mentions both a Project and Resource calendars but not Task calendars. Most planning and scheduling software, including Microsoft Project, allow Tasks to be assigned different Task calendars and these are used when:

- Resources are not assigned to tasks but the tasks require different calendars, or

- When all resources assigned to a task use the same calendar and individual resource calendars are not required.

5.2 Assigning a Calendar to a Project

A new project is assigned by default the **Standard** calendar as the **Project Calendar** when it is created. The **Project Calendar** is changed using the **Project Information** form, which is opened by selecting:

- **Project**, **Project Information…**, and

- The alternative calendar from the **Calendar:** drop-down box:

The **Project Calendar** is identified in the **Change Working Time** form as the calendar with **(Project Calendar)** written after the name. This form is covered in the next paragraph.

When a **Project Calendar** is changed or edited, the end date of all tasks assigned with the **Project Calendar** will be recalculated based on the new calendar. This may make a considerable difference to your project schedule dates.

5.3 Editing Calendar Working Days

To edit a calendar, select **Tools**, **Change Working Time...** to open the **Change Working Time** form:

- To make **Nonwork Days** into **Work Days**, highlight the day(s) you want to edit by:
  - ➤ Click on an individual day, or
  - ➤ Ctrl-click to select multiple days, or
  - ➤ Click and drag to select multiple days, or
  - ➤ Click on a column or columns of days by clicking the day of the week box, which is located below the month and year.
  - ➤ Then click on the **Nonworking time** radio button to make these days NonWorking.
- To make **Work Days** into **Nonwork Days**, highlight the day(s) you want to edit as described in the paragraph above and then click on the **Nondefault working time** radio button to make these days working days.

5.4 Adjusting Working Hours

To adjust the working hours of one or more days:

- Open the **Change Working Time** form,

- Highlight the days you want to edit, and

- Edit the working hours in the **From:** and **To:** section on the right-hand side of the screen.

The form below shows how three 7-hour shifts are entered with one shift (the first and fourth entries in the **From:** & **To:** mini-table) spanning midnight and therefore having two entries:

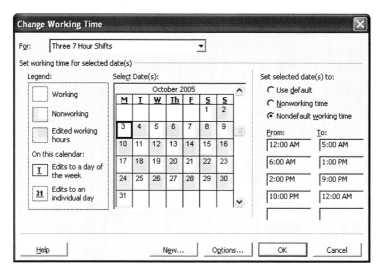

5.5   Creating a New Calendar

Select **Tools**, **Change Working Time...**, to open the **Change Working Time** form and click on the [New...] button to open the **Create New Base Calendar** form:

- To create a new calendar, click on the **Create new base calendar** radio button which will be a copy of the Global.mpt base calendar, type in the new calendar name in the **Name:** box and click on the [OK] button to create it, or

- To copy an existing calendar, click on the **Make a copy of** radio button and select the calendar you want to copy from the drop-down box and type in the new calendar name.

5.6   Renaming a Calendar

To rename a calendar:

- Select **Tools**, **Organizer…**, and select the **Calendars** tab.

- Highlight the calendar you want to rename and click on the ⬚Rename… button to open the **Rename** form and type in the new name.

5.7   Deleting a Calendar

To delete a calendar:

- Select **Tools**, **Organizer…**, and select the **Calendars** tab.

- Highlight the calendar you want to delete and click on the ⬚Delete… button.

-

5.8   Copying a Base Calendar to Global.mpt for use in Future Projects

Global.mpt is the default project template and all new projects copy their default settings from the Global.mpt. Once you have set up a calendar with all the holidays for your location or business, it is suggested that you copy it to the Global.mpt. This calendar will then be available in all new schedules.

- Select **Tools**, **Organizer…**, and select the **Calendars** tab.

- Select the **Standard** calendar from your project and click on the ⬚<< Copy button.

5.9 Copying Calendars Between Projects

To copy a calendar between projects:

- Open both projects,

- Select **Tools**, **Organizer…**, and select the **Calendars** tab,

- From the drop-down boxes at the bottom of the tab under Calendars available in: select the projects that you want to copy to and from, and

- Select the calendar you want to copy and click on the [<< Copy] button.

5.10 Resource Calendars

Individual Resources are allocated a Base Calendar when they are created. The resource Base Calendar may be changed and edited to reflect the availability of the resource. This feature is covered in the **CREATING RESOURCES** chapter.

5.11 Selecting Dates

Microsoft Project 2003 has a function to enable the user to quickly scroll though days, months and years when editing dates from a column. A calendar form may be displayed by clicking on a date cell with the mouse pointer:

- To change the day, click on the required day.

- To change month either:

  ➢ Scroll a month at a time by clicking on the arrows on the top left hand or top right hand side of the form, or

  ➢ Click on the month at the top of the form and a drop down list will be displayed to allow any month of the year to be selected.

- To change the year, click on the year in the top of the form and scrolling arrows will be displayed allowing scrolling one year at a time.

 When a date is selected from a column Microsoft Project 2003 will set a constraint without informing the user. This may result in an incorrect constraint being set.

WORKSHOP 3

Maintaining the Calendars

Preamble

The normal working week at OzBuild Pty Ltd is Monday to Friday, 8 hours per day excluding Public Holidays. The installation staff works Monday to Saturday, 8 hours per day.

Assignment

The company observes the following Australian holidays:

	2005	2006	2007	2008
New Years Day	3 January*	2 January*	1 January	1 January
Good Friday	25 March	14 April	6 April	21 March
Easter	28 March	17 April	9 April	24 March
Christmas Day	26 December*	25 December	25 December	25 December
Boxing Day	27 December*	26 December	26 December	26 December

* These holidays occur on a weekend and the dates in the table above have been moved to the next weekday.

Boxing Day is a religious holiday, the day after Christmas, celebrated in many countries.

Assignment

1. Edit the **Standard Calendar** to ensure that only the holidays in 2006 and 2007 above are present.

2. Create a new calendar titled **6 Day Working Week** for the 6-day week by:

   ➤ Copying the **Standard (Project Calendar)**, and then

   ➤ Clicking on the **S** for Saturday in the **Change Working Time** form and then clicking on the **Nondefault working time** radio button to make all Saturdays work days.

3. Save your **OzBuild Bid** project.

6   ADDING TASKS

It is appreciated that the Work Breakdown Structure would normally be created before the activities required to deliver the WBS deliverables are developed. It is simpler to demonstrate adding Activities first, in this chapter, and creating the WBS using Outlining second, in the next chapter. Once these skills are understood then either may be entered first.

Activities, should be well-defined, measurable pieces of work with a measurable outcome. Task descriptions containing only nouns such as "Specification" have confusing meanings. Does this mean Draft, Review, Approve, Issue, or all of these?

Adequate task descriptions always have a verb-noun structure to them. A more appropriate task description would be "Specification Approved" or "Specification Issued" The limit for task names is 255 characters, but try to keep task descriptions meaningful yet short and concise so they are easier to print.

When tasks are created they may be organized under a Summary task which would often represent a WBS Component and have logic added to calculate their start and finish dates. Summary or Detailed tasks may be created first and logic added once the relevant tasks have been created.

The *PMBOK® Guide* covers this topic under section **6.1 Activity Definition**.

This chapter will cover the following topics:

Topic	Menu Command
• **Adding New Tasks**	Select a line in the schedule and strike the **Ins** (**Insert Key**) or click on a blank line.
• **Reordering** tasks	Select and drag the task(s) or cut and paste into the required location.
• **Copying** tasks in Microsoft Project 2003	Select the tasks and copy & paste to the required location.
• **Copying** tasks from other Programs	Display the required columns and paste the data.
• **Elapsed** duration tasks	Type "e" after the duration & before the Units, e.g. 5edays.
• **Milestones**	Assign a zero duration, or Check the **Mark task as milestone** box on the **Advanced** tab in the **Task Information** form.
• **Task Information** form	Double-click anywhere on the task line, or Highlight the task line click on the ⬛ button.
• Assigning **Calendars** to tasks	Set a task calendar in the **Advanced** tab in the **Task Information** form or display the **Task Calendar** column.

6.1 Adding New Tasks

There are several methods of adding a task.

Method 1

The first and easiest is to:

- Click on the first blank line under the title **Task Name** and type the task description.

- The duration of the new task is completed with a default duration, this may have a "?" after to indicate it has been assigned an **Estimated Duration**. Overtype the default duration with the required duration task. The option of assigning and/or displaying a new task with an **Estimated Duration** is controlled in the **Schedule** tab of the **Options** form by checking or un-checking **New tasks have estimated durations**.

	❶	Task Name	Duration	Start	Finish	17 Oct '05							24 Oct '05				
						S	S	M	T	W	T	F	S	S	M	T	W	T	F
1		First Task	1 day?	Wed 19/10/05	Wed 19/10/05					■							

- Click into the second row and enter a second Task Name. A sequential **Task Number**, starting from "**1**" will be created in the column to the left of the **Task Name**.

	❶	Task Name	Duration	Start	Finish	17 Oct '05							24 Oct '05				
						S	S	M	T	W	T	F	S	S	M	T	W	T	F
1		First Task	5 days	Wed 19/10/05	Tue 25/10/05					▓▓▓▓							
2		Second Task	1 day?	Wed 19/10/05	Wed 19/10/05					▓							

The task **Start** and **Finish** dates will be calculated from the **Project Start Date** and the task duration. This information is displayed in the **Start** and **Finish** columns.

Method 2

The second method of adding a task, which may be used for inserting a task between two other tasks is to highlight a task where you want to insert a new task, the highlighted task will be moved down and:

- Select **I**nsert, **N**ew Task, or

- Press the **Insert Key** on the keyboard, or

- Highlight the entire task row by clicking on the Task ID, then right-click and select **N**ew **task** from the sub-menu.

	❶	Task Name	Duration	Start	Finish	17 Oct '05							24 Oct '05				
						S	S	M	T	W	T	F	S	S	M	T	W	T	F
1		First Task	5 days	Wed 19/10/05	Tue 25/10/05					▓▓▓▓							
2		Inserted Task	3 days	Wed 19/10/05	Fri 21/10/05					▓▓							
3		Second Task	2 days	Wed 19/10/05	Thu 20/10/05					▓							

 Do not type in a Start or Finish date into the **Start** or **Finish** column unless you want to set a constraint, which overrides the logic. Microsoft Project 2003 is programmed to set an Early Constraint when dates are typed into these columns and there is no warning message that these constraints have been set, except when using Windows XP and a Graphical Indicator or Smart Tag that will warn you that constrain has been set.

6.2   Reordering Tasks by Dragging

You may move one or more tasks up or down the schedule by:

- Highlighting any one or more adjacent tasks by using the Task ID column; this will ensure you have selected the whole task and not just cells of the task,

- Moving the cursor to the top line of the selected tasks until it changes to an ⟨icon⟩ icon,

- Then left-clicking and holding down the mouse to drag the row up or down. A gray line will indicate where the tasks will be inserted.

The tasks will be renumbered when in their new location.

6.3   Copying Tasks in Microsoft Project 2003

Tasks may also be copied from another project or copied from within the same project using the normal Windows commands, **Copy** and **Paste**, by using the menu commands **Edit**, **Copy Task** and **Edit**, **Paste** or **Ctrl+C** and **Ctrl+V**.

You may also copy one or more adjacent tasks by using the **Ctrl Key** and dragging as follows:

- Select the whole task or tasks, not just a cell,

- Hold down the **Ctrl Key**, and

- Drag the tasks to the location you want to insert them. This will create a copy of the original tasks.

6.4   Copying Tasks from other Programs

Task data may be copied to and from, or updated from other programs such as Excel, by cutting and pasting. The columns and rows in your spreadsheet will need to be formatted in the same way as in your schedule before they may be pasted into your schedule. It is recommended that you first display the data that you want to import or update in your schedule. If you have no tasks then create a dummy task and data, then copy and paste this dummy data into your spreadsheet, update the data and paste it back into the schedule. The data headings are not brought across from the schedule; therefore it is also recommended that you type the headings into the spreadsheet above the imported data, which will assist you in typing the data in the correct columns.

When you copy and paste dates into the schedule, you may find that activities are assigned constraints, which you may not desire. It is recommended that you display the **Indicators** column, which will show an icon if a constraint has been applied.

6.5 Milestones

A Milestone normally has a zero duration and is used to mark the start or finish of a major event. A Task is assigned a zero duration to create a milestone and is then normally displayed in the bar chart with a "♦".

The *PMBOK® Guide* discusses **Milestone lists** in section 6.1.3.3 and **Milestone charts** in section 6.5.3. These are extracts from a schedule usually created using filters, showing the key milestones of a project. It is considered good practice check a contract for all contractual milestones and ensure all these Milestones are listed in the contract schedule.

Microsoft Project 2003 also has the ability to display a task with a non-zero duration as a Milestone as follows:

- Highlight the task with a duration that you want to be a milestone,

- Open the **Task Information** form by double-clicking on the task,

- Select the **Advanced** tab, and

- Click the **Mark task as milestone** check box.

	❶	Task Name	Duration	Start	Finish	17 Oct '05 S M T W T F S S	24 Oct '05 M T W T
1		First Task	5 days	Wed 19/10/05	Tue 25/10/05		
2		Inserted Task	3 days	Wed 19/10/05	Fri 21/10/05		
3		Second Task	2 days	Wed 19/10/05	Thu 20/10/05		
4		Milestone	0 days	Wed 19/10/05	Wed 19/10/05	♦ 19/10	
5		Milestone with Duration	4 days	Wed 19/10/05	Mon 24/10/05	♦ 19/10	

Microsoft Project 2003 does not allow the user to assign a Milestone as a **Start Milestone** or a **Finish Milestone**. Therefore a Milestone without a predecessor is automatically set as a Start Milestone and commences at the start of a work period, e.g. at 8:00am in the morning and is set as a Finish Milestone when assigned a predecessor and scheduled at the end of a work period, e.g. at 5:00pm.

6.6 Elapsed Durations

A task may be assigned an **Elapsed** duration. The task will ignore all calendars and the task will take place 24 hours a day and 7 days per week. A 24-hour, 7-day/week calendar does not need to be created for these tasks. This is useful for tasks such as curing concrete.

To enter an elapsed duration, type an "e" between the duration and units. The example below shows the difference between a 7-**Elapsed Day** task and a 7-day task on a **Standard** (5 day/week) calendar.

	❶	Task Name	Duration	17 Oct '05 S M T W T F S S	24 Oct '05 M T W T F S
1		7 Day task with Elapsed Duration	7 edays		
2		7 Day Task	7 days		

6.7 Task Information Form

The Task Information form may be opened by double-clicking on a task line or by clicking on the [button icon] button when the task is highlighted. You are able to make changes to a number of task parameters from this form. Once the form is open, it is not possible to move to another task without closing the form. There are five tabs on the form:

- **General** – This contains the basic information about a task that may be entered and displayed.
  - ➢ The **Estimated** check box is used to indicate the task has an **Estimated Duration**. The task duration will be displayed with a "?" which disappears when a duration is entered against a task.
  - ➢ **Priority** is used in leveling. 1000 is the highest and 0 the lowest.
  - ➢ The **Bar** options are covered in the **Formatting Bars** section.

- **Predecessors** – This is where the task's predecessors are displayed. This is covered in the **ADDING THE DEPENDENCIES** chapter.

- **Resources** – This is where resources may be created, assigned to tasks and assignment information displayed. This topic is covered in the **RESOURCES** chapters.

- **Advanced** – Options are covered in the **CONSTRAINTS** chapter.

- **Notes** – This is where notes about a task may be recorded, such as the **Scope Definition**.

- **Custom Fields** – Any **Custom Fields** that have been customized will be displayed in this tab. **Custom Fields** will not be covered in detail in this book. They are existing yet undefined fields that may be customized by selecting **Tools, Customize, Fields...** These fields may hold different types of project information such as text, times, values, etc. and are there to make the software more suitable for any given user. There are options on how these fields are summarized at the summary bar level.

6.8 Indicators Column

The **Indicators** column will display an icon when a task contains a non-default setting such as a Note, Constraint, or a Task calendar. Placing the mouse over the icon will display information about the task.

6.9 Assigning Calendars to Tasks

Tasks often require a different calendar from the **Project Calendar**. This is assigned in the **Project Information** form. Microsoft Project 2003 allows each task to be assigned a unique calendar. A Task Calendar may be assigned by using the **Task Information** form or displaying the **Task Calendar** column.

6.9.1 Assigning a Calendar Using the Task Information Form

- Select one or more tasks that you want to assign to a different calendar by using Shift-Click or Ctrl-Click.

- Open the **Task Information** form when selecting a single task, by double-clicking on a task.

- Open the **Task Information** form when selecting multiple tasks by:
  - ➢ Select **Project**, **Task Information**, or
  - ➢ **Shift+F2**, or
  - ➢ Right-click and select **Task Information**.

- Then select the Advanced tab:

- From the **Calendar:** drop-down box select the calendar you want to assign to the task or tasks.

6.9.2 Assigning a Calendar Using a Column

You may also display the **Task Calendar** column and edit the task calendar from this column. The process of displaying a column is covered in the **FORMATTING THE DISPLAY** chapter. After a calendar has been assigned, an icon will appear in the **Indicators** column as displayed beside the **Bid Strategy Meeting** activity below:

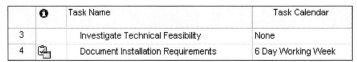

	❶	Task Name	Task Calendar
3		Investigate Technical Feasibility	None
4	📋	Document Installation Requirements	6 Day Working Week

WORKSHOP 4

Adding Tasks

Preamble

If you do not have the standard Microsoft Project settings loaded on your computer or your Global.mpt has been edited then you may not have the same results as displayed in this workshop.

Assignment

1. Use the columns to enter the Name and Original Duration of the Products as below.
2. Assign the 6-Day Working Week calendar using the **Task Information** form, **Advanced** tab. Double-click on the task to open this form.
3. The task will become a milestone by assigning a zero duration.

Task Name	Duration	Calendar Assignment
Bid Request Documents Received	0 days	
Bid Strategy	1 day	
Technical Feasibility Study	8 days	
Installation Requirements	4 days	Assign the 6 Days Working Week calendar
Component Bids	3 days	
Project Schedule	4 days	Assign the 6 Days Working Week calendar
Technical Details Schedule	9 days	
Component Bids Costs	2 days	
Draft Bid Document	3 days	
Reviewed Draft Bid Document	1 day	
Design Validation	1 day	
Revised Bid Document	1 day	
Component Work Packages Negotiated	6 days	
Bid Document Final	1 day	
Bid Submitted	0 days	

4. Save your **OzBuild Bid** project.
5. Check your answer with the example over the page.

ANSWER TO WORKSHOP 4

6. Your schedule may look like this:

	❶	Task Name	Duration	Start	Finish	3 Dec '06 S M T W T F S	10 Dec '06 S M T W T
1		Bid Request Documents Received	0 days	4 Dec '06	4 Dec '06	◆ 4/12	
2		Bid Strategy	1 day	4 Dec '06	4 Dec '06	▪	
3		Technical Feasibility Study	8 days	4 Dec '06	13 Dec '06	▬▬▬▬▬▬▬	
4	📅	Installation Requirements	4 days	4 Dec '06	7 Dec '06	▬▬▬	
5		Component Bids	3 days	4 Dec '06	6 Dec '06	▬▬	
6	📅	Project Schedule	4 days	4 Dec '06	7 Dec '06	▬▬▬	
7		Technical Details Schedule	9 days	4 Dec '06	14 Dec '06	▬▬▬▬▬▬▬▬	
8		Component Bids Costs	2 days	4 Dec '06	5 Dec '06	▬	
9		Draft Bid Document	3 days	4 Dec '06	6 Dec '06	▬▬	
10		Reviewed Draft Bid Document	1 day	4 Dec '06	4 Dec '06	▪	
11		Design Validation	1 day	4 Dec '06	4 Dec '06	▪	
12		Revised Bid Document	1 day	4 Dec '06	4 Dec '06	▪	
13		Component Work Packages Negotiated	6 days	4 Dec '06	11 Dec '06	▬▬▬▬▬	
14		Bid Document Final	1 day	4 Dec '06	4 Dec '06	▪	
15		Bid Submitted	0 days	4 Dec '06	4 Dec '06	◆ 4/12	

The icon in the Information column on the Left-Hand Side indicates that tasks 4 and 6 have a non-standard calendar which is the 6-Day Working Week calendar set in the last workshop.

7   ORGANIZING TASKS USING OUTLINING

Outlining is used to summarize and group tasks under a hierarchy of **Parent** or **Summary Tasks**. They are used to present different views of your project during planning, scheduling and statusing. These headings are normally based on your project **Work Breakdown Structure (WBS)**, **Control Accounts** or **Planning Packages**. The development of the **WBS** is covered in *PMBOK® Guide* Knowledge Area **Project Scope Management** and the development of the **WBS** is covered in detail in section **5.5 Create WBS**.

Defining the project's breakdown structures can be a major task for project managers. The establishment of templates may make this operation simpler because a standard breakdown is predefined and does not have to be typed in for each new project.

Projects should be broken into manageable areas by using a structure based on a breakdown of the project deliverables, systematic functions, disciplines or areas of work. The Outline structure created in your project should reflect the primary breakdown of your project and is normally the **WBS**.

Microsoft Project 2002 introduced a new feature titled **Grouping**, which is similar to the **Organize** function in Primavera P3 and SureTrak software. This feature allows the grouping of tasks under headings other than the "Outline Structure." Unlike Primavera software, **Grouping** is not the primary method of organizing tasks and is covered in the **GROUPING TASKS, OUTLINE CODES AND WBS** chapter and may be used to represent other project breakdown structures.

7.1   Creating an Outline

To create an **Outline**:

- A **Summary** task which could represent a **WBS Component** is placed above your **Detailed tasks** which could represent your activities:

- Then **Demote** the **Detailed tasks** below **Summary task**. (Demoting is explained in Section 7.2, below.):

The start and finish dates of the **Summary task** are adopted from the earliest start date and latest finish date of the **Detailed tasks**.

The duration of the **Summary** is calculated from the adopted start and finish dates over the **Summary** task calendar, which is initially the **Project Calendar**.

7.2 *Promoting and Demoting Tasks*

Demoting or **Indenting** tasks may be achieved in a number of ways. Select the task or tasks you want to **Demote**. Ensure you have selected the whole task and not just some cells. You may use any of the following methods to **Demote a selected task**:

- Click on the Indent ⇨ button, or

- Right-click on the **Task Id** column to open the task shortcut menu, click on the ⇨ Indent button, or

- Move the mouse until you see a double-headed horizontal arrow in the task name, left-click and drag the task right. A vertical line (see lower of the two pictures below) will appear indicating the outline level you have dragged the task(s) to, or

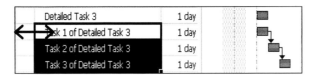

- Hold down the **Alt** and **Shift keys** and press the **Right Arrow Key** on your keyboard.

Demoting or **Outdenting tasks** uses the same principle as promoting tasks. Select the task or tasks you want to demote, ensure you have selected the whole task and not just some cells, then you may:

- Click on the Outdent ⇦ button, or

- Right-click on the **Task Id** column to open the task shortcut menu, click on the ⇦ Outdent button, or

- Move the mouse until you see a double-headed horizontal arrow in the task name column, left-click and drag the tasks left, or

- Hold down the **Alt** and **Shift keys** together and press the **Left Arrow Key** on your keyboard.

Tasks may be added under a **Detailed** task and demoted to a third level and so on.

In earlier versions on Microsoft Project 2003 the Outlining function did not operate correctly and it was not possible to outdent some tasks. A Hotfix Package (software patch) is available from the Microsoft website to correct this problem.

7.3 Summarizing Tasks

Once you have created summary tasks, the detailed tasks may be rolled up or summarized under the summary tasks. Rolled up tasks are symbolized by the + sign to the left of the summarized task description:

- This picture shows **Detailed Task 3** rolled up.

	ⓘ	Task Name	Duration	17 Oct '05							24 Oct '05					
				S	M	T	W	T	F	S	S	M	T	W	T	F	S
1		⊟ **Summary Task**	8 days													
2		Detailed Task 1	3 days													
3		Detailed Task 2	2 days													
4		⊞ **Detailed Task 3**	3 days													

- This picture shows **SUMMARY TASK** rolled up.

	ⓘ	Task Name	Duration	17 Oct '05							24 Oct '05					
				S	M	T	W	T	F	S	S	M	T	W	T	F	S
1		⊞ **Summary Task**	8 days													

7.3.1 To Rollup Summary Tasks and Show Tasks

Select the task you want to rollup:

- Click on the ⊟ to the left of the Task Name, or

- Click on the **Hide Subtasks** ⊟ icon, or

- Double-click on the **Task ID** (not the **Task Name** as this will open the **Task** form).

Displaying rolled-up tasks is similar to rolling them up. To do this, select the task you want to expand. Then:

- Click on the to ⊞ to the left of the Task Name, or

- Click on the **Show Subtasks** ⊞ icon, or

- Double-click on the **Task ID**.

The Outline Symbols, ⊞ and ⊟, in front of the tasks may be hidden and displayed from the **Tools**, **Options…**, **View** tab, **Show outline symbol**.

7.3.2 Roll Up All Tasks to an Outline Level

A schedule may be rolled up to any Outdent Level by selecting the desired Outdent Level from the $\boxed{\text{Show} \cdot}$ drop-down box on the **Formatting Tool Bar**.

7.3.3 Show All Tasks

Select the $\boxed{\text{\scriptsize +} \text{ All Subtasks}}$ option at the top to display all tasks.

7.4 Project Summary Task

A project summary task may be displayed by checking the **Show project summary task** box from the **Tools**, **Options…**, **View** tab. This task spans from the first to the last task in the project and is in effect a built-in Level 1 outline. The description of the Summary Task is the Project Title entered in the **File**, **Properties** form:

WORKSHOP 5

Maintaining the Task Codes

Preamble

A review of the internal reporting requirements shows that you need to identify the following Work Breakdown Structure Components:

1 – OzBuild Bid
1.1 – Research
1.2 – Estimation
1.3 – Proposal

Assignment

1. Go to the **View** tab in the **Tools**, **Options...** form and check the option to display the Project summary task and observe how it is formatted.
2. Remove the Project summary task.
3. Create an Outline Level 1 for the whole project entitled "OzBuild Bid" and
4. Create an Outline Level 2 for each of the three WBS Components: Research, Estimation and Proposal. Try using the various alternative methods for indenting and outdenting tasks.
5. Your schedule may look like this:

	❶	Task Name	Duration	Start	Finish	
1		⊟ **OzBuild Bid**	**9 days**	**4 Dec '06**	**14 Dec '06**	
2		⊟ **Research**	**8 days**	**4 Dec '06**	**13 Dec '06**	
3		Bid Request Documents Received	0 days	4 Dec '06	4 Dec '06	◆ 4/12
4		Bid Strategy	1 day	4 Dec '06	4 Dec '06	
5		Technical Feasibility Study	8 days	4 Dec '06	13 Dec '06	
6		⊟ **Estimation**	**9 days**	**4 Dec '06**	**14 Dec '06**	
7	📇	Installation Requirements	4 days	4 Dec '06	7 Dec '06	
8		Component Bids	3 days	4 Dec '06	6 Dec '06	
9	📇	Project Schedule	4 days	4 Dec '06	7 Dec '06	
10		Technical Details Schedule	9 days	4 Dec '06	14 Dec '06	
11		Component Bids Costs	2 days	4 Dec '06	5 Dec '06	
12		⊟ **Proposal**	**6 days**	**4 Dec '06**	**11 Dec '06**	
13		Draft Bid Document	3 days	4 Dec '06	6 Dec '06	
14		Reviewed Draft Bid Document	1 day	4 Dec '06	4 Dec '06	
15		Design Validation	1 day	4 Dec '06	4 Dec '06	
16		Revised Bid Document	1 day	4 Dec '06	4 Dec '06	
17		Component Work Packages Negotiated	6 days	4 Dec '06	11 Dec '06	
18		Bid Document Final	1 day	4 Dec '06	4 Dec '06	
19		Bid Submitted	0 days	4 Dec '06	4 Dec '06	◆ 4/12

6. Save your **OzBuild Bid** project.

8   FORMATTING THE DISPLAY

This chapter shows you how to set up the on-screen presentation so that the schedule will be easier to read and more consistent. These are the basic building blocks to create reports that would be distributed to the project stakeholders. This chapter covers the following display customizing topics:

Topic	Menu Command
• **Table** – formatting the columns of data	**V**iew, Ta**b**le:Entry, **M**ore Tables... or Select a column and right-click to insert or delete a column.
• **Formatting Columns**	Double-click on the column title.
• **Inserting Columns**	Highlight a column and strike the **Ins Key**, or Select **I**nsert, **C**olumn..., or Right-click and select Insert **C**olumn....
• **Deleting Columns**	Highlight a column and strike the **Delete** key, or Select **E**dit, Hi**d**e Column, or Right-click and select Hide **C**olumn.
• **Format Bars**	F**o**rmat, **B**ar Styles... or double-click on a bar.
• **Row Height**	Drag with the mouse.
• **Format Text Font**	F**o**rmat, **F**ont... to format columns and F**o**rmat, **T**ext Styles... to format all other fonts.
• **Timescale**	F**o**rmat, T**i**mescale... or Double-click on the timescale.
• **Gridlines**	F**o**rmat, **G**ridlines....
• **Relationship Lines**	F**o**rmat, **L**ayout....

The formatting is applied to the current **View** and is automatically saved as part of the View when another View is selected. Views are covered in the **VIEWS, TABLE AND DETAILS** chapter.

8.1   Formatting the Columns

There are two methods of formatting the columns:

- Using **Table** function, this is where you set up the data columns in the way you want to see the information on the screen and in printouts. You may edit, create and delete **Tables** and select which one is used display the data.

- Inserting and/or deleting columns of data without using the **Tables** function.

8.1.1   Formatting Columns Using the Table Function

- Select **View**, **Table:Entry** and select from the list of predefined **Tables** you want to display:

- Select **View**, **Table:**, **More Tables…** to open the **More Tables** form:

- To create a new Table.

   Edit…   – To edit the highlighted Table.

   Copy…   – To copy the highlighted Table.

   Organizer…   – Opens the **Organizer** form which enables you to copy a Table from one opened project to another or to the Global Project.

   Apply   – Applies the selected Table making it visible on the screen.

- When you select [New...], [Edit...] or [Copy...] you will be presented with the **Table Definition** form:

> ➤ Click on the **Show in menu** box to display the Table in the menu found under **View, Table:**.
> ➤ The columns of data will be displayed on screen from left to right in the same order as the rows in the form.
> ➤ Highlight a row and then you may use the [Cut Row], [Copy Row], [Paste Row], [Insert Row] and [Delete Row] buttons.
> ➤ The data to be displayed may be selected from the drop-down box in the **Field Name** column.
> ➤ **Align Data** and **Width** are used for formatting the data in the columns.
> ➤ The Microsoft Project 2003 **Field Name** may be replaced by typing your own title in the **Title** box.
> ➤ The **Date format:** drop-down box is used to change the format for this table only.

- **Row Height:** sets the default height of all the rows in this table. A row height may be changed by dragging the cell boundary line once a task has been created.
  > ➤ **Lock first column** prevents the first column from scrolling and is useful when the first column contains the Task Name.
  > ➤ **OK** takes you back to the **More Tables** form where you may click on the **Apply** button to commit the new or edited Table.

If you want to save a table for use in all your new projects then copy the table to the **Global.mpt** template using **Tools**, **Organizer...** and select the **Tables** tab.

You may also copy a **Table** to another project or rename a **Table** using **Tools**, **Organizer...** and selecting the **Tables** tab.

8.1.2 Formatting Columns

When you use this function, you are editing the **Table** currently in use and your changes are saved when you select a different table. Double-click on a column description to open the **Column Definition** form where you may edit the selected column in a similar way to the **Table Definition** form.

The IME Mode button allows the customization of the **Input Mode Editor** for some fields. This feature will only be displayed if it is installed with the Eastern Asian operating systems.

8.1.3 Inserting Columns

Insert a column by clicking on the column title where you require the new column. This will highlight the column. To insert a new column:

- Select **Insert**, **Column…**, or
- Hit the **Ins** Key, or
- Right-click and select **Insert Column…**.

8.1.4 Deleting Columns

Delete a column by highlighting the column or by clicking on the title. Then:

- Select **Edit**, **Hide Column**, or
- Hit the **Delete** key, or
- Right-click and select **Hide Column**.

1. There will be no confirmation of deleting a column, but you are allowed to undo the deletion.
2. The term "hide" means "delete" and the column is removed from the Table in this project.

8.1.5 Adjusting the Width of Columns

You may adjust the width of the column either manually or automatically. For manual adjustment, move the mouse pointer to the nearest vertical line of the column. A ↔ icon will then appear and enable the column to be adjusted. For automatic adjustment, once again position the mouse pointer to the nearest vertical line of the column, and double right-click the mouse. The column width will automatically adjust to the best fit.

8.1.6 Adding a Space Between the Value and Label

Select **Tools**, **Options…**, **Edit** and check on the **Add space before label** check box to add a space between the value and label in date columns.

8.2   Formatting the Bar Style

The bars in the Gantt Chart may be formatted to suit your requirements for display. Microsoft Project 2003 has the option to:

- Format all the Task Bars, or

- Format one or more specific Task Bars.

8.2.1   Formatting All Task Bars

To format all the bars you must open the Bar Style form by selecting:

- **Format**, **Bar Styles…**, or

- Double-click anywhere in the Gantt Chart area, but not on an existing bar, as this will open the **Format Bar** form for formatting an individual bar.

The following notes are the main points for using this function. Detailed information is available in the help facility by searching for "Bar styles dialog box".

- Each bar listed in the table will be displayed on the bar chart.

- Bars may be deleted with the Cut Row button, pasted using Paste Row button and new bars inserted using the Insert Row.

- The **Name** is the title you may assign to the bar and is displayed in the printout legend. To hide the bar on the legend precede the **Name** with an *.

- The appearance of each bar is edited in the lower half of the form. The bar's start point, middle and end point may have their color, shape, pattern, etc. formatted.

- **Show For … Tasks** allows you to select which tasks are displayed. More than one task type may be displayed by separating each type with a ",". Bar types not required are prefixed with "**Not**" For example Normal,Rolled Up,Split,Not Summary bar would not display a bar for a summary task. Should you leave this cell blank then all task types will be displayed in this format.

- The bars may be placed on one of four rows numbered from 1 to 4, top to bottom. If multiple bars are placed on the same row, the bar at the top of the list will be drawn first and the ones lower down the list will be drawn over the top.

- **From** and **To** allow you to establish where the bars start and finish. The picture below shows how to format Total Float and Negative Float. Unlike other planning and scheduling software, the Negative Float is drawn from the Start Date of a task and not the Finish Date.

- The **Text** tab allows you to place text inside or around the bar:

- It is not possible to format the font in this **Bar Styles** form. Select **Format**, **Text Styles...** to format the bar text font.

If you want to show Critical and Non-critical tasks, then the bars should be formatted as shown below, with particular attention paid to the **Show For ... Tasks** column Non-critical Tasks are formatted as **Normal, Non-critical** and Critical Tasks as **Normal, Critical**.

There is also a **Gantt Chart Wizard** available by clicking on the ⬚ icon but this wizard will overwrite any formatting you may have created. This is a straightforward method of formatting your bars.

8.2.2 Layout Form – Format Bars Options

Select **Format**, **Layout...** to open the **Layout** form. This form has some additional bar formatting options for users to customize the appearance of the Gantt Chart.

- **Date format:** sets the format for dates displayed on bars only. Dates are displayed on bars using **Format, Bar...** or **Format, Bar Styles....**

- **Bar height:** sets the height of all the bars. Individual bars may be assigned different heights by selecting a bar shape in the styles form.

- **Always roll up Gantt bars** and **Hide rollup bars when summary expanded** works as follows:

  ➤ Tasks before rollup:

  ➤ With **Always roll up Gantt bars** checked and **Hide rollup bars when summary expanded** unchecked:

  ➤ With **Always roll up Gantt bars** and **Hide rollup bars when summary expanded** checked:

  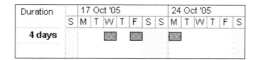

  ➤ An individual bar may be rolled up to a summary task using the **Roll up Gantt bar to summary** option in the **Task Information** form.

- Round bars to whole days:
  - ➤ When this option is unchecked, the length of the task will be shown in proportion to the total number of hours worked per day over the 24-hour time span. For example, an 8-hour working duration bar is shown below:

Duration	Tuesday	Wednesday	Thursday
1 day		▓	

  - ➤ When this option is checked, the task bar will be displayed and spanned over the whole day irrespective of working time:

Duration	Tuesday	Wednesday	Thursday
1 day		▓▓▓▓	

- **Splitting Tasks**
  - ➤ An unstarted task may be split using the Split Task icon [icon] on the Task Bar, then highlighting the bar to be split and dragging the section of the bar with the mouse to the location where it is planned to conduct the work. The picture below shows Task 10 – Draft Technical Details Schedule being split. Splits may be removed using the same process.

  - ➤ In-progress tasks may be split manually by dragging the incomplete portion to the right or a split may be created automatically by commencing a task before its predecessor is complete. Splitting of in-progress tasks is covered in both the **TRACKING PROGRESS** and **OPTIONS** chapters. The two pictures below are of the same task, first with the option checked and then unchecked:

- **Show bars splits**
  - ➤ When checked, the activity bar will display splits:

  - ➤ When unchecked, the activity bar will not display splits:

  - ➤ Tasks will only split however when the option in **Tools**, **Options…**, **Schedule** tab, **Spilt in-progress tasks** is checked.

8.2.3 Format One or More Specific Task Bars

Individual bars may be formatted to make them look different from other bars.

To format one or more bars:

- Select:
  - ➢ One task bar by clicking on it, or
  - ➢ Multiple bars by Ctrl-clicking each bar or left-clicking and dragging with the mouse, then
- Open the **Format Bar** form by:
  - ➢ Selecting **Format**, **Bar...**, or
  - ➢ Moving the mouse over a bar in the bar chart until the mouse changes to a ✥ and double-clicking. When more than one bar has been selected you will need to hold the **Ctrl Key** down when double-clicking on a bar.
- Then select the required bar formatting options from the **Format Bar** form:

- The ⬚ Reset ⬚ is used to restore the default bar formatting to selected bars.

The bar shape may be formatted and text information added in the same way as formatting all the bars described earlier in this chapter.

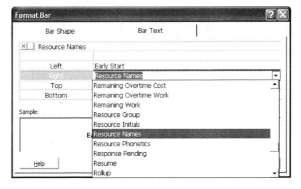

- Select **Format**, **Text styles...** to format the text font.

- A Tasks Bar may be hidden by checking the **Hide task bar** option in the **Task Information** form.

8.3 Row Height

Row heights may be adjusted to display text that would otherwise be truncated by a narrow column.

The row height may be set in the **Table Definition** form by select **View**, **Table:**, **More Tables…**, from this view select the table you wish to edit the row height in and click on the ⌐ Edit… ⌐ button. Once the **Table Definition** form is open select the row height from the drop down box next to **Row height:**.

The row height of one or more columns may also be adjusted in a similar way to adjusting row heights in Excel, by clicking on the row and dragging with the mouse:

- Highlight one or more rows that need adjusting by dragging or Ctrl-clicking. If all the rows are to be adjusted, then click on the **Select All** button above row number 1, to highlight all the tasks.

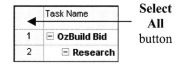

- Then move the mouse pointer to the Left-Hand Side of a horizontal row divider line. The pointer will change to a double-headed arrow ⇕. Click and hold with the left mouse button and drag the row or rows to the required height.

8.4 Format Fonts

8.4.1 Format Font Command

The **Format**, **Font…** function allows you to format any selected text in rows or columns:

- Select all the rows by clicking on the **Select All** button, box above row number 1, or

- Select one or more rows or columns by Ctrl-clicking or dragging, then

- Select **Format**, **Font…** to open the **Font** form:

- You may select the font style, font size, and color of the text from the **Font** dialog box.

Once formatted, the selected font style and type will be applied to the data column or task row in any table.

8.4.2   Format Text Style

The **Format**, **Text Styles...** command opens the **Text Styles** form and allows you to select a text type from the **Item to Change:** drop-down box and apply formatting to the selected text style:

Text may formatted by using any of the styles listed below:

- **All**: This is all text including columns and rows,

- **Noncritical**, **Critical**, **Milestone**, **Summary**, **Project Summary**, **Marked**, **Highlighted** and **External tasks**,

- **Row** and **Column** titles,

- **Top**, **Middle** and **Bottom Timescale Tiers**, and

- **Bar Text** left, right, below, above and inside.

8.5   *Format Colors*

Colors are formatted in a number of forms and there is no single form for formatting all colors:

- **Non-working time** colors in the Gantt Chart are formatted in the **Timescale** form, double-click on the timescale.

- **Text** colors are formatted in the **Text Styles** and **Font** forms, found under the **Format** command.

- **Gridline** colors are formatted in the **Gridlines** form, also found under the **Format** command.

- **Hyperlink** colors are formatted under **Tools**, **Options...**, **Edit**.

- **Timescale** colors are formatted with the system color scheme used in the **Start**, **Settings**, **Control Panel**, **Display** option.

- The **Logic Lines**, also known as **Dependencies**, **Relationships**, or **Links**, inherit their color from the predecessor's bar color.

8.6   Format Timescale

8.6.1   Format Timescale Command

The **Timescale** form provides a number of options for the display of the timescale, which is located above the Bar Chart, and the shading of **Non-working** time. This function has was enhanced with the release of Microsoft Project 2003 to have three tiers and not two.

To open the **Timescale** form:

- Double-click on the timescale, or

- Select **Format, Timescale…**.

There are many options here, which are intuitive and will not be described in detail.

Top Tier, Middle Tier and Bottom Tier Tab

- These three time scales may have different scales. These are often set at "weeks and days" or "months and weeks." By default, the Top Tier time scale has been disabled. You may enable the three tiers together by selecting Three Tiers (Top, Middle, Bottom) from the **Timescale options, Show:**.

- The **Label** will affect how much space the timescale will occupy, so the selection of a long label will result in longer Task bars.

- **Tick lines** and **Scale separator** hide and display the lines between the text.

- **Size:** controls the horizontal scale of the timescale and in association with the **Label:** are the two main tools for scaling the horizontal axis in the Gantt Chart.

- If you choose to use the **Use fiscal year** function to display the financial year, then you will need to select the **Tools, Options…, Calendar** tab to choose the month on which the fiscal year starts.

- Should you wish to say number the time periods say **Week 1, Week2**, etc, there are a number of sequential numbering options for the time periods available at the bottom of the label list.

Non-working Time Tab

The **Non-working time** tab allows you to format how the non-working time is displayed. You may select only one calendar. The non-working time may be presented as shading behind the bars, in front of the bars or hidden.

8.6.2 View Zoom

The **View**, **Zoom...** function is used to adjust the horizontal scale of the Gantt Chart only. It does not work like most other Windows products, which scale the whole work area.

 The **View**, **Zoom...** function is not a temporary change and overwrites any customized timescale settings.

8.6.3 Format Timescale Font

To format the Timescale font, select **Format**, **Text styles...** to open the **Text Styles** form:

The timescale fonts may be formatted separately by selecting the appropriate line item under **Item to Change:**.

8.7 Format Gridlines

Gridlines are important to help divide the visual presentation with dividing lines on the Bar Chart. This example shows **Middle Tier Gridlines** every week and **Bottom Tier Gridlines** every day.

To format the Grid Line select **Format**, **Gridlines…** to open the Gridlines form:

- Select the gridline from the dropdown box under **Line to change:**.
- Select color and type from under **Normal**.
- Some gridlines may be set to occur at intervals under the **At interval** option.

Some of the titles for the gridlines are not intuitive, so some interpretation is given below:

- For Data Column and Row dividing lines, use **Sheet Rows** and **Sheet Columns**.
- For Timescale and Column Titles, use **Title Horizontal** and **Title Vertical**.
- Gantt Chart area, including lines for Project Start and Finish Date, Current and Status Date, are clearly described.
- Page Breaks will only display manually-inserted breaks. A page will only break if the **Manual page breaks** check box in the **Print** form is checked.

 Many laser printers will not print light gray lines clearly, so it is often better to use dark gray or black Sight Lines for better output.

8.8 *Format Links, Dependencies, Relationships, or Logic Lines*

The Links, also known as Dependencies, Relationships, or Logic Lines, may be displayed or hidden by using the **Layout** form.

- Select **Format**, **Layout…** to open the **Layout** form and click on one of the three radio buttons under **Links** to select the style you require:

➢ The color of the **Link** is inherited from the color of the predecessor task.
➢ To display critical path on the relationship lines you will need to format the bars with a different color. This is often set to red.

  The color of the successors' relationship lines is adopted from the task bar color. Therefore, re-formatting critical bars with the **Format Bar** form will also re-format the color of the successors' relationship lines and they will no longer display the Critical Path color on the Logic Lines. This will effectively mask the critical path and could provide misleading results.

WORKSHOP 6

Formatting the Bar Chart

Preamble

Management has received your draft report and requests some changes to the presentation.

Format your schedule as follows:

1. Create a new **Table** titled **Review** by copying the **Entry** table.

2. Add **Task Calendar** column between **Duration** and **Start** columns in the **Table Definition** form.

3. Left Align the Task Calendar data.

4. Check the **Show in menu** option.

5. Apply the Review Table.

6. Click on the **Duration** column and right-click to display a menu, then hide this column.

7. Format the **Middle Tier Timescale** with **Units:** of **Months** with **Label:** of **January** and the **Bottom Tier Timescale** with **Units:** of **Days** with **Label:** of **M,T,W,…** and **Size:** of 120%. These are titled **Major Columns** and **Minor Gridlines** in Microsoft Project 2000.

8. Format the Gridlines with **Middle Tier Columns** to solid black lines and **Bottom Tier Columns** to dotted black lines. These are titled **Major Columns** and **Minor Gridlines** in Microsoft Project 2000.

9. Remove the date from the milestones.

10. Add the task **Name** to the right of each **Task** bar.

11. Save your **OzBuild Bid** project.

12. Check your result with the example shown on the next page.

ANSWER TO WORKSHOP 6

	❶	Task Name	Task Calendar	Start	Finish
1		⊟ OzBuild Bid	None	4 Dec '06	14 Dec '06
2		⊟ Stage 1 - Research	None	4 Dec '06	13 Dec '06
3		Bid Request Documents Received	None	4 Dec '06	4 Dec '06
4		Bid Strategy	None	4 Dec '06	4 Dec '06
5		Technical Feasibility Study	None	4 Dec '06	13 Dec '06
6		⊟ Stage 2 - Estimation	None	4 Dec '06	14 Dec '06
7		Installation Requirements	6 Day Working Week	4 Dec '06	7 Dec '06
8		Request Component Bids	None	4 Dec '06	6 Dec '06
9		Project Schedule	6 Day Working Week	4 Dec '06	7 Dec '06
10		Technical Details Schedule	None	4 Dec '06	14 Dec '06
11		Component Bids Costs	None	4 Dec '06	5 Dec '06
12		⊟ Stage 3 - Proposal	None	4 Dec '06	11 Dec '06
13		Draft Bid Document	None	4 Dec '06	6 Dec '06
14		Reviewed Draft Bid Document	None	4 Dec '06	4 Dec '06
15		Design Validation	None	4 Dec '06	4 Dec '06
16		Revised Bid Document	None	4 Dec '06	4 Dec '06
17		Component Work Packages Negotiated	None	4 Dec '06	11 Dec '06
18		Bid Document Final	None	4 Dec '06	4 Dec '06
19		Bid Submitted	None	4 Dec '06	4 Dec '06

9   ADDING TASK DEPENDENCIES

The next phase of a schedule is to add logic to the tasks. There are two types of logic that you may use:

- **Dependencies**, (**Relationships** or **Logic** or **Links**) between tasks, and

- Imposed **Constraints** to task start or finish dates. These are covered in the **CONSTRAINTS** chapter.

The *PMBOK® Guide* section **6.2 Activity Sequencing** describes both **Precedence Diagramming Method** (**PDM**) and **Arrow Diagramming Method** (**ADM**). Microsoft Project is a **PDM** software package.

Microsoft Project 2003's Help file and other text uses the terms "**Dependencies, Relationships** and **Links**" for Dependencies but does not use the term "**Logic**."

There are a number of methods for adding, editing and deleting task **Dependencies**. We will look at the following techniques in this chapter:

Topic	Notes for creating a SF Dependency
• Graphically in the Gantt, Calendar or Network Diagram Views	Drag the 4-headed mouse pointer from one task to another to create an FS dependency.
• Through the **Link** and **Unlink** icon on the Standard toolbar	Select the tasks in the order they are to be linked and click on the Link icon.
• By using the Menu command	Select the tasks in the order they are to be linked and select **Edit**, **Link Tasks**, or **Ctrl+F2**.
• By opening the **Task Information** form	Predecessor only may be added and deleted.
• Through the **Predecessor** and **Successor Details** forms	Open the bottom pane, **Windows, Split** and then select **Format, Details, Predecessors and Successors**.
• By editing or deleting a dependency using the **Task Dependency** form	Double-click on a task link (relationship line) in the **Bar Chart** or **Network Diagram** view.
• **Autolink** new inserted tasks and moved tasks	Select **Tools, Options…, Schedule** tab and check the **Autolink Inserted or Moved Tasks** box.
• By displaying the **Predecessor** or **Successor** column	Edit the relationships in the columns.

Dependencies

Generally, there are two types of dependencies that may be entered into the software:

- **Mandatory dependencies** also referred to as **Hard Logic** are dependencies that may not be avoided: for example, a footing excavation has to be prepared before concrete may be poured into it.

- **Discretionary dependencies** also referred to as **Soft Logic** or **Sequencing Logic** or **Preferred Logic**, which often may be changed at a later date to reflect planning changes: for example, determining in which order the footing holes may be dug.

There is no simple method of documenting which is hard and which is soft logic. A schedule with a large amount of soft logic has the potential of becoming very difficult to maintain when the plan is changed. You will also find that as a project progresses, soft logic converts to hard logic as commitments are made and tasks are started.

Constraints

Constraints are applied to Tasks when relationships do not provide the required result. Typical applications of a constraint are:

- The availability of a site to commence work.

- The supply of information by a client.

- The required finish date of a project.

Constraints are often entered to represent contract dates and may be directly related to contract items.

External dependencies may be created in a project schedule by creating a milestone and applying a constraint.

Constraints are covered in detail in the **CONSTRAINTS** chapter.

9.1 Understanding Dependencies

There are four types of dependencies available in Microsoft Project 2003:

- Finish-to-Start (**FS**) (also known as conventional)

- Start-to-Start (**SS**)

- Start-to-Finish (**SF)**

- Finish-to-Finish (**FF**)

Two other terms you must understand are:

- **Predecessor**, a task that controls the start or finish of another immediate subsequent task.

- **Successor**, a task whose start or finish depends on the start or finish of another immediately preceding task.

The following pictures show how the dependencies appear graphically in the **Gantt Chart** and **Network Diagram** (PERT) views.

The **FS** (or conventional) dependency looks like this:

While the **SS** dependency is like this:

The **SF** dependency looks like:

The **FF** dependency would be:

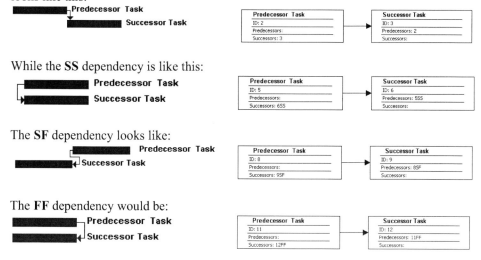

9.2   Understanding Lags and Leads

A **Lag** is a duration that is applied to a dependency to make the successor start or finish earlier or later.

- A successor task will start later when a positive **Lag** is assigned. Therefore, a task requiring a 3-day delay between the finish of one task and start of another will require a positive lag of 3 days.

- Conversely, a lag may be negative (also called a **Lead)** when a new task can be started before the predecessor task is finished.

- **Leads** and **Lags** may be applied to any relationship type including Summary Task relationships.

An example of a **FS** with positive lag

An example of a **FS** with negative lag:

Here are some important points to understand about Lags.

- Lags are normally calculated on the **Successor Calendar**. (Primavera P3 and SureTrak software uses the predecessor's calendar.)

- Lags may be assigned **Elapsed** durations, therefore they will be based on a 24-hour, 7-day/week. To enter an elapsed lag type an "e" before the unit, e.g. **5ed**.

- Lags may be expressed in terms of % and in this situation the lag is a percentage of the predecessor's duration. The example below shows a FS dependency +250%; the predecessor is 1day so the Lag is 2.5days.

You must be careful when using a lag to allow for delays such as curing concrete when the Base Calendar is not a seven-day calendar. Since this type of activity lapses non-work days, the activity could finish before Microsoft Project 2003's calculated finish date. You may want to use elapsed durations in a lag in this situation.

9.3 Restrictions on Summary Task Dependencies

Dependencies may be made between Summary and Detailed tasks of a different Summary task. Consider the following points when using dependencies at Summary Task level:

- There is a built-in dependency between Summary and Detailed tasks. Detailed tasks may be considered as Start-to-Start successors and Finish-to-Finish predecessors of their Summary Task.

- Summary tasks may only have **FS** and **SS** dependencies; you will receive a warning message when you attempt to enter an illegal dependency.

 It is recommended that dependencies be maintained at the detail level. This is particularly important when moving tasks from one summary task to another since the dependencies will still be valid. Again, be aware that there is a function found under **Tools**, **Options…**, **Schedule** tab which will Autolink moved tasks and this function should be turned off if you wish to move a task and keep the existing logic.

9.4 Displaying the Dependencies on the Gantt Chart

The dependencies may be displayed or hidden with the **Layout** form.

- Select **Format**, **Layout…** to open the **Layout** form and click on the radio button under the style you require:

- The color of the dependency line is inherited from the color of the predecessor task.

- To display a critical path on the relationship lines you will need to format the bars as critical.

9.4.1 Graphically Adding a Dependency

You may graphically add a **Finish-to-Start** dependency only by:

- Selecting the **Gantt**, **Calendar** or **Network Diagram** views from the **View Bar** on the right-hand side of the screen or selecting **View**, **Gantt Chart**, **Calendar** or **Network Diagram**, then:

- Move the mouse pointer over a task until the mouse pointer changes to a ⊹, left-click and drag to the successor task. The cursor will change to a ⊖ shape during this operation.

9.4.2 Using the Link and Unlink Icon on the Standard Toolbar

The ⊟ **Link Tasks** icon on the toolbar may be used for linking tasks with a Start-to-Finish dependency:

- Highlight one of more tasks using Ctrl-left-click to select one task at a time and Shift and left-click to select a contiguous group of tasks.

- Then click the ⊟ **Link Tasks** icon on the toolbar and the tasks will be linked with Start-to-Finish dependencies in the order that they were selected.

To remove a dependency, select the tasks and click on the ⊟ **Unlink Tasks** icon.

9.4.3 Linking Using the Menu Command

The menu may be used for linking tasks with a Start-to-Finish dependency:

- Highlight one or more tasks using Ctrl-left-click to select one task at a time or Shift and left-click to select a group of tasks.

- Then select **Edit**, **Link Tasks**, or **Ctrl+F2** and the tasks will be linked with Start-to-Finish dependencies in the order that they were selected.

Dependencies may be removed using the menu using **Edit**, **Unlink Tasks**.

 Primavera P3 and SureTrak software links tasks that have been highlighted from top to bottom. Microsoft Project 2003 links the tasks in the order they are highlighted.

9.4.4 Adding and Deleting Predecessors with the Task Information Form

The **Task Information** form may be used for adding and deleting predecessors only.

- Double-click on a task to open the **Task Information** form,

- Select the **Predecessor** tab,

- To select the predecessor, you may either:
  - ➢ Type in the Predecessor Task ID in the first line under ID, or
  - ➢ Use the drop-down box under task name:

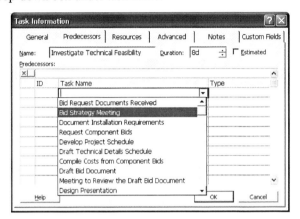

- Now enter the Relationship Type from the **Type** drop-down list and the lag, if required, from the **Lag** drop-down list.

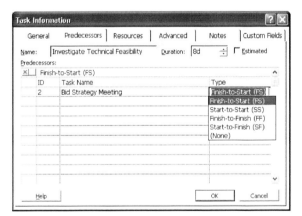

- To enter another relationship click on the next line.

- You are not able to scroll up or down to another task while the **Task Information** form is open.

To complete your operation, either:

- Press the **Enter Key** or click on the [OK] button to commit the changes, or

- Click on the **Esc Key** or click on the [Cancel] button to abort any changes.

9.4.5   Predecessor and Successor Details Forms

The Predecessor and Successor Details form may be displayed by:

- Opening the bottom pane by selecting **Window**, **Split**,

- Then make the lower pane active by clicking anywhere in the lower pane. The bar on the left-hand side of the lower pane will turn blue when it is active.

- Then select **Format**, **Details**, **Predecessors and Successors** to display the **Predecessors and Successors Detail** form:

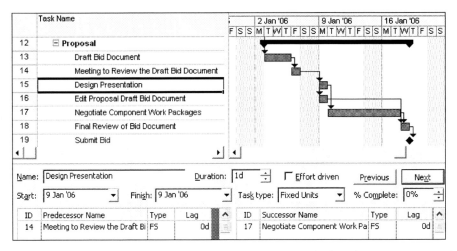

Predecessors and successors may be added using the same method as the **Task Information** form.

9.4.6   Editing or Deleting Dependencies Using the Task Dependency Form

To use the **Task Dependency** form, a logic link between tasks must already exist. To open the **Task Dependency** form, double-click on a task link (relationship line) in the Bar Chart or Network Diagram.

A Link may only be edited or deleted from this form.

9.4.7 Autolink New Inserted Tasks or Moved Tasks

This function automatically creates predecessors to tasks above it and successors below it when a task is moved or inserted. This option may be activated by selecting **Tools**, **Options…**, **Schedule** tab and check the **Autolink inserted or moved tasks** box. When activated you must ensure that:

- You have selected the whole task by clicking on the task ID and highlighting all the columns before you drag the task to a new location. Otherwise, you will only move the cell contents.

 When the task is moved, **Autolink New Tasks or Moved** tasks will delete the existing predecessor and successor logic without warning. This function potentially makes substantial changes to your project logic and may affect the overall project duration.

9.4.8 Editing Relationships Using the Predecessor or Successor Columns

The **Predecessor** or **Successor** column may be displayed and edited following the example below.

	❶	Task Name	Predecessors	Successors	17 Oct '05 S M T W T F S
1		Predessor		2SS+3 days,3	
2		Successor 1	1SS+3 days	3	
3		Successor 2	1,2		

9.4.9 Viewing Relationships Using the Unique ID Predecessor or Unique ID Successor Columns

Each task is assigned a Unique ID when it is created and this number is not used again in the schedule, even if the task is deleted. There are two other columns that may be used to edit and display relationships using the Unique ID:

- The **Unique ID Predecessor**, and
- The **Unique ID Successor**.

9.4.10 Editing Relationships Using WBS Predecessor or WBS Successor Columns

There are two other columns that may be used only to display (and not edit) the **Predecessors** and **Successors**:

- The **WBS Predecessor**, and
- **WBS Successor**.

9.5 Scheduling the Project

Once you have your tasks and the logic in place, Microsoft Project 2003 calculates the tasks' dates/times. More specifically, Microsoft Project 2003 has **Scheduled** the project to calculate the **Early Dates**, **Late Dates** and the **Total Float**. This will allow you to review the **Critical Path** of the project. Microsoft Project 2003 uses the term **Slack** instead of the standard term **Float**. Both terms are used interchangeably throughout this book.

Sometimes it is preferable to prevent the **Automatic Calculation** of your project's start/end dates. To do this, select **Tools**, **Options…**, **Calculation** tab. Click on **Manual**.

To calculate the schedule with the calculation mode set to manual:

- Press the **F9 Key**, or

- Click on the **Select All** button, top left hand corner of the Gantt Chart view, right-click to open a menu and select **Calculate Project**.

WORKSHOP 7

Adding the Relationships

Preamble

You have determined the logical sequence of tasks, so you may now create the relationships.

Assignment

1. Format the **Middle Tier Timescale** to **Weeks – 31 Jan '01** and **Bottom Tier Timescale** to **Days – M,T,W,… Timescale size** to **70%** and remove the Middle Tier Gridlines.
2. Remove the Task **Name** from the bars.
3. Apply the **Entry** table.
4. Input the logic below using the several of the methods detailed in this chapter.

	❶	Task Name	Predecessors
1		⊟ **OzBuild Bid**	
2		⊟ **Research**	
3		Bid Request Documents Received	
4		Bid Strategy	3
5		Technical Feasibility Study	4
6		⊟ **Estimation**	
7	📑	Installation Requirements	5
8		Component Bids	7
9	📑	Project Schedule	7
10		Technical Details Schedule	5
11		Component Bids Costs	8
12		⊟ **Proposal**	
13		Draft Bid Document	9,10,11
14		Reviewed Draft Bid Document	13
15		Design Validation	14
16		Revised Bid Document	14
17		Component Work Packages Negotiated	15
18		Bid Document Final	16,17
19		Bid Submitted	18

5. Hide and Display the Logic Links using **F<u>o</u>rmat**, **<u>L</u>ayout…**.
6. Check your results against the diagram on the next page.
7. Save your **OzBuild Bid** project.

ANSWER TO WORKSHOP 7

	❶	Task Name	Duration	Start	Finish	Predecessors
1		⊟ **OzBuild Bid**	**30 days**	**4 Dec '06**	**17 Jan '07**	
2		⊟ **Research**	**9 days**	**4 Dec '06**	**14 Dec '06**	
3		Bid Request Documents Received	0 days	4 Dec '06	4 Dec '06	
4		Bid Strategy	1 day	4 Dec '06	4 Dec '06	3
5		Technical Feasibility Study	8 days	5 Dec '06	14 Dec '06	4
6		⊟ **Estimation**	**9 days**	**15 Dec '06**	**29 Dec '06**	
7	📵	Installation Requirements	4 days	15 Dec '06	19 Dec '06	5
8		Component Bids	3 days	20 Dec '06	22 Dec '06	7
9	📵	Project Schedule	4 days	20 Dec '06	23 Dec '06	7
10		Technical Details Schedule	9 days	15 Dec '06	29 Dec '06	5
11		Component Bids Costs	2 days	27 Dec '06	28 Dec '06	8
12		⊟ **Proposal**	**12 days**	**2 Jan '07**	**17 Jan '07**	
13		Draft Bid Document	3 days	2 Jan '07	4 Jan '07	9,10,11
14		Reviewed Draft Bid Document	1 day	5 Jan '07	5 Jan '07	13
15		Design Validation	1 day	8 Jan '07	8 Jan '07	14
16		Revised Bid Document	1 day	8 Jan '07	8 Jan '07	14
17		Component Work Packages Negotiated	6 days	9 Jan '07	16 Jan '07	15
18		Bid Document Final	1 day	17 Jan '07	17 Jan '07	16,17
19		Bid Submitted	0 days	17 Jan '07	17 Jan '07	18

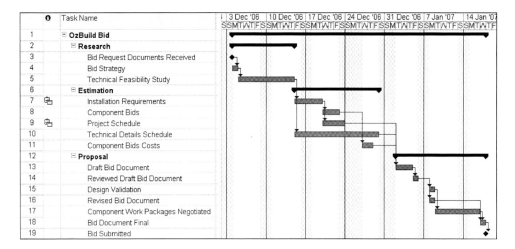

You will notice that tasks with a 6 Day Working Week Calendar are scheduled to work on Saturdays.

10 NETWORK DIAGRAM VIEW

The **Network Diagram View** is an enhancement of the earlier versions of Microsoft Project **PERT View** and displays tasks as boxes connected by the relationship lines. This chapter will not cover this subject in detail but will introduce the main features.

To view your project in the Networking View:

- Select **View**, **Networking Diagram**, or

- Click on the **Networking Diagram** icon ⬚⬚ on the **View Bar** on the left-hand side of the screen.

Many features available in the **Gantt Chart View** are also available in the **Network Diagram View**, including:

Topic	Menu Command
• Add new tasks	Click and drag into a blank area. This will add a new Task with a Finish-to-Start relationship, or Use the **Insert Key** or selecting **Insert**, **New Task**. These tasks are added after the highlighted task without a relationship.
• Delete Tasks	Select the task and press the **Delete** key.
• Display the **Task Information** form	Double-click on a Task Box, or Highlight a task and right-click on it and select **Task Information…** for the menu.
• Format Dependencies	Select **Format**, **Layout…**
• Display the **Task Dependency** form	Double-click on a relationship line.
• Display information in the lower pane	Select **Window**, **Split**, or Drag the dividing bar.
• Format Task Boxes	Select **Format**, **Box Styles…**, or Double-click on the outside edge of a box.
• Format an individual Task Box	Select **Format**, **Box…**
• Change the scale of the display	Select **View**, **Zoom…** which displays the **Zoom** form.

The **Network Diagramming View** may be used to create and display a **Network Diagram** and used in the *PMBOK® Guide* **Schedule Network Analysis** discussed in section 6.5.2.

10.1 Understanding the Network Diagram View

The following list describes the main display features of the Network Diagram View:

- Summary Tasks, Detail Tasks and Milestones are normally formatted with a different shape. Typical shape examples are provided as follows:
  - ➢ Summary Tasks are Trapezoidal –
  - ➢ Detail Tasks are Rectangular –
  - ➢ The Milestone Task is an elongated diamond –

- Summary Tasks are positioned to the left and at the same level or above Detail Tasks.

- Summary Tasks may be rolled up by clicking on the ⊟ above the Task and expanded by clicking on the ⊞ above a rolled-up summary task.

- All relationship lines are drawn as **Finish-to-Start** even when they are not linked as a **Finish-to-Start** relationship. The link type may be displayed on the arrow. See **Link style** later in this chapter.

- Critical Tasks may be formatted to have different borders and backgrounds.

- The contents of the Task Boxes and relationship lines may also be formatted.

10.2 Adding and Deleting Tasks in the Network Diagramming View

- A **New Task** may be created with a **Finish-to-Start** relationship by dragging from the center of a Task Box into a blank part of the screen.

- A **New Task** may be created without a relationship below the tasks position in the Gantt Chart by:
  - ➢ Using the **Insert Key**, or
  - ➢ Selecting **Insert**, **New Task**.

10.3 Adding, Editing and Deleting Dependencies

Dependencies may be added, deleted or edited using the following methods:

- Graphically add a relationship by clicking on the center of one task and dragging to the successor.

- Hold the **Ctrl Key** to select two or more tasks and then use the **Link** function.

- The **Unlink** removes dependencies between selected tasks.

- Open the **Task Information** form by double-clicking on a task and selecting the **Predecessors** tab.

- Double-click on a **Relationship line** to open the **Task Dependency** form and edit or delete a dependency.

- Create a split window by selecting **Window**, **Split**. Display the predecessors and successors in the lower pane by selecting **Format**, **Details**, **Predecessors and Successors**.

10.4 Formatting the Task Boxes

Task Boxes may be formatted from the **Box Styles** form, which is displayed by:

- Selecting **Format**, **Box Styles...**, or

- Double-clicking on the outside edge of a box.

10.5 Formatting Individual Boxes

One highlighted **Task Box** may be formatted differently than all others by selecting **Format**, **Box...** to open the **Format Box** form.

The button is used to set the formatting back to default.

10.6 Formatting the Display and Relationship Lines

Most formatting, except formatting the boxes, is set within the **Layout** form. Select **Format**, **Layout...** to open the **Layout** form:

- The **Layout Mode** allows you to drag a Task Box to a new position. When **Allow manual box positioning** is selected, place the mouse over the Task Box. When it changes to a ✛, drag the box to the required location.

- **Box Layout** allows you to specify how the Task Boxes are arranged. This option will only work when **Layout Mode** is set to **Automatically position all boxes**. For example, when "Top Down by Week" is selected, all the Tasks that start in the first week will be placed in the first column. The other options under **Box Layout** should be self-explanatory.

- **Link style** is an option to display relationships. Checking **Show link labels** will place the Relationship Type and Lag on the relationship line and is useful when all your relationships are not Finish-to-Start. See below.

- **Link color** allows you to specify the color of the critical links and other link types. Selecting the option **Match predecessor box border** sets the format of the relationship lines to the predecessor's box border format.

- **Diagram Options** are self-explanatory. The **Hide all fields except ID** will display the Task Boxes, as below. In the example, note that **Show link labels** has also been checked:

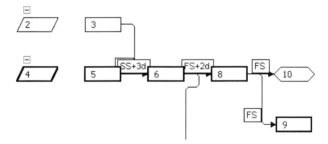

10.7 Early Date, Late Date and Float/Slack Calculations

To help understand the calculation of late and early dates, float and critical path, we will now manually work through an example. The boxes below represent tasks.

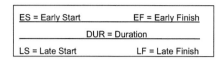

The forward pass calculates the early dates: EF = ES + DUR – 1

Start the calculation from the first task and work forward in time.

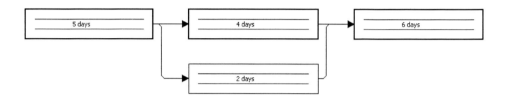

The backward pass calculates the late dates: LS = LF – DUR + 1

Start the calculation at the last task and work backwards in time.

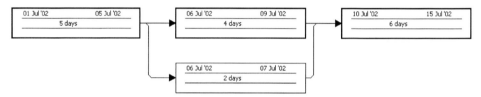

The **Critical Path** is the path where any delay causes a delay in the project and runs through the top row of tasks.

Total Float is the difference between either the **Late Finish** and the **Early Finish** or the difference between the **Late Start** and the **Early Start**. The lower 2 days' task has float of 9 – 7 = 8 – 6 = 2 days. None of the other tasks has float.

A task may not be on the Critical Path and may have more than one predecessor. A **Driving Relationship** is the predecessor that determines the Task Early Start. Microsoft Project 2003 does not identify the difference between **Driving** and **Non-driving Relationships**, which may often make analyzing a schedule difficult.

WORKSHOP 8

Scheduling Calculations

Preamble

We want to practice calculating Early and Late dates with a simple manual exercise.

Assignment

Calculate the early and late dates for the following tasks, assuming a Monday to Friday working week and the first task starts on 1 May 06.

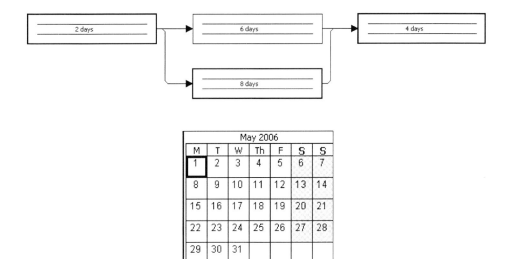

ANSWER TO WORKSHOP 8

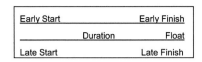

Forward Pass $EF = ES + DUR - 1$

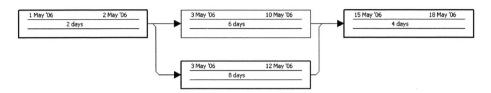

Backward Pass $LS = LF - DUR + 1$

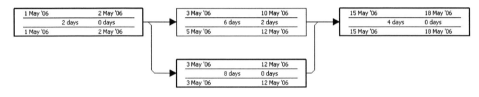

May 2006						
M	T	W	Th	F	S	S
1	2	3	4	5	6	7
8	9	10	11	12	13	14
15	16	17	18	19	20	21
22	23	24	25	26	27	28
29	30	31				

11 CONSTRAINTS

Constraints are used to impose logic on tasks that may not be realistically scheduled with logic links. Microsoft Project 2003 will only allow one constraint against a given task. This chapter will deal with the following constraints in detail:

- **Start No Earlier Than**

- **Finish No Later Than**

These are the minimum number of constraints that are required to effectively schedule a project.

These two constraints may be applied to summary and detailed tasks; all other constraints may only be applied to detailed tasks.

Start No Earlier Than (also known as an "Early Start" constraint) is used when the start date of a task is either known precisely or approximately. Microsoft Project 2003 will not calculate the task start date prior to this date.

Finish No Later Than (also known as "Late Finish" constraint) is used when the latest finish date is stipulated. Microsoft Project 2003 will not calculate the task's late finish date after this date.

The following chart summarizes the methods used to assign Constraints to Tasks:

Topic	Notes for Creating a Constraint
• Open the **Task Information** form.	Double-click on the Task and select the **Advanced** tab.
• Display the **Constraint Type** and **Constraint Date** column.	Apply the **Constraint Table** or insert the columns in an existing table.
• Type a date into a date field of the **Task Information** form or the **Details** form or a column.	Type a date in an Early Start box will apply an **Start No Earlier Than** of that date, without warning. A date typed into an Early Finish box will apply a **Finish No Later Than** constraint, without warning.
• Display a **Combination** view displaying the **Task Details** form in the lower pane.	Open the bottom pane, select <u>V</u>iew, **More** **Views…**, highlight the **Task Details** and click on ⌐ Apply ⌐.

There is an option found under the <u>T</u>ools, <u>O</u>ptions…, **Schedule** tab titled <u>T</u>asks will always honor their constraint dates. This function is described in detail in the **OPTIONS** chapter, **Schedule** section. When this option is checked, which is the default, constraints override a logic link. When unchecked, a logic link will override a constraint and a task may be delayed.

 Only one constraint may be applied to an activity except when a **Deadline Date** is assigned to an activity. This topic is discussed in this chapter.

A full list of **constraints** available in Microsoft Project 2003 is:

- **As Soon As Possible**   This is the default for a new task. A task is scheduled to occur as soon as possible and does not have a Constraint Date.

- **As Late As Possible**   A Task will be scheduled to occur as late as possible and does not have any particular Constraint Date. The Early and Late dates have the same date. A task with this constraint has no Total Float and delays the start of all the successor activities.

- **Start No Earlier Than**   This constraint sets a date before which the task will not start.

- **Start No Later Than**   This constraint sets a date after which the task will not start.

- **Must Start On**   This constraint sets a date on which the task will start. Therefore the task has no float. The early start and the late start dates are set to be the same as the Constraint Date.

- **Must Finish On**   This constraint sets a date on which the task will finish and therefore has no float. The early finish and the late finish dates are set to be the same as the Constraint Date.

- **Finish No Earlier Than** This sets a date before which the task will not finish.

- **Finish No Later Than**   This sets a date after which the task will not finish.

- **Deadline Date**   This is similar to applying a **Finish No Later Than** constraint. This offers the opportunity of putting a second constraint on a task.

Earlier Than constraints operate on the **Early Dates** and **Later Than** constraints operate on **Late Dates**. The picture below demonstrates how constraints calculate Total Float (Total Slack) of tasks (without predecessors or successors) against the first task of 10 days' duration:

	Duration	Constraint Date	Constraint Type	Total Slack	Late Start	Late Finish	
1	10 days	NA	As Soon As Possible	0 days	18 Oct '05	31 Oct '05	
2	3 days	NA	As Late As Possible	0 days	27 Oct '05	31 Oct '05	
3	3 days	24 Oct '05	Start No Earlier Than	3 days	27 Oct '05	31 Oct '05	
4	3 days	25 Oct '05	Start No Later Than	5 days	25 Oct '05	27 Oct '05	
5	3 days	24 Oct '05	Must Start On	0 days	24 Oct '05	26 Oct '05	
6	3 days	21 Oct '05	Must Finish On	0 days	19 Oct '05	21 Oct '05	
7	3 days	25 Oct '05	Start No Earlier Than	2 days	27 Oct '05	31 Oct '05	
8	3 days	26 Oct '05	Finish No Later Than	4 days	24 Oct '05	26 Oct '05	

1. An **Expected Finish** is used in Primavera P3 and SureTrak software to calculate the remaining duration of a task. There is no equivalent of this constraint in Microsoft Project 2003.

2. An activity assigned with an **As Late as Possible** constraint in Primavera P3 and SureTrak software will schedule the activity so it absorbs only **Free Float** and will not delay the start of successor activities. In Microsoft Project 2003, a task assigned with an **As Late as Possible** constraint will be delayed to absorb the Total Float and delay all its successor activities, not just the activity with the constraint.

11.1 Assigning Constraints

11.1.1 Open the Task Information Form

To assign a constraint using the **Task Information** form:

- Double-click on a task to open the form,

- Select the **Advanced** tab,

- Select the **Constraint type:** from the drop-down box,

- Select the **Constraint date:** from the calendar, or type the date in the box, and

- Click on the OK button to accept the constraint.

11.1.2 Displaying the Constraint Type and Constraint Date Column

To assign a constraint using the **Constraint Type** and **Constraint Date** columns:

- Either
  - ➢ Insert the **Constraint Type** and **Constraint Date** columns in your existing table by selecting **Insert**, **Column…**, or
  - ➢ Select the **Constraint Dates** table by selecting **View**, **Table:**, **More Tables…**.

- Assign your **Constraint Type** and **Constraint Date** from the drop-down boxes in the columns.

11.1.3 Typing a Date into the Task Information or Details Form

You may assign some constraints from the **Task Information** or **Task Details** form:

- A **Start No Earlier** constraint is assigned by overtyping the Start date, and

- A **Finish No Earlier** constraint is assigned by overtyping the Finish date.

You may overtype or select a date from the drop-down box.

 This function provides no warning that a constraint has been set and new users need to be careful when they enter a date into a Start or Finish box.

11.1.4 Display a Combination View Through the Task Details Form

There are a number of forms where constraints may be set, including the **Task Details** form, which is covered in detail in the **VIEWS, TABLES AND DETAILS** chapter. The **Task Details** form may be displayed by:

- Splitting the screen by selecting **Window**, **Split**,

- Make the bottom pane active by clicking in the bottom half anywhere, or

- Select **View**, **More Views…**, and select the **Task Details** form from the drop-down list:

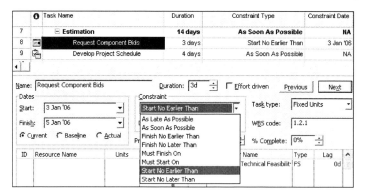

11.2 Deadline Date

Deadline Date was a new Microsoft Project 2000 feature, which allows you to set a date by when a task should be completed. A **Deadline Date** is similar to placing a **Finish No Later Than** constraint on a task and affects the calculation of the **Late Finish** date and float of the activity:

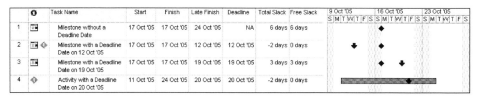

The Deadline Date may be displayed as a column and the display on the bar chart may be formatted as such. This is covered in the **FORMATTING THE DISPLAY** chapter. An Indicator icon is placed in the Indicator column.

11.3 Schedule From Project Finish date

You are able to impose an absolute project finish date by setting the **Schedule from:** option to **Project Finish Date** in the project using the **Project Information** form.

This option may be set after tasks have been added to the schedule. From the time that the project is set to schedule from the Project Finish date all new tasks will be assigned with an **As Late As Possible** (ALAP) constraint as they are created.

Any original tasks which may be set as **As Early As Possible** (AEAP) may either be:

- Reset as ALAP, and calculated with all new tasks as ALAP, or

- Left as AEAP.

When the original tasks are left as AEAP, the tasks will be scheduled as AEAP with a Start No Earlier constraint which is calculated either:

- With no float when their combined durations are greater than the ALAP tasks, or

- Will not start earlier than the earliest Early Start of the ALAP tasks when their combined durations are greater than the ALAP tasks.

11.4 Task Notes

It is often important to note why constraints have been set. Microsoft Project 2003 has functions that enable you to note information associated with a task, including the reasons associated for establishing a constraint.

The **Task Information** form has a **Note** tab, which has some word processing type formatting functions.

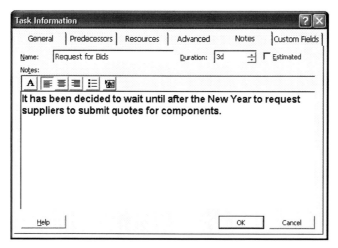

The notes may be displayed by:

- Inserting a column (The formatting of rows is covered in the **FORMATTING THE DISPLAY** chapter.):

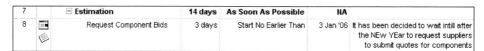

- Displaying on the bar chart (This topic is covered in the **FORMATTING THE DISPLAY** chapter.):

- There is an option for printing task notes in the **Page Setup...**, **View** form.

WORKSHOP 9

Constraints

Preamble

Management has provided further input to your schedule.

Assignment

1. Insert the **Total Slack** column, right of the **Finish** column in the **Entry** table.

2. Format the timescale to Months - January, Weeks - 28, 4... and Scale at 130%.

3. Format the Minor Timescale Gridlines to dotted black.

4. Run the **Gantt Chart Wizard** found under the **F̲ormat** command, and display Critical Path in the Gantt Chart. Do not choose to display resources and dates, and show the link lines between dependent tasks.

5. Add a **Total Float** bar to all tasks as shown below.

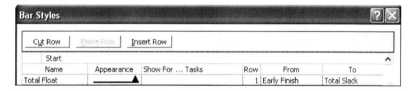

6. Observe the calculated finish date and the critical path of the project.

7. The client has said that they require the submission on 22 Jan 07. Apply a **Finish No Later Than** constraint and assign a constraint date of 22 Jan 07 to the **Bid Submitted** task and review float, this should have not changed. Should you be presented with an error message, read the message and then set the constraint.

8. Due to proximity to Christmas, management has requested we delay the **Component Bids** until first thing in the New Year (02 Jan 07). Consensus is that a better response and sharper prices will be obtained after the Christmas rush. Record this in the task notes.

   • To achieve this, set a **Start No Earlier Than** constraint and a constraint date of 02 Jan 07 on the **Component Bids** task. Should you be presented with an error message, allow scheduling conflict and set the constraint.

   • Now observe the impact on the critical path and end dates. Notice the negative float is not displayed on the Total Float bars. This bar would need to be added separately.

9. After review, it is agreed that two days can be deducted from **Component Work Packages Negotiated** task. Change the duration of this task to 4 days. Press **F9** to ensure the schedule is recalculated.

10. Save your **OzBuild Bid** project.

11. Save the project as **OzBuild No Resources** and close it. We will require a copy of this schedule later for Workshop 15.

ANSWER TO WORKSHOP 9

Before delaying the **Request Component Bids** until 02 Jan 07:

	Task Name	Duration	Start	Finish	Total Slack
1	OzBuild Bid	30 days	4 Dec '06	17 Jan '07	0 days
2	Research	9 days	4 Dec '06	14 Dec '06	0 days
3	Bid Request Documents Received	0 days	4 Dec '06	4 Dec '06	0 days
4	Bid Strategy	1 day	4 Dec '06	4 Dec '06	0 days
5	Technical Feasibility Study	8 days	5 Dec '06	14 Dec '06	0 days
6	Estimation	9 days	15 Dec '06	29 Dec '06	0 days
7	Installation Requirements	4 days	15 Dec '06	19 Dec '06	1 day
8	Component Bids	3 days	20 Dec '06	22 Dec '06	1 day
9	Project Schedule	4 days	20 Dec '06	23 Dec '06	4 days
10	Technical Details Schedule	9 days	15 Dec '06	29 Dec '06	0 days
11	Component Bids Costs	2 days	27 Dec '06	28 Dec '06	1 day
12	Proposal	12 days	2 Jan '07	17 Jan '07	0 days
13	Draft Bid Document	3 days	2 Jan '07	4 Jan '07	0 days
14	Reviewed Draft Bid Document	1 day	5 Jan '07	5 Jan '07	0 days
15	Design Validation	1 day	8 Jan '07	8 Jan '07	0 days
16	Revised Bid Document	1 day	8 Jan '07	8 Jan '07	6 days
17	Component Work Packages Negotiated	6 days	9 Jan '07	16 Jan '07	0 days
18	Bid Document Final	1 day	17 Jan '07	17 Jan '07	0 days
19	Bid Submitted	0 days	17 Jan '07	17 Jan '07	0 days

After delaying the **Request Component Bids** until 02 Jan 07:

	Task Name	Duration	Start	Finish	Total Slack
1	OzBuild Bid	35 days	4 Dec '06	24 Jan '07	-2 days
2	Research	9 days	4 Dec '06	14 Dec '06	3 days
3	Bid Request Documents Received	0 days	4 Dec '06	4 Dec '06	3 days
4	Bid Strategy	1 day	4 Dec '06	4 Dec '06	3 days
5	Technical Feasibility Study	8 days	5 Dec '06	14 Dec '06	3 days
6	Estimation	14 days	15 Dec '06	8 Jan '07	-2 days
7	Installation Requirements	4 days	15 Dec '06	19 Dec '06	5 days
8	Component Bids	3 days	2 Jan '07	4 Jan '07	-2 days
9	Project Schedule	4 days	20 Dec '06	23 Dec '06	7 days
10	Technical Details Schedule	9 days	15 Dec '06	29 Dec '06	3 days
11	Component Bids Costs	2 days	5 Jan '07	8 Jan '07	-2 days
12	Proposal	12 days	9 Jan '07	24 Jan '07	-2 days
13	Draft Bid Document	3 days	9 Jan '07	11 Jan '07	-2 days
14	Reviewed Draft Bid Document	1 day	12 Jan '07	12 Jan '07	-2 days
15	Design Validation	1 day	15 Jan '07	15 Jan '07	-2 days
16	Revised Bid Document	1 day	15 Jan '07	15 Jan '07	4 days
17	Component Work Packages Negotiated	6 days	16 Jan '07	23 Jan '07	-2 days
18	Bid Document Final	1 day	24 Jan '07	24 Jan '07	-2 days
19	Bid Submitted	0 days	24 Jan '07	24 Jan '07	-2 days

After trimming 2 days from **Component Work Packages Negotiated**:

	Task Name	Duration	Start	Finish	Total Slack
1	OzBuild Bid	33 days	4 Dec '06	22 Jan '07	0 days
2	Research	9 days	4 Dec '06	14 Dec '06	5 days
3	Bid Request Documents Received	0 days	4 Dec '06	4 Dec '06	5 days
4	Bid Strategy	1 day	4 Dec '06	4 Dec '06	5 days
5	Technical Feasibility Study	8 days	5 Dec '06	14 Dec '06	5 days
6	Estimation	14 days	15 Dec '06	8 Jan '07	0 days
7	Installation Requirements	4 days	15 Dec '06	19 Dec '06	8 days
8	Component Bids	3 days	2 Jan '07	4 Jan '07	0 days
9	Project Schedule	4 days	20 Dec '06	23 Dec '06	10 days
10	Technical Details Schedule	9 days	15 Dec '06	29 Dec '06	5 days
11	Component Bids Costs	2 days	5 Jan '07	8 Jan '07	0 days
12	Proposal	10 days	9 Jan '07	22 Jan '07	0 days
13	Draft Bid Document	3 days	9 Jan '07	11 Jan '07	0 days
14	Reviewed Draft Bid Document	1 day	12 Jan '07	12 Jan '07	0 days
15	Design Validation	1 day	15 Jan '07	15 Jan '07	0 days
16	Revised Bid Document	1 day	15 Jan '07	15 Jan '07	4 days
17	Component Work Packages Negotiated	4 days	16 Jan '07	19 Jan '07	0 days
18	Bid Document Final	1 day	22 Jan '07	22 Jan '07	0 days
19	Bid Submitted	0 days	22 Jan '07	22 Jan '07	0 days

12 FILTERS

This chapter covers the ability of Microsoft Project 2003 to control which activities are displayed, both on the screen and in printouts, by using **Filters**.

12.1 Understanding Filters

Microsoft Project 2003 has an ability to display tasks that meet specific criteria. You may want to see only the incomplete Tasks, or the work scheduled for the next couple of months, or the Tasks that are in-progress.

Microsoft Project 2003 defaults to displaying all tasks. It has a number of pre-defined filters available that you may use or edit. You can also create one or more of your own.

A filter may be applied to display or to highlight only those tasks that meet a criteria.

There are two types of filters:

- The first is where you select a **Filter** which exists or has been created on the **More Filters** form.

- The second is to create an **AutoFilter** which is very similar to the Excel **AutoFilter** (Drop-down filter) function.

Topic	Menu Command
• Apply a **Filter**	Select **Project**, **Filter for: All Tasks**, or With the **Formatting** toolbar displayed, select from the drop-down list.
• Create or modify a **Filter**	Select **Project**, **Filter for: All Tasks**, **More Filters...** to open the **More Filters...** form.
• Turn on **AutoFilter**	Select **Project**, **Filter for: All tasks**, **AutoFilter**, or Click on the **AutoFilter** [▽=] icon on the **Formatting** toolbar.
• Apply an **AutoFilter**	Click on the [▾] icon in the column headers.

12.2 Applying a Filter

Filters may be applied using several methods:

Method 1
Select **Project**, **Filter for: All Tasks**, and select the filter required from the menu.

Only filters established in the **Filter Definition** form are displayed. The currently applied filter is always written after **Filtered for:** in the menu. See above.

This may not be a complete list of filters as only filters chosen to be displayed in the menu when they are created will be displayed in this list.

Method 2
Display the **Formatting** toolbar, and select the filter you require from the drop-down list:

Select **View**, **Toolbars**, **Formatting** to display the formatting toolbar.

This may not be a complete list of filters since only filters chosen to be displayed in the menu when they are created will be displayed in this list.

Method 3
Select **P̲roject**, **F̲ilter for: All Tasks**, **More Filters...** to open the **M̲ore Filters...** form:

- The two radio buttons at the top of the form allow you to select filters that operate either on a **Task** criteria or on a **Resource** criteria.
  - ➤ **Task** criteria will operate on the criteria of most data such as costs, dates, durations, text columns, number columns, outline and WBS.
  - ➤ **Resource** criteria will operate on a similar criteria as Tasks but will select the resource value and not the task value.
- Select the required filter from the drop-down list, and
- You have a choice of selecting:
  - ➤ **Highlight** to highlight the tasks that meet the criteria, or
  - ➤ **Apply** to display only the tasks that meet the criteria.

12.3 Creating and Modifying Filters

Select **Project**, **Filter for: All Tasks**, **More Filters…** to open the **More Filters** form where you may create or modify a filter:

- Click on Organizer… to copy a filter from another file.

- Click on:

  ➢ New… to create a new filter, or

  ➢ Edit… to edit an existing filter, or

  ➢ Copy… to copy an existing filter.

- The **Filter Definition** form will be displayed. The one-line example below will only display critical tasks.

- The filter may then be edited to display or highlight the required tasks.

- Checking the **Show in menu** box will place the **filter** in the menu.

- Checking **Show related summary rows** will display any associated Summary Tasks.

- Select OK to return to the **More Filters** form.

12.4 Defining Filter Criteria

The filter criteria is determined by four columns of information in the **Filter Definition** form:

- **And/Or**, this function operates when you have two or more lines of data in the **Filter Definition** form to operate on.

- **Field Name** defines the data field you want to operate on.

- **Test** sets the criteria such as "Greater Than" or "Less Than."

- **Value(s)** is/are a date, number or text for the **Test** field to operate on. If more than one value is to be considered, for example when a **Test** is "Between," the two values are separated by a comma ",". The example below is a filter that will only display detail activities that will start between 24 Nov and 1 Dec 02.

This chapter will not cover all the aspects of filter definitions but will cover the major principles, so you may experiment when you require a filter.

There are a number of predefined filters with a standard Microsoft Project 2003 installation. You should inspect these to gain an understanding of how filters are constructed and applied.

12.4.1 Simple Filters, Operator and Wild Cards

A simple **Filter** contains one line of data and therefore the **And/Or** function is not used. These are the most common filters and meet most common filtering requirements.

These filters are used for such purposes as displaying tasks which:

- Are not started, complete, or in-progress tasks.

- Have a Start or Finish before or after a particular date.

- Contain specific text.

- Are within a range of dates.

There are some operands you should be aware of:

- The **Value(s)** field may have "Yes" or "No" entered. These are used for data items such as Milestones and Critical Tasks. The filter below will select all tasks that are not Milestones:

The **Wildcard** functions are similar to the DOS Wildcard functions and are mainly used for filtering text:

- You may replace a single character with a "**?**". Thus, a filter searching for a word containing "b?t" will display words like "bat", "bit" and "but."

- You may replace a group of characters with an *****. Thus, a filter searching for a word containing "b*t" will display words like "blot", "blight" and "but."

12.4.2 Calculated Filters

A calculated filter compares one value with another. The **Value(s)** field is selected from the drop-down box. The example below will display those tasks that are scheduled to start later than the baseline:

12.4.3   And/Or Filters

The **And/Or** function allows you to search for tasks which:

- Meet more than one criteria by using the **And/Or** option. The filter below displays tasks with Slack less than 5 days **Or** contain the word "Bid" and display the summary tasks:

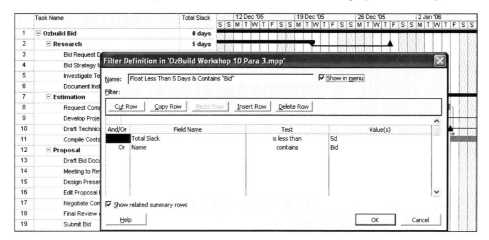

- Meet one criteria or a second by using the **And** function. The filter below displays tasks with Slack less than 5 days **And** contain the word "Bid" and do not display the summary tasks:

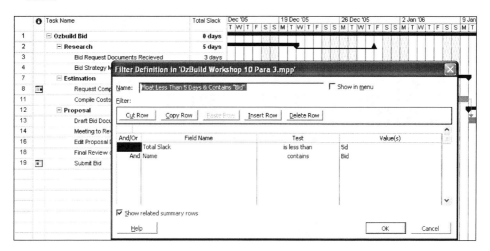

12.5 Multiple And/Or

Multiple **And/Or** statements are possible by placing a line with only an **And/Or** statement. The filter below selects tasks that contain the word "Bid" and start after 1 Jan 04 or are critical:

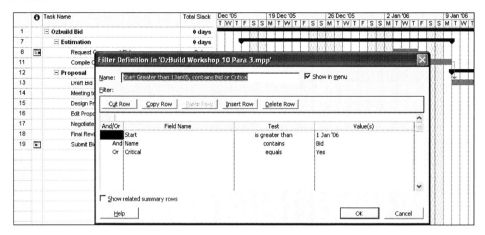

12.5.1 Interactive Filter

These filters allow you to enter the **Value(s)** of the filtered field after applying the filter. The filter is tailored each time it is applied via a user-prompt. The filter below will ask you to enter a word in the task name.

For this function to operate properly, the text in the **Value(s)** field must commence with a double quote " and end with a double quote and question mark "? :

After the filter is applied, you will be presented with the **Interactive Filter** form to enter the required text:

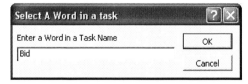

12.6 AutoFilters

AutoFilters in Microsoft Project 2003 are similar to the Excel **AutoFilter** function and allow you to select the filter criteria from drop-down menus in the column headers.

To create an **AutoFilter** based on one parameter:

- Use one of the following methods to turn on the **AutoFilter** function:
    - ➤ **Project**, **Filter for: All tasks**, **AutoFilter**, or
    - ➤ Click on the **AutoFilter** 🔽 icon located on the Formatting toolbar.
- The column headers will display the 🔽 icon in the column header. Click on this icon in one of the columns to display a drop-down box:

- Select the required criteria from the drop-down box.

You may now select another column and create a filter based on a second parameter to further reduce the number of tasks displayed.

To create a **Custom AutoFilter**, which is based on two parameters:

- Click on the 🔽 icon in the column headers.
- Select the **(Custom…)** option to open the **Custom AutoFilter** form:

- Select the parameters you want to operate on from the four drop-down boxes and check the **And** or **Or** radio button.

- To save a drop-down filter as a normal filter, click on the ⌊ Save… ⌋ button, which opens the **Filter Definition** form.

WORKSHOP 10

Filters

Preamble

Management has asked for reports on tasks to suit their requirements.

Assignment

Your will require the **OzBuild Bid** project to complete this exercise.

1. They would like to see all the critical tasks.
    ➢ Apply the **Critical** tasks filter. The Filter command is found under the **Project** menu item.
    You will see only tasks that are on the critical path and their associated summary tasks.

2. They would like to see all the tasks with float less than 5 days:
    ➢ Make a copy of the Critical filter and edit it:
    ➢ Assign a title to the filter: **Float Less Than 5 Days**.
    ➢ Change the condition to display a total slack of less than 5 days.
    ➢ Show the filter in the menu.
    You should find that one extra task is now shown.

3. They would like to see all the tasks with float less than 5 days or contain the word "Bid."
    ➢ Copy the **Float Less Than 5 Days** filter.
    ➢ Assign a title to the filter: **Float Less Than 5 Days & Contains "Bid"**.
    ➢ Add the condition: **Or** Name (Task Name) contains **Bid**, and
    ➢ Do not show in the menu.
    ➢ Apply the filter.
    There will be additional activities shown.

4. We now wish to create an **AutoFilter** that displays all the activities containing the word "Meeting."
    ➢ Apply the **All Tasks** Filter.
    ➢ Click on the ⊽= icon to activate the Auto Filters.
    ➢ Create a filter to select tasks containing the word "Technical."

5. Now apply the **All Tasks** Filter, remove the **AutoFilter** and save your **OzBuild Bid** project.

ANSWERS TO WORKSHOP 10

After applying the Critical Filter:

Creating the **Float Less Than 5 Days** Filter:

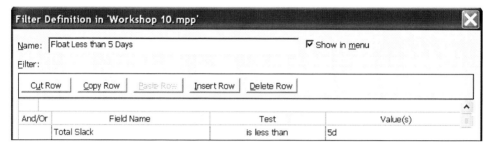

After applying the **Float Less Than 5 Days & Contains "Bid"** Filter:

Creating an AutoFilter that displays Tasks Name containing **Technical**:

13 VIEWS, TABLES AND DETAILS

A **View** is a function where parameters such as the **Table**, **Details** and **Bar** formatting are saved. A **View** may be saved and reapplied later on. A filter may be saved as part of a **View**.

Typically a **View** would be created for each report that has been defined in the **Communications Plan**. A **View** would applied to a schedule and used to create a report. The use of **Views** in this way saves a considerable amount time as the alternative would be to spend a significant amount of time reformatting the current View for each report.

The views displayed in the menu and on the **View Bar** with a standard load of Microsoft Project 2003 are listed below. There are more views available from the **More Views** form which will not be covered in this book.

View Name	Notes on the View
• Calendar	This may be applied to the top window only and displays the tasks overlaid on a calendar.
• Gantt	Displays a Table on the left of the screen and Gantt Chart on the right.
• Network Diagram	This view is a PERT-style display and is covered in the **NETWORK DIAGRAM VIEW** chapter.
• Task Usage*	Similar to Resources Usage, displays a Table with Tasks with associated Resources on the left and the Resources usage data apportioned over time on the right.
• Tracking Gantt	Similar to the **Gantt** view.
• Resource Graph*	A split table displaying the Resource name on the left-hand side and resource usage in bar chart format on the right-hand side.
• Resource Sheet*	A single table displaying Resource information such as costs and calendars.
• Resource Usage*	Similar to the Task usage, displays a Table with Resources with associated Tasks on the left and the Resources usage data apportioned over time on the right.

* The Views containing resource information are covered in more detail in the **STATUSING PROJECTS WITH RESOURCES** chapter.

The **Calendar** view is not covered in detail in this book and **Network** views are covered in the **NETWORK DIAGRAM VIEW** chapter.

13.1 Understanding Views

There are two types of Views:

- A **Single View** is normally applied to the top pane only; when the pane is split, the **Details** form is displayed in the bottom pane.

- A **Combination View** is comprised of two **Single Views**, one displayed in the top pane and one in the bottom pane.

Views may be created for each report identified in the **Communications Plan** and this function makes the creation of reports much simpler. It is highly recommended that a View is created for each frequently created report.

All **Single Views** may be applied to the top pane and when the window is split, most may be applied to the bottom pane. When a **Single View** is applied to the bottom pane, it will only display the information attributed to the task that is highlighted in the top pane.

When a **Single View** is applied to the top or bottom pane, the other pane is left with the contents of the previous **Combination View**.

A **View** is based on a **Screen** when it is created. The **Screen** may not be changed after the **View** is created. There are 14 **Screens**:

- Calendar
- Network Diagram
- Resource Form
- Resource Name Form
- Resource Usage
- Task Form
- Task Sheet

- Gantt Chart
- Relationship Diagram
- Resource Graph
- Resource Sheet
- Task Details Form
- Task Name Form
- Task Usage

The Table in **APPENDIX 1 – SCREENS USED TO CREATE VIEWS** lists the Screens and provides further detail about formatting the screens. A few important points to consider are:

- The **Calendar** screen may only be displayed in the top pane.

- The **Gantt Chart**, **Network Diagram** and **Relationship Diagram** screens are best displayed in the top pane and have limited use when displayed in the bottom pane.

- The **Forms** are best displayed in the bottom pane and display **Task** or **Resource** information about a task that is highlighted in the top pane. **Forms** may be further formatted by selecting **Format, Details**.

- The **Task Sheet** is similar to the **Gantt Chart** but does not display bars and is best displayed in the top pane.

- The **Resource** and **Task Usage** screens display resource information and are further discussed in the **RESOURCE HISTOGRAMS AND TABLES** chapter.

13.2 Applying a View

Views may be applied by either:

- Selecting **View** from the menu and then selecting the required View from the list above **More Views…**:

- Displaying the **View Bar** and clicking on the icon of the required View. To display or hide the **View Bar**, select **View**, **View Bar**. The **View Bar** will be displayed on the left-hand side of the screen, and will display the same list of Views as those in the menu.

- Selecting **View**, **More Views…** to open the **More Views** form and select the required View from the drop-down list.

Some Views are displayed in the menu and **View Bar** and these are available from the **More Views** form. To display a View in the menu and the **View Bar**, the View should be edited and the **Show in menu** box checked.

13.3 Creating a New View

A new View may be created by copying and editing an existing View, or by choosing **Copy...** to generate a View.

13.3.1 Creating a New Single View

To create a new Single View:

- Select **View**, **More Views...** to open the **More Views** form,

- Click on the New... button to open the **Define New View** form:

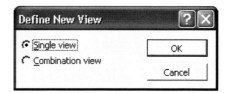

- Click on the **Single view** radio button to open the **View Definition** form:

- You may now enter:
  - ➤ The new View name in the **Name:** box by overtyping the "**View 1**" name assigned by Microsoft Project 2003,
  - ➤ Select the **Screen:** View, see **APPENDIX 1** for more information on the screens. A list of available screens is displayed below:

  - ➤ Select the **Table:** you want to apply with the view.

- ➤ You may not want to display your tasks using the Outline display mode. The **Group:** function allows you to group your tasks by other data items such as a **Text Column** or **Constraint Type** and is covered in the **GROUPING TASKS** chapter.
- ➤ You may also select a filter to apply with the layout from the **Filter:** drop-down box.
- ➤ Click the **Highlight filter** box to highlight the tasks that meet the filter specification as opposed to applying the filter.
- ➤ Click on the **Show in menu** box to display the View in the **View** menu.

- Click on the [OK] button to create the new **View**.

- From the **More Views** form click on the [Apply] button to apply the new **View**.

13.3.2 Creating a Combination View

To create a new Single View:

- Select **View**, **More Views…** to open the **More Views** form,

- Click on the [New…] button to open the **Define New View** form:

- This will open the **View Definition** form:

- Enter your View Name and the Views you want to display in the top and bottom pane,

- Click on **Show in menu** to display the View in the menu and on the **View Bar**, and

- Click on the [OK] button to create the new **View**.

It is a useful technique to create a View, and associated Table and Filter all with the same name and keep them together as a set. For example a Layout created to show Critical tasks would have a View, with Table and Filter all titled say Critical.

13.3.3 Copying and Editing a View

To copy an existing View:

- Select **View**, **More Views…**:

- Select the View you want to copy from the drop-down list and click on the [Copy…] button to open the **View Definition** form. This form is different for Single and Combination Views. The example below is a **Single View** created from the **Gantt Chart** Screen:

- The **Screen:** may not be changed in an existing or copied view and the screen option is shown as gray. See picture above.

- Change the name and any other parameters and then click on [OK] to create the **View**.

13.3.4 Copying a View To and From Another Project

Views may be copied from one project to another with the **Organizer** function. This may be accessed by selecting:

- [Organizer…] from the **More Views** form, or

- **Tools**, **Organizer…**, and selecting the **Views** tab.

13.4 Tables

A table selects and formats the columns displayed with a view. **Tables** are covered in the **FORMATTING THE DISPLAY** chapter. A table is applied to some **Views**. You may change the table applied to a view:

- When the view is active and you assign a different table, or

- By editing the **View**.

There are both Task and Resource tables and these are applied to the relevant view.

When you format a table by adding or removing columns, etc., you are editing the current table. These changes will appear when the table is next applied, even if it is associated with a **View** that is different from the current View. It is therefore recommended that you assign one Table to only one View.

13.4.1 Applying a Table

A **Table** may be applied by:

- Selecting **View**, **Table:** and selecting from the list in the menu, or

- Selecting **View**, **Table:**, **More Tables…** and selecting a table from the list and clicking on [Apply], or

- You may display a menu with the table options by clicking the **Select All** button, the box above the row 1 number, then right-clicking the mouse to display a sub-menu.

13.4.2 Create and Edit a Table

A **Table** may be created or edited by:

- Selecting **View**, **Table:**, **More Tables…** to open the **More Tables** form:

- Clicking on [New…] to create a new table, [Edit…] to edit an existing table or [Copy…] to create a copy of an existing table. All these buttons open the **Table Definition** form shown below:

- The functions in this form are similar to those in many other forms. The functions that are unique to this form are listed below:

  ➤ **Date format:** – Changes the format of the dates in this project and table only.

  ➤ **Row height:** – Allows you to specify the row height for this table.

  ➤ **Lock first column** – Ensures the first column is always displayed when scrolling to the right.

  ➤ **Auto-adjust header row heights** – Automatically adjusts the header height when the width of the column is adjusted so the column text wraps.

- [Organizer…] – Allows a table to be copied from one schedule to another.

- [Apply] – Applies the table to a view.

13.5 Details Form

Details forms are the third level of formatting that may be assigned in some views. An extensive list of the Details forms is outlined in **APPENDIX 1 – SCREENS USED TO CREATE VIEWS**.

Each view has a number of Details options, which tends to make this aspect of Microsoft Project 2003 difficult for all levels of users.

The **Details** forms may be selected by:

- Selecting **Format**, **Details**, or

- Right-clicking in the active pane to open the menu.

Example of Details forms:

- Task Form with Resource Costs Details form:

- Task Details with Predecessors and Successors Details form:

WORKSHOP 11

Organizing your Data

Preamble

Having completed the schedule you may report the information with different views.

Assignment

Display your project in the following formats, noting the different ways you may represent the same data. Open your **OzBuild Bid** project from previous workshops to complete the following exercise.

1. Display the **Calendar** view and scroll through a few months and see the holidays. Right Click and explore the menu options.
2. Display the **Network Diagram** view and zoom to 50%, then scroll around the schedule.
3. Display the **Relationship Diagram** view and scroll around the schedule by double-clicking on tasks.
4. Display the **Gantt Chart** view and split the screen.
5. Apply the **Task Details Form** view in the bottom screen.
6. Apply each one of the following **Details** forms to the **Task Details** view in the bottom screen.

7. Apply the following Tables to the **Gantt Chart** view in the top pane:
   ➢ Entry, then
   ➢ Tracking, then
   ➢ Schedule.
8. Close the split.

Continued over…

9. We now will create a Combination View to show only Critical Tasks with the Task Details form in the lower pane.

➤ Copy the Entry table and create a table titled **Critical** with the following columns:
   o ID
   o Indicators
   o Name
   o Start
   o Finish
   o Total Slack

➤ Create a Single Pane Gantt Chart View titled **Critical Top Pane**

➤ Create a Single Pane View titled **Critical Bottom Pane** using the Task Details form and All Tasks filter.

➤ Create a Combination View titled **Critical** and apply it.

➤ Apply the **Critical** View:

14 PRINTING AND REPORTS

You are now at the stage to print the schedule so people may review and comment on it. This chapter will examine one of the many options for printing your project schedule.

There are two tools available to output your schedule to a printer:

- The **Printing** function prints the data displayed in the current View.

- The **Reporting** function prints reports, which are independent of the current View. Microsoft Project 2003 supplies a number of predefined reports that may be tailored to suit your own requirements. Reports will not be covered in detail in this book.

 It is recommended that you consider using a product such as Adobe Acrobat to output your schedule in pdf format. You then will be able to email high quality outputs that recipients may print or review on screen without needing a copy of Microsoft Project 2003.

14.1 Printing

When a View is split, only the active View may be printed. The active view has a blue bar down the left-hand side of the screen. Views created from **Forms** (for example, the Task Form) may be not printed so the printing options are shown in gray.

Print settings are applied to the individual Views and the settings are saved with currently applied View.

There are three commands used when printing:

- **File**, **Page Setup...**
- **File**, **Print Preview**
- **File**, **Print...** or **Ctrl+P**

Each of these functions will be discussed only for printing the Gantt Chart. Printing all other Views is a similar process.

Some Views will have additional options and others reduced functionality. These other options should be easily mastered once the basics covered in this chapter are understood.

 Each time you report to the client or management, it is recommended that you save a complete copy of your project and change the name slightly (perhaps by appending a date to the file name or using a version number) or create a subdirectory for this version of the project. This allows you to reproduce these reports at any time in the future and an electronic copy is available for dispute resolution purposes at a later date. You may save the project into the same directory provided you change the file name.

14.2 *Print Preview*

To preview the printout, use Microsoft Project 2003's **Print Preview** option:

- Select <u>F</u>ile, **Print Pre<u>v</u>iew**, or

- Click the Print Preview 🔲 icon on the toolbar to view the printout in the window, or

- Click on the ⌐ Preview ⌐ button from the **Print** form. The **Print** form is covered later in this chapter, or

- Click on the ⌐ Print Preview... ⌐ button in the **Page** tab of the **Page Setup** form.

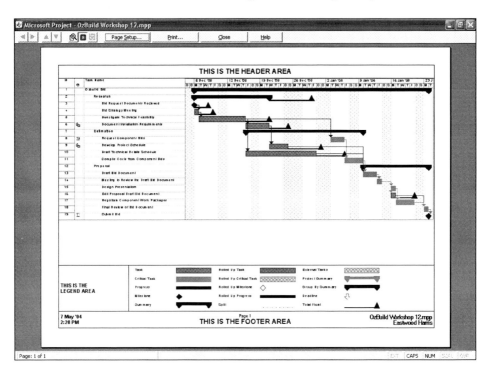

The following paragraphs describe the functions of the icons at the top of the Print Preview screen from left to right:

- The first four icons on the left, ◄ ► ▲ ▼, allow scrolling when a printout has more than one page.

- The magnifying glass 🔍 zooms in only. You will need to click on the preview screen to zoom out again. You may also click on the preview screen to zoom in.

- The next two icons, 🔲 and 🔳, display one or all pages, respectively.

- The next four are self-explanatory buttons labeled ⌐ Page <u>S</u>etup... ⌐, ⌐ <u>P</u>rint... ⌐, ⌐ <u>C</u>lose ⌐ and ⌐ <u>H</u>elp ⌐.

14.3 Page Set-up

To open the **Page Setup** form:

- Click the [Page Setup...] button on the **Print Preview** toolbar, or

- Select **File**, **Page Set_up...** to display the **Page Setup** form:

The **Page Setup** form contains the following tabs:

- Page

- Margins

- Header

- Footer

- Legend

- View

Depending on the View being printed, some options in the **Print Setup** form will be unavailable and shown in gray.

The [Options...] button opens the printer setup/options form.

14.3.1 Page Tab

The Microsoft Project 2003 options in the **Page** tab are:

- **Scaling** allows you to adjust the number of pages the printout will fit onto:
  - ➤ **Adjust to:** – Allows you to choose the scale of the printout that both the bars and column text are scaled to. Microsoft Project 2003 will calculate the number of pages across and down for the printout.
  - ➤ **Fit to:** – Allows you to choose the number of pages across and down and Microsoft Project 2003 will scale the printout to fit.
- The **First page number:** – Allows you to choose the first page number of the printout. This is useful when enclosing the printout as a follow-on to another document.
- Pages are numbered down first and then across:

14.3.2 Margins Tab

With this option you may choose the margins around the edge of the printout.

- Type in the margin size around the page. It is best to allow a wider margin for an edge that is to be bound or hole punched. 1" or 2.5cm is usually sufficient. The units of measurement, in. or cm, are adopted from the operating system **Control Panel**, **Regional and Language Option** settings.

- Microsoft Project 2003 will print a border around the Gantt Chart bars and Columns. **Borders around** places a border line around the outside of all text in the Headers and Footers. There are three options:

  ➢ **Every page** – This places a border around every page.
  ➢ **Outer pages** – This capability is only available with a **Network Diagramming** View. It allows you to join all the pages into one large printout with a border only on the outside edge of all the pages once they are joined up.
  ➢ **None** – Does not place a border on any sheets of the printout.

14.3.3 Header and Footer Tabs

Headers appear at the top of the screen above all schedule information and footers are located at the bottom, below the **Legend** if it is displayed. Both the headers and footers are formatted in the same way. We will discuss the setting-up of footers in this chapter.

Click on the **Footer** tab from the **Page Setup** form. This will display the settings of the default footers and headers. You should modify the output to suit your requirements.

- **Preview:** – The box at the top of the form shows how your Footer will be displayed.

- Text may be placed in all three positions in the Footer and Header – on the Left, Center and Right. Click on the required tab to the right of **Alignment:** to select the alignment position and insert new text or remove existing text in the box below.

- Text may be added by using a number of methods:
  - ➢ Freeform text may be typed into the footer box below **Alignment:**
  - ➢ You may click one of these icons, ⊞ **Page Number**, ⊞ **Total Page Count**, ⊞ **Current Date**, ⊙ **Current Time**, ⊟ **File Name** or ⊡ **Insert Picture**, to add data in the footer.
  - ➢ To insert Microsoft Project field-type information to your footer, click on ⌞Add⌟ to insert the field into the footer. You may select from the drop-down box to the right of **General:** or **Project fields:**
  - ➢ To format the text you must first highlight the text and then click on the **Format Text Font** icon ⎣A⎦ to open the **Font** form.
  - ➢ ⌞Print Preview...⌟ – Returns you to the **Print Preview** form.
  - ➢ ⌞Options...⌟ – Opens the **Printer Properties** form.
  - ➢ ⌞Print...⌟ – Opens the **Print** form.
  - ➢ ⌞OK⌟ – Accepts the changes.
  - ➢ ⌞Cancel⌟ – Cancels any recent changes that have not yet been saved.

14.3.4 Legend Tab

The **Legend Text** is printed to the left of the **Legend**:

The **Legend Text** is formatted in the same way as the **Header** and **Footer**.

The **Legend** has three additional options not available in the **Header** and **Footer**.

- Click on the radio button below **Legend on:**
  - ➢ **Every page** will print the legend at the bottom of every page.
  - ➢ **Legend page** will print the legend on a separate page with no detailed schedule data, bars, or columns.
  - ➢ **None** will not print a legend.
- **Width:** sets the width of the **Legend Text**.
- **Legend Labels...** Opens the **Font** form for formatting the font of the text in the legend next to each of the bars and milestones.
- To hide a bar type, type an * in front of the description in the **Bar Styles** form and this bar will not be displayed in the Legend:

14.3.5 View Tab

The View tab has five options:

- **Print all sheet columns:** – This option applies to the top-most horizontal pages only when there is more than one page across a printout.

  ➢ When checked, this option will print all the sheet columns displayed by the current table in the Gantt Chart, even if the columns are hidden by the vertical divider in the normal view.

  ➢ When unchecked, this option will only print the visible columns.

- **Print first … columns on all pages** – Applies to all pages. The greater of the number of columns between this option and the options above will be printed on the first page.

  ➢ **When checked**, this will allow repetitiously printing the selected number of columns on all pages.

  ➢ **When unchecked**, this will not print any columns on the second and subsequent pages across.

- **Print notes** will allow the printing of any **Notes** such as **Task Notes** on a separate page.

- **Print blank pages** will allow the printing of all pages in the Gantt Chart, even when there are no bars.

- **Fit timescale to end of page** will extend the timescale and associated bars so they fit to the end of a page:

  ➢ Option is unchecked, the bars stop in the middle of a page:

  ➢ Option is checked, bars and timescale extend to the end of a page:

- **Print row totals for values within date range** and **Print column totals** options become available when tabular data is selected for printing such as a Resource Sheet view.

14.4 Print Form

The **Print** form may be opened by:

- Selecting **File**, **Print…**, or

- Executing the keystrokes **Ctrl+P**, while

- Clicking on the ![print icon] print icon normally found on the Standard toolbar will automatically print out the document .

The following options are available:

- The **Printer** options are only available when this form is accessed from the main menu and are shown in gray when accessed from **Print Preview**.

- **Print range** allows you to choose the pages to be printed.

- **Copies** specifies the number of copies to be printed.

- **Timescale** allows specifying a Gantt Chart date range that will be printed. It does not filter out tasks. It is used to reduce the range of the Gantt Chart that will be printed. Unlike earlier versions of Microsoft Project, this setting is saved with a View when the project is saved.

- **Print left column of pages only** will print only the left pages of a printout that are more than one page wide.

- **Manual page breaks:**
  - ➢ Manual page breaks are inserted by highlighting the row above where a page break is required. Then, select **Insert**, **Page Break**. A dotted line will indicate the location of the manual page break.
  - ➢ To remove a manual page break, highlight the row above where there is a page break and select **Insert**, **Remove Page Break**.
  - ➢ The **Manual page breaks** check box in the **Print** form must be checked to acknowledge manual page breaks in the printout.

14.5 Reports

Select **View**, **Reports…** to open the **Reports** form which displays six icons.

- Select a Report option by:
  - ➢ Double-clicking on any one of the icons, or
  - ➢ Clicking on an icon and clicking on the [Select] button.
- This will open up a menu of reports under the chosen heading. The picture below displays the **Current Activities…** menu. The remaining five headings are done similarly and therefore are not explained in detail:

Double-click on any report and it will be sent to **Print Preview**. Here the print settings may be edited prior to printing.

Select **Critical Tasks** and click on the [Edit…] button to open the **Task Report** form. Some of the report parameters may be edited here:

WORKSHOP 12

Reports

Preamble

We want to issue a report for comment by management.

Assignment

Open your **OzBuild Bid** project from the previous workshop to complete the following steps:

1. Apply the **Gantt Chart** view.
2. Select the top pane and apply the Entry Table.
3. Delete the Resource Name column.
4. Adjust the columns to the best fit.
5. We wish to fit all the activities on one A4 or Letter size landscape page by:
    - Adjusting the middle tier unit of timescale to **Months** and minor bottom tier to **Weeks**.
    - Selecting Print Preview and showing all data columns.
    - Setting the page size to fit to 1 page wide by 1 page tall.
6. Hide the Legend by selecting **Legend on: None**.
7. Add the Project Title and Company Name in the footer with a font of Arial Bold 14 on the left hand side.
8. Compare your result with the picture on the next page.

ANSWERS TO WORKSHOP 12

15 TRACKING PROGRESS

The process of tracking progress is used once you have completed the plan, or have completed sufficient iterations to reach an acceptable plan, and the project is progressing. Now the important phase of regular monitoring begins. Monitoring is important to help catch problems as early as possible, and thus minimize the impact of problems on the successful completion of the project.

The *PMBOK® Guide* sections **4.4 Direct and Manage Project Execution** and **4.5 Monitoring and Control Project Work** would use the tracking progress function of Microsoft Project to assist in these processes.

The main steps for monitoring progress are:

- Set the **Baseline Dates**, also known as **Target Dates**. These are the dates against which progress is compared.

- Authorizing the work to proceed in accordance with the schedule.

- Record or mark-up progress as of a specific date, often titled the **Data Date**, **Status Date**, **Current Date** and **As-Of-Date**.

- **Update** or **Status** the schedule with **Actual Start** and **Actual Finish** dates where applicable, and adjust the task durations and percent complete.

- Compare and **Report** actual progress against planned progress and revise the schedule, if required.

- Add additional tasks as a result of **Change Requests**.

- Authorize further work in accordance with the current schedule.

By the time you get to this phase you should have a schedule that compares your original plan with the current plan, showing where the project is ahead or behind. If you are behind, you should be able to use this schedule to plan appropriate remedial measures to bring the project back on target.

This chapter will cover the following topics:

Topic	Menu Command
• Setting the **Baseline**	Select **T**ools, Trac**k**ing, **S**ave Baseline...
• Recording Progress	Guidelines on how to record progress.
• **Current Date** and **Status Date**	May be edited from the **Project**, **P**roject **Information...** form.
• Updating the Schedule	Select **T**ools, Trac**k**ing, Update **P**roject...
• Move the **Incomplete Work** of an **in-progress** task into the future	Select **T**ools, Trac**k**ing, Update **P**roject...
• Updating the Tasks	Select **T**ools, Trac**k**ing, Update **T**asks...

15.1 Setting the Baseline

Setting the Baseline copies the following information into new fields in the existing file:

- **Early Start** and **Finish** dates into fields titled **Baseline Start** and **Baseline Finish**.

- **Original Duration** into the **Baseline Duration**.

- Each resource's **Costs** and **Work** into **Baseline Costs** and **Baseline Work** (the number of hours) when resources are assigned to tasks.

Once the Baseline is set you will be able to compare your progress with your original plan. You will be able to see if you are ahead or behind schedule and by how much.

Some important points you should understand before setting the Baseline:

- The Baseline Dates should be established before you status the schedule for the first time.

- The Baseline Dates and Duration fields are not calculated fields and may be edited in columns and forms. Caution should be used before changing a Baseline Date or Duration, since it is the basis for all project deviation measurements.

- Setting the Baseline Date does not store the logic, float/slack times, or constraints.

- A Baseline is normally applied to all tasks irrespective of their Outline levels.

15.1.1 Setting Baseline Dates

To set the Baseline select **Tools**, **Tracking**, **Save Baseline...** to display the **Save Baseline** form.

- The **Save baseline** option copies the **Early Start** and **Finish** dates into the **Baseline Start** and **Finish** date fields respectively.

- You may highlight some tasks before opening the **Save Baseline** form and clicking on the **Selected tasks** radio button to set the Baseline for the specified tasks only.

This operation will overwrite any previous Baseline settings.

The **Save Baseline** form shows the default settings, which selects **All Tasks** and the **Early dates** which are titled **Start/Finish**. This is the normal method of setting the Baseline.

After establishing the Baseline, you can input the progress data without fear of losing the original dates. This will also enable you to compare the progress with the original plan.

15.1.2 Setting an Interim Baseline

This function was introduced in Microsoft 2002.

It may be necessary to save an interim baseline as a result of **Change Requests**. This would occur when the scope of a project has changed so much that the original Baseline is no longer viable and a new baseline is required to measure progress against, but at the same time you may also want to keep a copy of the original baseline. This process may also be used to display the effect of scope changes on an original project plan by comparing one baseline with another.

There are two types of data fields to save interim baselines:

- Using one of the 10 additional baselines titled **Baselines 1** to **10**. These Baselines will save start date, finish date, work and cost information.

- Using one of the 10 sets of **Start Date, Finish Date** and **Duration** fields. This function will only save the start and finish date information. This is termed an **Interim Plan** by Microsoft Project 2003.

To set the Interim Baseline or Interim Plan, select **Tools**, **Tracking**, **Save Baseline...** to display the **Save Baseline** form, select either:

- **Save baseline** to save the current schedule to one of the 11 Baselines, or

- **Save interim plan** then:
  - ➤ Select the dates you want to copy from using the **Copy:** drop-down box, and then
  - ➤ Select where you want to copy the dates to using the **Into:** drop-down box.

The **Baseline** data may be reviewed in some Views such as the **Task Details Form** and in columns. You will be able to display the **Baseline 1** to **10** and **Interim Plan** dates and durations in columns and as a bar on the Gantt Chart but not in the forms. Therefore, it is recommended that the current baseline be saved as **Baseline** since the data is more accessible that way. Previous baselines are copied to **Baselines 1** to **10**.

Date fields may be renamed with the **Customize Fields** form. Select **Tools**, **Customize**, **Fields...** to open this form.

15.1.3 Summary Task Interim Baseline Calculation

When a Detailed task is moved from one Summary task to another, the Detailed task Baseline dates are moved with the task. It is possible, however, that the original Summary Baseline data will no longer be valid if the Detailed task that has been moved established either the start or the finish date of the Summary task.

When a schedule has costs or work then any movement of a detailed task from one summary task to another summary task should result in a change to the baseline value of the summary tasks. The Costs and Work Baseline calculations are covered in the **STATUSING PROJECT WITH RESOURCES** chapter, paragraph **20.9 Summary Task Interim Baseline Calculation**.

In the picture below, the task Detailed 2.3 was moved from below Detailed 2.2 to below Detailed 1.3 and the baseline of tasks Parent 1 and Parent 2, the lower bar on each task, are no longer an accurate summary of the detailed tasks. When the task was moved in the example below, the option **Autolink inserted or moved tasks** found under **Tools**. **Options...**, **Schedule** tab is unchecked.

A new function in Microsoft Project 2002 may recalculate the Summary Task Baseline data (but not Interim Plan dates) when a Detailed task is moved by using the **Roll up baselines** option in the **Save Baseline** form:

- **Entire project** – Will recalculate the entire project baseline and recalculate all Summary tasks. This is effectively resetting the baseline.

- **Selected tasks: - Roll up Baselines:** – This has two options which operate on selected tasks:
  - ➤ **To all summary tasks** – This option resets the baseline of selected tasks to the current schedule. This does not reset the summary tasks baseline to reflect the new baseline of detailed tasks.
  - ➤ **From subtasks to selected summary task(s)** – This option will allow a summary task baseline to be updated to reflect the original baseline of moved tasks.

In the example below a new task Detail 1.4 was added below the Parent 1 task.

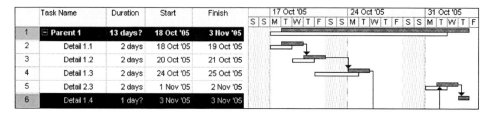

Parent 1 and Detail 1.4 were highlighted and the option **From subtasks to selected summary task(s)** applied. The baseline of Parent 1 now accurately reflects the detailed tasks which it summarizes. See below:

 It is recommended to set a revised baseline when a new detailed activity has been added. The new activity and the associated Parent tasks should be highlighted and the option **From subtasks to selected summary task(s)** applied.

15.1.4 Clearing and Resetting the Baseline

You may clear some or all of the Baseline fields using the **Clear Baseline** form. This is opened by selecting **Tools**, **Tracking**, **Clear Baseline…**:

15.1.5 Displaying the Baseline Data

The Baseline dates data may be displayed by:

- Displaying the Baseline columns where the data may be edited, or

- Displaying the dates in a form such as the Resources Details Form. This will only display the **Baseline** data and not for **Baseline 1** to **10**, or

- Show a baseline bar on the Bar Chart.

The Baseline Start Dates, Finish Dates and Durations may be edited and are not linked by logic. Therefore, a change to a Baseline Duration will not affect either the Baseline Start Date nor the Baseline Finish date.

15.2 Authorizing Execution of Work

Normally Views such as a "2 Week Look Ahead" is created to assist in identifying work that should be executed in the immediate future.

The person responsible for the Task, who may not be performing the work, could be identified in a Custom Outline Code leaving the Resource function available for assigning the work to people.

This View could be Grouped by the responsible person with a manual page break inserted at each responsible person, thus allowing a page to be printed for each responsible person. See the picture below:

15.3 Practical Methods of Recording Progress

Normally a project is statused once a week, bi-weekly, or monthly. Very short projects could be statused daily or even by the shift or hour. As a guide, a project would typically be statused between 12 and 20 times. Progress is recorded on or near the **Data Date** and the scheduler updates the schedule upon the receipt of the information.

The following information is typically recorded for each task when statusing a project:

- The task start date and time if required,

- The number of days/hour the **Task** has to go or when the task is expected to finish,

- The percentage complete, and

- If complete, the task finish date and time, if required.

A marked-up copy recording the progress of the current schedule is often produced prior to updating the data with Microsoft Project 2003. Ideally, the mark-up should be prepared by a physical inspection of the work or by a person who intimately knows the work, although that is not always possible. It is good practice to keep this marked-up record for your own reference at later date. Ensure that you note the date of the mark-up (i.e. the data date) and, if relevant, the time.

Often a Statusing Report or mark-up sheet, such as the one below, is distributed to the people responsible for marking up the project progress. The marked-up sheets are returned to the scheduler for data entry into the software system.

The View, such as the one below, may have a filter applied. In this case, only tasks in-progress or due to start in the next few weeks are displayed. A manual page break could be placed at each responsible person's band, and when the schedule is printed each person would have a personal listing of their tasks that are either in-progress or due to commence. This is particularly useful for large projects.

Other electronic methods, discussed next, may be employed to collect the data, but irrespective of the method used, the same data needs to be collected.

	Task Name	Early Start	Act. Start	Early Finish	Act. Finish	% Comp.	Act. Dur.	Rem. Dur.
	⊟ Responsibility: Angela Low	02 Jan '02	NA	08 Jan '02	NA	0%	0 days	5 days
8	Request Component Bids	02 Jan '02	NA	04 Jan '02	NA	0%	0 days	3 days
11	Compile Costs from Bids	07 Jan '02	NA	08 Jan '02	NA	0%	0 days	2 days
	⊟ Responsibility: Carol Peterson	03 Dec '01	NA	19 Jan '02	NA	0%	0 days	32 days
3	Bid Document Received	03 Dec '01	NA	03 Dec '01	NA	0%	0 days	0 days
14	Draft Bid Meeting	14 Jan '02	NA	14 Jan '02	NA	0%	0 days	1 day
19	Submit Bid	19 Jan '02	NA	19 Jan '02	NA	0%	0 days	0 days
	⊟ Responsibility: David Williams	03 Dec '01	NA	18 Jan '02	NA	0%	0 days	32 days
4	Bid Strategy Meeting	03 Dec '01	NA	03 Dec '01	NA	0%	0 days	1 day
13	Draft Bid Documents	09 Jan '02	NA	11 Jan '02	NA	0%	0 days	3 days
15	Design Presentation	15 Jan '02	NA	15 Jan '02	NA	0%	0 days	1 day
18	Final Bid Meeting	18 Jan '02	NA	18 Jan '02	NA	0%	0 days	1 day
	⊟ Responsibility: Melinda Young	15 Jan '02	NA	17 Jan '02	NA	0%	0 days	3 days
16	Edit Proposal Draft	15 Jan '02	NA	15 Jan '02	NA	0%	0 days	1 day
17	Finalise Bid Package	16 Jan '02	NA	17 Jan '02	NA	0%	0 days	2 days
	⊟ Responsibility: Scott Morrison	04 Dec '01	NA	28 Dec '01	NA	0%	0 days	17 days
5	Investigate Technical Feasibility	04 Dec '01	NA	13 Dec '01	NA	0%	0 days	8 days
6	Document Installation Requirements	14 Dec '01	NA	18 Dec '01	NA	0%	0 days	4 days
9	Develop Project Schedule	19 Dec '01	NA	22 Dec '01	NA	0%	0 days	4 days
10	Draft Technical Details Schedule	14 Dec '01	NA	28 Dec '01	NA	0%	0 days	9 days

The previous View has been created by:

- Entering the responsible person in Text 1,

- Renaming Text 1 as Responsibility using **Tools**, **Customize**, **Fields...** and

- Grouping by Text 1, which has been renamed **Responsibility**.

There are several methods of collecting the project status:

- By sending a sheet to each responsible person to mark up and return to the scheduler.

- By cutting and pasting the data from Microsoft Project 2003 into another document, such as Excel, and emailing the data to them as an attachment.

- By giving the responsible party direct access to the schedule software to update it. This approach is not recommended, however, unless the project is broken into subprojects. By using the subproject method, only one person updates each part of the schedule.

- Microsoft Central, a companion Microsoft Project product that allows collaborative scheduling, could be implemented. This topic is beyond the scope of this book.

Some projects involve a number of people. In such cases, it is important that procedures be written to ensure that the status information is collected:

- In a timely manner,

- Consistently,

- In a complete manner, and

- In a usable format.

It is important for a scheduler to be aware that some people have great difficulty in comprehending a schedule. When there are a number of people with different skill levels in an organization, it is necessary to provide more than one method of updating the data. You even may find that you have to sit down with some people to obtain the correct data, yet others are willing and comfortable to email you the information.

15.4 Understanding the Concepts

There are some terms and concepts used in Microsoft Project 2003 that must be understood before we update a project schedule:

15.4.1 Task Lifecycle

There are three stages of a task's lifecycle:

- **Not Started** – The **Early Start** and **Early Finish** dates are calculated from the logic, **Constraints** and **Task Duration**.

- **In-Progress** – The task has an **Actual Start** but is not complete.

- **Complete** – The task is in the past, the **Actual Start** and **Actual Finish** dates have been entered into Microsoft Project 2003, and they override the logic and constraints.

15.4.2 Actual Start Date Assignment of an In-Progress Task

This section will explain how Microsoft Project 2003 assigns the **Early Start** of an **In-Progress** task.

- A task **Duration** is the duration from the **Early Start** or **Actual Start** to the **Early Finish** or **Actual Finish** and is calculated over the **Task Calendar**.

- When an **Actual Start** is entered into the **Actual Start** field, this date overrides the **Early Start date**. The predecessor logic and start date constraints are ignored.

- An un-started task **Actual Start date** is set to equal the **Early Start** date when:
  - ➢ A **% Complete** between 1% and 99% is entered,, or
  - ➢ An **Actual Duration** is entered, or
  - ➢ An **Actual Finish** is entered, or
  - ➢ When a % Complete of 100% is entered, then an Actual Start date equal to the Early Start and an Actual Finish date equal to the Early Finish date are both set.

15.4.3 Calculation of Actual and Remaining Durations of an In-Progress Task

- The **Actual Duration** is the worked duration of a task and **Remaining Duration** is the unworked duration of a task.

- **Duration** = **Actual Duration** + **Remaining Duration**. Before a task is commenced the **Actual Duration** is zero and the **Remaining Duration** equals the **Duration** assigned to the task.

- There is an in-built proportional link between **Duration, Actual Duration, Remaining Duration** and **% Complete**. It is not possible to unlink these fields (as in other scheduling software) and therefore not possible to enter the **Remaining Duration** independently of the **% Complete**.
  - ➢ Change the **Duration**, the **Actual Duration** remains constant and the **% Complete**, and the **Remaining Duration** changes proportionally.
  - ➢ Change the **% Complete**, the **Duration** remains constant and the **Actual Duration** and the **Remaining Duration** change proportionally.
  - ➢ Change the **Actual Duration**, the **Duration** remains constant and the **% Complete** and the **Remaining Duration** changes proportionally.
  - ➢ Change the **Remaining Duration**, the **Actual Duration** remains constant and the **% Complete** and the **Duration** changes proportionally.

- When a **% Complete** is assigned, then the **Actual Start** date is set to be equal to the **Early Start** date and durations are recalculated as per the above rules.

- When the **% Complete** is set to 100 or the **Remaining Duration** is set to zero, the **Actual Finish** date is set to the **Early Finish date** and the **Actual Duration is** set to the **Duration**.

- An **Actual Finish** date overrides an **Early Finish** date, and finish date constraints are ignored.

The example below shows three tasks, the first unstarted, the second in-progress and the third complete. You should observe:

- The relationship between the **Duration**, **Actual Duration**, **Remaining Duration** and **% Complete** in each of the tasks, and

- How the **Actual Start** and **Actual Finish** are set.

	Start	Actual Start	Early Finish	Actual Finish	% Complete	Duration	Actual Duration	Remaining Duration			
1	18 Oct '05	NA	31 Oct '05	NA	0%	10 days	0 days	10 days			
2	18 Oct '05	18 Oct '05	31 Oct '05	NA	25%	10 days	2.5 days	7.5 days			
3	18 Oct '05	18 Oct '05	31 Oct '05	31 Oct '05	100%	10 days	10 days	0 days			

 Unlike other scheduling software, it is not possible in Microsoft Project 2003 to unlink the **Remaining Duration** and **% Complete**. This will prove frustrating to some schedulers as you will not be able use the **% Complete** column to represent the amount of work complete when the task is not progressing at a linear rate.

15.4.4 Calculating the Early Finish Date of an In-Progress Task

Retained Logic and Progress Override are not terms used by Microsoft Project 2003 documentation. These terms are used by other scheduling software and are used here to help clarify how Microsoft Project 2003 performs its calculations. In the example below, there are two tasks with a Finish-to-Start relationship:

	Actual Start	Actual Finish	% Complete			
1	NA	NA	0%			
2	NA	NA	0%			

There are two options for calculating the finish date of the successor when the successor task starts before the predecessor task is finished:

- **Retained Logic**. In the example below, the logic relationship is maintained between the predecessor and successor for the unworked portion of the Task, the Remaining Duration, and continues after the predecessor has finished.

	Actual Start	Actual Finish	% Complete			
1	19 Oct '05	NA	50%			
2	21 Oct '05	NA	10%			

This option will operate when the following conditions are met:
  ➢ The Project Option **Split in-progress tasks** is checked, and
  ➢ There is an **Actual Start**, and
  ➢ A **% Complete** between 1% and 99% is assigned to the successor task.

- **Progress Override**. In the example below, the Finish-to-Start relationship between the predecessor and successor is disregarded, and the unworked portion of the Task, the Remaining Duration, continues before the predecessor has finished:

	Act. Start	Act. Finish	% Comp.	17 Oct '05							24 Oct '05					
				M	T	W	T	F	S	S	M	T	W	T	F	S
1	19 Oct '05	NA	50%													
2	21 Oct '05	NA	10%													

Progress Override option will operate when:

➢ The Project Option **Split in-progress tasks IS NOT** checked,

or

➢ The task has an **Actual Start** and 0% Complete and Project Option **Split in-progress tasks IS** checked.

This function may result in some problems in reporting a schedule when the **Split in-progress tasks** option is used in combination with some Tasks set to 0 % Complete and other tasks set between 1% and 99% Complete. The two examples below are from the same schedule, both with the **Split in-progress tasks** option checked, one with 0% and one with 1%. You will notice the task assigned 0% has an earlier Finish Date than the task assigned 1% complete, which has split.

	Act. Start	Act. Finish	% Comp.	17 Oct '05							24 Oct '05							31 Oct '05					
				M	T	W	T	F	S	S	M	T	W	T	F	S	S	M	T	W	T	F	S
1	19 Oct '05	NA	50%																				
2	19 Oct '05	NA	0%																				

	Act. Start	Act. Finish	% Comp.	17 Oct '05							24 Oct '05							31 Oct '05					
				M	T	W	T	F	S	S	M	T	W	T	F	S	S	M	T	W	T	F	S
1	19 Oct '05	NA	50%																				
2	19 Oct '05	NA	1%																				

You therefore need to pay careful attention to any warning messages Microsoft Project 2003 presents.

15.4.5 Summary Bars Progress Calculation

Summary bars are not normally statused by entering the **Actual Start** date, **Actual Finish** date, or **% Complete** against them. This is possible in Microsoft Project and is covered later in this chapter in the section titled **Marking Up Summary Tasks**.

This status information is usually entered against the detailed tasks, and the summary tasks inherit the status data from the detailed tasks.

- An **Actual Start** is assigned against a Summary Task when any Child Task has an **Actual Start**.

- A Summary Task's **% Complete** is calculated from the total of all the child tasks' **Actual Durations** divided by the total of all the child tasks' **Durations**.

- A Summary Task's **Actual** and **Remaining Durations** are calculated from the **Duration** and **% Complete**.

- An **Actual Finish** is assigned against a Summary task when all Detail tasks have an **Actual Finish**.

15.4.6 Understanding the Current Date, Status Date and Update Project Date

Microsoft Project 2003 has two project data date fields that may be displayed as vertical lines on the schedule, and these dates may be edited from the **Project**, **Project Information...** form:

- **Current Date** – This date is set to the computer's date each time a project file is opened. It is used for calculating **Earned Value** data when a **Status Date** has not been set.

- **Status Date** – This field is blank by default. When this date is set, it will not change when the project is saved and reopened at a later date. When set, this date overrides the **Current Date** for calculating **Earned Value** data.

It is recommended that the **Status Date** be set and displayed as a vertical line on a progressed schedule, and that the **Current Date** not be displayed, as the **Current Date** represents the date today and does not normally represent any scheduling significance.

The **Update Project Date** may also influence how Microsoft Project 2003 calculates the end date of some activities. This date may not be displayed as a vertical line on the screen but may be used in conjunction with the **Reschedule Uncompleted Work To Start After** function covered later in this chapter.

NEITHER the **Current Date** nor the **Status Date** is used to calculate the **Early Finish** of an **In-Progress** task of a schedule using **F9** or **Automatic Scheduling**, unless one of the following two functions is used:

- The **Tools**, **Tracking**, **Update Project...**, **Reschedule incomplete to start after: Current Date**, or

- The **Status Date** may be used to move the start of incomplete and the finish of completed parts of a task back or forward to the **Status Date** with the new to Microsoft Project 2002 function **Status Date Calculation Options**. This option will be discussed at the end of this chapter. It also has restrictions which could make the function difficult to use on a project.

Ideally, scheduling software has one **Data Date** and its function is to:

- Separate the completed parts of tasks from incomplete parts of tasks,

- Calculate or record all costs and hours to date before the data date, and to forecast costs and hours to go after the data date.

- Calculate the **Finish Date** of an in-progress task from the **Data Date** plus the **Remaining Duration** over the **Task Calendar**.

Therefore, it is relatively simple in Microsoft Project 2003 to be in a situation where you have complete or in-progress tasks with start dates later than the data date, and/or incomplete or un-started tasks with a finish date earlier than the data date. This is an unrealistic situation, which is more difficult to achieve in other scheduling software packages. Care should be taken to avoid this situation.

15.5 *Updating the Schedule*

The next stage is to update the schedule by entering the mark-up information against each task.

When dealing with large schedules it is normal to create a look-ahead schedule by creating a filter to display incomplete and un-started tasks commencing in the near future only.

Microsoft Project 2003 provides several methods of statusing the schedule:

- **Update Project** – This is an automated process that assumes all tasks have progressed as planned. After updating a project, you may adjust the dates and percent complete to the recorded progress.

- **Update Tasks** – This function is used to status tasks one at a time.

- Update tasks using the **Task** or **Task Details** form.

- Update tasks by displaying the appropriate tracking columns by:
  - ➤ Selecting the **Tracking** table, or
  - ➤ Creating your own table, or
  - ➤ Inserting the required columns in an existing table.

Each of these four methods is discussed in the following sections. Then we will discuss the following two functions which are designed to assist you in moving tasks to their logical places in relation to the **Status Date**:

- **Move Incomplete Work into the Future**, and

- **Status Date Calculation Options**.

15.5.1 Using Update Project

Microsoft Project 2003 has a facility titled **Update Progress** for updating a project as if it had progressed according to plan. This function sets **Actual Start** and **Actual Finish** dates, **% Complete** and **Renaming Durations** in proportion to a user-assigned date.

Select **Tools**, **Tracking**, **Update Project...** to open the **Update Project** form:

There are two options under **Update work as complete through:** which apply to in-progress tasks only.

- **Set 0% – 100 % Complete**:
  - ➢ This option sets the **Actual Start** to the **Early Start**, and
  - ➢ Sets the **% Complete** and **Actual Duration** in proportion to the amount of time worked for any in-progress tasks.
  - ➢ Sets the **Status Date** to the date you have nominated as the update date, the vertical line in the picture below:

- **Set 0% or 100 % Complete only**. This option sets:
  - ➢ The **Actual Start** to the **Early Start** but leaves the **% Complete** and **Actual Duration** at zero.
  - ➢ The **% Complete** is set to 100% only when the task is complete.
  - ➢ Does not set the **Status Date** (or reset if it has be set in a previous update) to the date you have nominated as the update date. Therefore is no vertical line representing the **Status Date** in the picture below:

You may use the **Selected tasks** option when you highlight the tasks to be progressed before opening the **Update Project** form. Unselected tasks will not be progressed, but these tasks may be scheduled to occur after the **Status Date** by using the **Reschedule uncompleted work to start after:** function. This is covered later in this section.

You may not reverse progress with this option.

15.5.2 Update Tasks

Microsoft Project 2003 has a function that may be used for updating tasks one at a time or may be used for updating selected tasks to be updated with the same information. For example, there may be several tasks with the same Actual Start or % Complete.

- Select one or more tasks that you want to update with the same information such as the same Actual Start date.

- Select **Tools**, **Tracking**, **Update Tasks…** to open the **Update Tasks** form:

- Enter the required data and click on the ⬚ OK ⬚ button to close the form.

 Using the **Update Tasks** form is a cumbersome method for updating a large number of individual tasks since the form has to be closed after each task has been updated, the cursor moved to the next task and the form reopened. If you have a large number of tasks to be updated, it is quicker to use columns or a **Detailed** form in the lower pane.

15.5.3 Updating Tasks Using the Task Information, Task or Task Details Form

You may use either the **Task Information**, **Task** form or the **Task Details** form to update progress:

- Open the **Task** form by double-clicking on a task:

- To open the **Task Details** form, open the dual-pane view by either:
  - ➢ Selecting **Window**, **Split**,
  - ➢ Dragging the divider line with the mouse, or
  - ➢ Selecting a **View** with a dual pane or right-click.
  - ➢ Then, click in the bottom pane to make it active. There will be a blue bar down the left-hand side when the bottom pane is active.

  Now select **View**, **More Views…**, **Task Details Form** if an acceptable view is not available:

- Updating a task:
  - ➢ Enter a **% Complete**. An **Actual Start** date will be set by Microsoft Project 2003 and may be edited from the **Start:** drop-down box.
  - ➢ The **Duration** may be edited in order to calculate a new finish date. You will note that the % Complete will change when the duration is edited.
  - ➢ When a date is typed into the **Finish:** drop-down box, a **Finish Constraint** will be set without warning. These may be edited from the **Task Information** form's **Advanced** tab.

Using the **Task Information** form function is a cumbersome method for updating a large number of tasks, since the form has to be closed after each task has been updated, the cursor moved to the next task and the form reopened. If you have a large number of tasks to be updated, it is quicker to use columns or a **Detailed** form in the lower pane.

15.5.4 Updating Tasks Using Columns

An efficient method of updating tasks is by displaying the data in columns. This may be achieved by:

- Applying the **Tracking Table**, or

- Creating your own table, or

- Inserting the required columns.

To apply the tracking table, select **View**, **Table:**, **Tracking** table. This table may not exist if you are working on a schedule that has had this table deleted or if you have a non-standard load of Microsoft Project 2003 in which this table has been deleted from the Global.mpt. If you do not use the tracking table, be sure to add the following columns: **Actual Start**, **Actual Finish**, **% Complete**, **Actual Duration**, and **Remaining Duration**.

The status data may now be entered in the columns.

15.5.5 Marking Up Summary Tasks

It is not normal to mark up Summary Tasks, and Actual Dates may not be entered against Summary tasks. % Complete may be entered against a Summary Task and all the subordinate tasks will be auto-statused to match the summary % Complete.

When a **% Complete** is entered against a Summary task, all subordinate tasks, both Summary and Detailed, inherit a value depending upon the setting of the **Updating task status updates resource status** option found in **Tools**, **Options…**, **Calculation** tab.

To explain this concept further, see the following example. Both schedules pictured below had 60% entered against Task 2, the Research Phase of the OzBuild Bid task. All other Actual dates and % Complete were calculated by Microsoft Project 2003.

- With the **Updating task status updates resource status CHECKED** the activities are statused as if they were completed according to plan:

- With the **Updating task status updates resource status UNCHECKED** all activities are assigned to 60% complete, which is not the logical progression of the project:

15.5.6 Reschedule Uncompleted Work To Start After

There is a feature available in the **Update Project** form titled **Reschedule uncompleted work to start after:** which will schedule the **Incomplete Work** of an **In-Progress** task to start on a specific date in the future.

- If you want to apply this operation to some of the tasks, then these should be selected first.

- Select **Tools**, **Options…**, **Schedule** tab and ensure the **Split in-progress tasks option** is checked. If this option is not checked, then this function will not operate.

- Select **Tools**, **Tracking**, **Update Project…** to open the **Update Project** form.

- Click on the **Reschedule uncompleted work to start after:** radio button.

- In the drop-down box to the right, specify the date after which incomplete work should commence. Then click on the OK button.

A task may be split without the split being displayed in the Gantt Chart by unchecking the **Show bar splits** in the **Layout** form. In the examples below, the **Incomplete Work** has been moved after 24 October:

- The task has been split in the picture below and the splits displayed:

	Act. Start	Act. Finish	% Comp.	17 Oct '05	24 Oct '05	31 Oct '05
				S M T W T F S	S M T W T F S	S M T W T F S
1	18 Oct '05	NA	20%			

- The task has been split in the picture below and the splits **NOT** displayed:

	Act. Start	Act. Finish	% Comp.	17 Oct '05	24 Oct '05	31 Oct '05
				S M T W T F S	S M T W T F S	S M T W T F S
1	18 Oct '05	NA	20%			

When a project is updated using the **Update Project** function, the **Status Date DOES NOT** change the **Project Update Date**. You may end up with two dates that represent the **Data Date**—the **Update Project** date and the **Status Date**, which may both reflect different dates. The picture below shows the Status Date in the black vertical line at 18 Dec 02 and the **Update Project** date set at 10 Nov 05, which has split the last activity.

	Act. Start	Act. Finish	% Comp.	Act. Dur.	Rem. Dur.	24 Oct '05	31 Oct '05	7 Nov '05	14 Nov '05
						S M T W T F S	S M T W T F S	S M T W T F S	S M T W T
1	18 Oct '05	24 Oct '05	100%	5 days	0 days				
2	25 Oct '05	31 Oct '05	100%	5 days	0 days				
3	1 Nov '05	NA	20%	1 day	4 days				

You may use the **Update Project** function to reschedule tasks that are behind schedule and reschedule them after the **Update Project** date. This date will effectively become the **Data Date**. It is not possible to show the **Update Project** date as a vertical line on the bar chart. You may set and display the **Status Date** at the same date to achieve a position where incomplete work is all scheduled after a line displayed on the Gantt Chart.

It is recommended when you use the **Update Project** function that you should open the **Project Information** form and set the **Status Date** to the same date as the **Update Project** date. This enables you to display a **Data Date** in the bar chart in the correct place.

15.5.7 Status Date Calculation Options - New Tasks

New functions were introduced in Microsoft Project 2002 intended to assist schedulers to place the new tasks as they are added in a logical position with respect to the **Status Date**. If the **Status Date** has not been set the **Current Date** is used. In the example below the vertical black line is the **Status Date**:

- Task 1 has complete work in the future which is not logical,

- Task 2 would normally be considered in the logical position with respect to the **Status Date**, and

- Task 3 has incomplete work in the past which is also not logical.

	Duration	Start	% Complete	17 Oct '05	24 Oct '05	31 Oct '05	7 Nov '05
1	6 days	1 Nov '05	50%				
2	6 days	25 Oct '05	50%				
3	6 days	18 Oct '05	50%				

Select **Tools**, **Options**, **Calculation** tab and the new options are found under the **Calculation options for 'Project 1'**:

New Calculation Options in this box with 2002.

For these options to operate:

- The **Split in-progress tasks** option in the **Schedule** tab must be checked, and

- The required option on the **Calculation** tab under **Calculation** tab must be checked before the task is added, and

- The **Updating task status updates resource status** option on the **Calculation** tab must be checked.

 The documentation found in the Microsoft Project help files is not precise and does not make it clear to the user that these options may NOT be turned on and off to recalculate all tasks. The options only work on new tasks when they are added to a schedule or when a Task is updated by changing the % Complete.

The following four options are available:

- Check only **Move end of completed task parts after status date back to status date** and this is the effect on task 1 in the picture on the previous page:

	Duration	Start	Finish
1	6 days	18 Oct '05	1 Nov '05

- The **And move start of remaining parts back to status date** option is only available after the option above is checked:

	Duration	Start	Finish
1	6 days	18 Oct '05	25 Oct '05

- The **Move start of remaining parts before status date forward to status date** may be checked at any time, the picture below shows the effect on task 3 in the picture on the previous page:

	Duration	Start	Finish
1	6 days	11 Oct '05	25 Oct '05

- The **And move end of completed parts forward to status date** may be checked after the option above is checked:

	Duration	Start	Finish
1	6 days	18 Oct '05	25 Oct '05

This function will ignore constraints even when the Schedule Option **Tasks will always honor their constraint date** has been set.

Experimentation by the author indicates that the activities will adopt the rules that are set in the options form when the task is added or when a task Percentage Complete is changed. Therefore this function may not be applied to existing schedules, but only to new tasks if the options are set before the tasks are added or when a task Percentage is updated.

This function in its current form has some restrictions that schedulers may find unacceptable:

- Existing schedules may not be opened and the function applied.

- When the **Move start of remaining parts before status date forward to status date** is used, it overrides any **Actual Start** date that you have entered prior to entering a % Complete.

This option should be used with caution and users should ensure they fully understand how this function operates by statusing a simple schedule multiple times.

15.5.8 Status Date Calculation Options - When Statusing a Schedule

The Status Date Calculation Options also operates when a schedule is statused by changing the Percent Completes of Tasks. The example below shows a task with the Status Date, the dark vertical line, is set to the next period:

Duration	% Complete	Start	Finish
5 days	0%	18 Feb '04	24 Feb '04

When all the **Status Date Calculation Option** options are checked and the percent complete is changed from 0% to 50% the task is aligned to the new Status Date:

Duration	% Complete	Start	Finish
5 days	50%	23 Feb '04	1 Mar '04

Now the status date has been moved to the next week and the tasks have not moved in respect to the Status date and will not move when the project is recalculated:

Duration	% Complete	Start	Finish
5 days	50%	23 Feb '04	1 Mar '04

After percent complete changed to 60% the task splits and the unworked portion of the task is set to be completed after the new Status Date:

Duration	% Complete	Start	Finish
5 days	60%	23 Feb '04	5 Mar '04

15.6 Comparing Progress with Baseline

There will normally be changes to the schedule dates and more often than not these are delays. The full extent of the change is not apparent without having a Baseline bar to compare with the statused schedule.

- To display the **Baseline Bar** in the **Bar Chart** you may use either the **Format, Bar Styles...** function covered in the **FORMATTING THE DISPLAY** chapter, or

- You may use the **Gantt Chart Wizard** as follows:
  - ➢ Select **Format, Gantt Chart Wizard...** to open the Gantt Chart Wizard.
  - ➢ Select the **Baseline** option. This will display both the current schedule and the baseline.

> ➢ Hit the [Next >] button and follow the remainder of the instructions to complete the formatting. You will be given options for applying text and relationships in the Gantt Chart.

This wizard will overwrite any customized formatting you have made using the **Format, Bar Styles...** option.

If you want to see the Start and Finish Date variances, they are available by displaying the **Start Variance** and **Finish Variance** columns. These variance columns use the **Baseline** data and variance columns and are not available for **Baseline 1** to **10**.

15.7 In-progress Schedule Check List

The following check list may be used to check an in-progress schedule.

Complete Activities
- Have all activities an Actual Start and an Actual Finish in the past.

In-Progress Activities
- Actual Start Dates should all be in the past and Early Finish dates in the future.
- Check activities with Constraints, are the constraints still valid?
- Do all activities have Finish successors?
- Are there any activities with progress greater than planned and require the duration shortened?
- Are there any activities that have progress slower than planned and require the duration lengthened or split and delayed using the **Reschedule uncompleted work to start** (after date) function.

Not Started Activities
- Check all the constraints on these activities are still valid.
- Do activities have Finish successors?

Open Ends & Total Float
- Confirm all activities have successors and review float. Activities with excessive float should be assigned dummy successors or delayed if they are not scheduled in a realistic timeframe with sequencing logic or Early Start constraints.

Critical And Near Critical Path
- Check the Critical Path, is the scheduled critical path realistic and aligned with what project personnel consider critical?

Baseline Comparison

- Review the Baseline dates with the current schedule and confirm that any delays are legitimate.

- Have there been many changes and delays and therefore should the schedule be re-baselined?

15.8 Corrective Action

There are two courses of action available with date slippage:

- The first is to accept the slippage. This is rarely acceptable, but it is the easiest answer.

- The second is to examine the schedule and evaluate how you could improve the end date.

Solutions to return the project to its original completion date must be cleared with the person responsible for the project, since they can have the most impact on the work.

Suggested solutions to bring the project back on track include:

- Reducing the durations of tasks on, or almost on, the critical path. When tasks have applied resources, this may include increasing the number of resources working on the tasks. Changing longer tasks is often more achievable than changing the length of short duration tasks.

- Changing calendars, say from a five-day to a six-day calendar, so that tasks are being worked on for more days per week.

- Reducing the project scope and deleting tasks.

- Changing task relationships so tasks takes place concurrently. This may be achieved by introducing negative lags to Finish to Start relationships which maintains a Closed Network.

- Introducing Start-to-Start relationships which has the potential of creating an open network. Should maintaining the critical path be important then this option should be avoided.

- Changing the logic or sequencing of tasks to reduce the overall length of the critical path. This may take a lot of work and reviews.

15.9 Simple Procedure for Statusing a Schedule

For those people who require just one simple method of statusing a schedule the following process should be considered, but may not suit all situations especially when a project is way off plan:

- Set the Baseline by selecting **Tools**, **Tracking**, **Save Baseline…**.

- Display the Baseline bars by selecting **Format**, **Gantt Chart Wizard…**.

- Display the Status Date Gridline, select **Format**, **Gridlines**…, select Status Date.

- Select **Tools**, **Tracking**, **Update Project…** to open the **Update Project** form and select **Set 0% – 100 % Complete**, set the date in the form to the new **Status Date**.

- The project should be statused as if it has progressed exactly as planned and the Status Date should now be displayed in the bar chart.

- Displaying the **Tracking Table** may assist here.

- Now adjust the task dates by dragging the bars or entering the dates in the appropriate column, the order that the actions take place is important:
  - ➢ **Complete** tasks should have the Actual Start and then the Actual Finish dates adjusted to when the task actually started and actually finished.
  - ➢ **In-Progress tasks** should have the Actual Start adjusted first, then the task bar dragged so the finish date is where it is expected to finish and finally the % Complete adjusted.
  - ➢ **Unstarted** tasks should have their logic and durations revised.

- Add any scope changes to the schedule.

- Save the project with a new filename.

WORKSHOP 13

Baseline Comparison

Preamble

At the end of the first week you have to update the schedule and report progress and slippage.

Assignment

Open your **OzBuild Bid** project file and complete the following steps:

1. Select **Tools**, **Options**, **Schedule,** and ensure **Split in-progress tasks** is checked.
2. Save the Baseline for all the tasks on your project using the **Tools**, **Tracking** command.
3. Display the Baseline Bars using the **Format**, **Gantt Chart Wizard…..** Do not display dates or resources and display links.

4. Before the Research work is commenced it is required to granulate the **Technical Feasibility Study** into more detail following the **Rolling Wave** Technique. The following Tasks should be added which are each 2 days long:
   ➤ Research Available Documents
   ➤ Conduct Technical Study
   ➤ Draft Technical Feasibility Study
   ➤ Publish Technical Feasibility Study
5. Connect up logic as per the picture over the page, with no logic from or to Parent tasks.

6. Set the Baseline for the new tasks only:

	Task Name	Duration	Start	Finish	Total Slack	Predecessors	December
							3 | 10 | 17 | 24
1	⊟ OzBuild Bid	33 days	4 Dec '06	22 Jan '07	0 days		
2	⊟ Research	9 days	4 Dec '06	14 Dec '06	5 days		
3	Bid Request Documents Received	0 days	4 Dec '06	4 Dec '06	5 days		
4	Bid Strategy	1 day	4 Dec '06	4 Dec '06	5 days	3	
5	⊟ Technical Feasibility Study	8 days	5 Dec '06	14 Dec '06	5 days	4	
6	Research Available Documents	2 days	5 Dec '06	6 Dec '06	5 days	4	
7	Conduct Technical Study	2 days	7 Dec '06	8 Dec '06	5 days	6	
8	Draft Technical Feasibility Study	2 days	11 Dec '06	12 Dec '06	5 days	7	
9	Publish Technical Feasibility Study	2 days	13 Dec '06	14 Dec '06	5 days	8	
10	⊟ Estimation	14 days	15 Dec '06	8 Jan '07	0 days		
11	Installation Requirements	4 days	15 Dec '06	19 Dec '06	8 days	9	
12	Component Bids	3 days	2 Jan '07	4 Jan '07	0 days	11	
13	Project Schedule	4 days	20 Dec '06	23 Dec '06	10 days	11	
14	Technical Details Schedule	9 days	15 Dec '06	29 Dec '06	5 days	9	

7. Apply the **Gantt Chart** view and the **Tracking** table.
8. Hide the **Physical %**, **Actual Cost** and **Actual Work** columns.
9. Use **Tools**, **Tracking**, **Update Project…** to update progress to 11 Dec 06.
10. Check the **Status date** in the **Project Information** form; it should be 11 Dec 06.
11. Display the Status Date as a solid RED line by selecting **Format**, **Gridlines**.
12. The project should now be statused as if it has gone exactly according to plan.

	Task Name	Act. Start	Act. Finish	% Comp.	Act. Dur.	Rem. Dur.	cember
							3 | 10
1	⊟ OzBuild Bid	4 Dec '06	NA	14%	4.71 days	28.29 days	
2	⊟ Research	4 Dec '06	NA	67%	6 days	3 days	
3	Bid Request Documents Received	4 Dec '06	4 Dec '06	100%	0 days	0 days	
4	Bid Strategy	4 Dec '06	4 Dec '06	100%	1 day	0 days	
5	⊟ Technical Feasibility Study	5 Dec '06	NA	63%	5 days	3 days	
6	Research Available Documents	5 Dec '06	6 Dec '06	100%	2 days	0 days	
7	Conduct Technical Study	7 Dec '06	8 Dec '06	100%	2 days	0 days	
8	Draft Technical Feasibility Study	11 Dec '06	NA	50%	1 day	1 day	
9	Publish Technical Feasibility Study	NA	NA	0%	0 days	2 days	

13. Update the following tasks using the table below and note there is no change in the end date of project as there is sufficient Float to absorbed the delay, but now an incomplete part of task 7 is in the past which is not logical:

	Task Name	Act. Start	Act. Finish	% Comp.	Act. Dur.	Rem. Dur.	cember
							3 | 10
7	Conduct Technical Study	6 Dec '06	NA	50%	1 day	1 day	
8	Draft Technical Feasibility Study	10 Dec '06	NA	25%	1 day	3 days	

14. Now use the **Reschedule uncompleted work to start after:** to schedule the **Incomplete Work** of an **In-Progress** task to start after 11 Dec 06. The tasks will only split if when the **Split in-progress** option is checked.

	Task Name	Act. Start	Act. Finish	% Comp.	Act. Dur.	Rem. Dur.	cember
							3 | 10
1	⊟ OzBuild Bid	4 Dec '06	NA	10%	3.44 days	29.56 days	
2	⊟ Research	4 Dec '06	NA	33%	4 days	8 days	
3	Bid Request Documents Received	4 Dec '06	4 Dec '06	100%	0 days	0 days	
4	Bid Strategy	4 Dec '06	4 Dec '06	100%	1 day	0 days	
5	⊟ Technical Feasibility Study	5 Dec '06	NA	29%	3.14 days	7.86 days	
6	Research Available Documents	5 Dec '06	6 Dec '06	100%	2 days	0 days	
7	Conduct Technical Study	6 Dec '06	NA	20%	1 day	4 days	
8	Draft Technical Feasibility Study	10 Dec '06	NA	20%	1 day	4 days	
9	Publish Technical Feasibility Study	NA	NA	0%	0 days	2 days	

15. Save your **OzBuild Bid** project.

16 GROUPING TASKS, OUTLINE CODES AND WBS

Outlining was discussed earlier as a method of organizing detailed tasks under summary tasks. There are alternative features available in Microsoft Project 2003 for organizing, grouping and displaying task information:

- Grouping
- Custom Outline Codes
- Outline Codes
- User-Defined WBS (Work Breakdown Structure)

These functions are addressed in this book but are not examined in detail.

We will discuss the following functions available in Microsoft Project 2003 to represent these structures in your schedule.

Topic	Menu Command
• Grouping	Select **Project**, **Group by:**
• Custom Outline Codes	Select **Tools**, **Customize**, **Fields…** and select the **Custom Outline Codes** tab to create a Custom Outline Code, Assign the codes by displaying a column and Select **Project**, **Group by:**, **More Groups…** option to create a grouping to display the tasks under the Custom Outline Code.
• Outline Codes	Displaying the **Outline Code** column or the **Outline Code** with the **Task Name** by selecting **Tools**, **Options…**, **View** tab and checking the **Show outline number**.
• WBS	Select **Project**, **WBS**, **Define Code…**

16.1 Understanding a Project Breakdown Structure

A Project Breakdown Structure represents a hierarchical breakdown of a project into logical functional elements. Some organizations have highly organized and disciplined structures with "rules" for creating and coding the elements of the structure. Some clients also impose a WBS code on a contractor for reporting and/or claiming payments. The following are other examples of such structures:

- PBS **Product Breakdown Structure**, the method utilized by the **PRINCE2**.
- OBS **Organization Breakdown Structure**, showing the hierarchical management structure of a project.
- CBS **Contract Breakdown Structure**, showing the breakdown of contracts.
- SBS **System Breakdown Structure**, showing the elements of a complex system.
- BOM **Bill of Materials**, showing the assemblies, sub assemblies and components of a piece of machinery.

Microsoft Project 2003 has functionality enabling you to represent your Project Breakdown structures using the **Grouping**, **Outlining** and the **WBS** functions.

16.2 *Grouping*

Grouping allows you to group tasks under data items such as Customized Outline Codes, Text columns, Durations, Constraints, etc. It is particularly useful when you have schedules with a large number of tasks and you want to work with a related group of tasks that are spread throughout a project. The picture below displays a simple project where the relationship between each Task is difficult to check by inspection of the Gantt Chart organized by Phase:

With the Grouping function it is possible to Group on a text field to reorganize the data. In this example, the schedule has been reorganized by the Text 1 and 2 fields, which have been renamed using the **Tools**, **Customize**, **Field…** to System & Building. You may now clearly see the logic between the Items:

When you group by a Text Field, the first few characters of the field determine the sort order. If you want the items to be ordered differently than the fields' text values, then you should place a number or letter at the start of the description to make the order of the groups suit your sorting requirements, or create a **Custom Outline Codes** which will take a little more effort but provide a more satisfactory result.

16.2.1 Customize Group

The **Customize Group** option allows you to create a temporary Group where the settings are not saved. Select **P**roject, **G**roup by: and there will be a predefined list of Groups for you to chose from:

Click on **Customize Group B**... to open the **Customize Group By** form:

A hierarchical multiple grouping is available by selecting how you require the Tasks to be Grouped. The form above produces the result below:

16.2.2 Using a Predefined Group

You may assign a predefined Group by:

- Selecting **Project**, **Group by:**

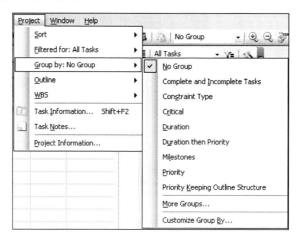

- Then, you may either:
  - ➤ Select a grouping from the list, or
  - ➤ Select **More Groups…** to open the **More Groups** form and then select one from the list after clicking on the **Task** or **Resource** radio button.

16.2.3 Creating a New Group

You may create a new Group by carrying out the following sequence:

- Selecting **Project**, **Group by:**, **More Groups…** to open the **More Groups** form,

- Click on the button to open the **Group Definition** form

- You may now create a "Grouping" which you may reapply at a later date or copy to another project using **Organizer**.

> **_i_** **Grouping** is similar to the Primavera P3 and SureTrak organize function. It is possible to mimic this Primavera function using the text columns as Activity Code dictionaries. Projects converted from Primavera P3 or SureTrak using the MPX format often translate Primavera's Activity Codes to Microsoft Project 2003's Text 1 through Text 10 fields. After conversion, the project may be **Grouped** by Text 1–10. **Custom Outline Codes** may produce a better result as bands may be ordered with this function.

16.2.4 Grouping Resources in the Resource Sheet

Resources may be created in the **Resource Sheet**. Then the resources may be grouped by a number of attributes. The standard options are shown below:

Resources are covered in more detail in the **RESOURCES** chapters.

16.3 Custom Outline Codes

Custom Outline Codes is a function new to Microsoft Project 2000 that allows the creation of up to 10 hierarchical Project Breakdown Structures. The process to use this function has three steps:

- Define the new Custom Outline Code structure, then

- Assign the codes to the tasks, then

- Create a Group to organize the tasks under the new Custom Outline Code structure.

16.3.1 Define a Custom Outline Code Structure

Select **Tools**, **Customize**, **Fields...** and select the **Custom Outline Codes** tab to open the form:

- An Outline Code may be created for either Task or Resource data by clicking on the appropriate radio button under the title **Outline Code**.

- The Import Custom Field... function allows you to copy a code structure from another project in a similar method to Organizer.

- The Rename... button opens a form to edit the name of the Outline Code. Two codes in the picture have been renamed Stage and System.

- The Define Code Mask... button opens the **Outline Code Definition** form where the code structure is defined.

  - As each **Level** is created it is assigned a number.
  - The **Sequence** defines the type of text that may be entered for the code: Numbers, Upper Case, Lower Case or Characters (text).
  - The **Length** specifies how many characters the Code Level may have: any, or a number between 1 and 10.
  - The **Separator** defines the character that separates each level in the structure.

- The [Edit Lookup Table...] opens a form to enter the codes and descriptions for the Outline Code.

- The picture shows three units at level 1 and their subsystems at level 2.

- The icons along the top of the form have a similar function to their use in outlining and may be used to indent and outdent codes and copy and paste code groups.

16.3.2 Assign Custom Codes to Tasks

The codes are assigned by displaying the appropriate column:

16.3.3 Organize Tasks Under a Custom Outline Code Structure

Select **Project**, **Group by:**, **More Groups…** option to create a grouping to display the tasks under the Custom Outline Code. The same process is used as outlined in the previous section to create a grouping:

The Summary Tasks are virtual tasks and may have resources and costs assigned to them.

16.4 Outline Codes

The Microsoft Project 2003 **Outlining** function may be used to mirror the Project Breakdown Structure. It is possible to display the Outline Code against each task in the schedule by:

- Displaying the **Outline Code** column, or

- Displaying the **Outline Code** with the **Task Name** by selecting **Tools**, **Options…**, **View** tab and checking the **Show outline number**.

An **Outline Level** displays how many levels down in the Outline Code structure the Task lies.

	Outline Number	Outline Level	Task Name
1	1	1	⊟ 1 OzBuild Bid
2	1.1	2	⊟ 1.1 Research
3	1.1.1	3	1.1.1 Bid Request Documents Received
4	1.1.2	3	1.1.2 Bid Strategy Meeting
5	1.1.3	3	1.1.3 Investigate Technical Feasibility
6	1.1.4	3	1.1.4 Document Installation Requirements
7	1.2	2	⊟ 1.2 Estimation
8	1.2.1	3	1.2.1 Request Component Bids
9	1.2.2	3	1.2.2 Develop Project Schedule
10	1.2.3	3	1.2.3 Draft Technical Details Schedule
11	1.2.4	3	1.2.4 Compile Costs from Component Bids
12	1.3	2	⊟ 1.3 Proposal
13	1.3.1	3	1.3.1 Draft Bid Document
14	1.3.2	3	1.3.2 Meeting to Review the Draft Bid Docu.
15	1.3.3	3	1.3.3 Design Presentation
16	1.3.4	3	1.3.4 Edit Proposal Draft Bid Document
17	1.3.5	3	1.3.5 Negotiate Component Work Packages
18	1.3.6	3	1.3.6 Final Review of Bid Document
19	1.3.7	3	1.3.7 Submit Bid

16.5 User Defined WBS Function

There are occasions when information must be presented under a predefined WBS Code structure. This structure could be a company standard, project-specific need, or defined by a client. This function is a method of tailoring the display of the **Outline Code** in a column titled **WBS**; but it does not provide an additional set of codes to organize your project tasks.

In a new project, the default WBS code is identical to the Outline Code. The example below displays both the WBS and Outline codes of the OzBuild schedule before doing any tailoring of the WBS code:

	WBS	Outline Number	Outline Level	Task Name
1	1	1	1	⊟ 1 OzBuild Bid
2	1.1	1.1	2	⊟ 1.1 Research
3	1.1.1	1.1.1	3	1.1.1 Bid Request Documents Received
4	1.1.2	1.1.2	3	1.1.2 Bid Strategy Meeting
5	1.1.3	1.1.3	3	1.1.3 Investigate Technical Feasibility
6	1.1.4	1.1.4	3	1.1.4 Document Installation Requirements
7	1.2	1.2	2	⊟ 1.2 Estimation
8	1.2.1	1.2.1	3	1.2.1 Request Component Bids
9	1.2.2	1.2.2	3	1.2.2 Develop Project Schedule
10	1.2.3	1.2.3	3	1.2.3 Draft Technical Details Schedule
11	1.2.4	1.2.4	3	1.2.4 Compile Costs from Component Bids

The WBS Codes structure may be tailored to suit your own requirements. Below is an example of a WBS code which has been tailored using the WBS code function. The Outline sequential numbers may be replaced by user-defined sequences of numbers or letters.

	WBS	Task Name
1	OzBuild1	⊟ Ozbuild Bib
2	OzBuild1.AA	⊟ Research
3	OzBuild1.AA-aaa	Bid Document Received
4	OzBuild1.AA-aab	Bid Strategy Meeting
5	OzBuild1.AA-aac	Investigate Technical Feasibility
6	OzBuild1.AA-aad	Document Installation Requirements
7	OzBuild1.AB	⊟ Estimation
8	OzBuild1.AB-aaa	Request Component Bids
9	OzBuild1.AB-aab	Develop Project Schedule
10	OzBuild1.AB-aac	Draft Technical Details Schedule
11	OzBuild1.AB-aad	Compile Costs from Bids
12	OzBuild1.AC	⊟ Proposal
13	OzBuild1.AC-aaa	Draft Bid Documents
14	OzBuild1.AC-aab	Draft Bid Meeting
15	OzBuild1.AC-aac	Design Presentation
16	OzBuild1.AC-aad	Edit Proposal Draft
17	OzBuild1.AC-aae	Finalise Bid Package
18	OzBuild1.AC-aaf	Final Bid Meeting
19	OzBuild1.AC-aag	Submit Bid

To create your own user-defined WBS codes, select **Project**, **WBS**, **Define Code…** to open the **WBS Code Definition** form:

- The **Project Code Prefix:** is where you enter a text string that will precede all **WBS** codes. See the example on the previous page.

- Each code level is defined in the **Sequence** column. There are four code types. Each is displayed above:
  - ➢ Numbers (ordered)
  - ➢ Uppercase Letters (ordered)
  - ➢ Lowercase Letters (ordered)
  - ➢ Characters (unordered)

  The **Numbers**, **Uppercase Letters** and **Lowercase Letters** are all numbered automatically.

  The **Characters** option will initially define all WBS codes at this level as an * and these may be overwritten with text. Microsoft Project 2003 will not renumber them.

- A **Length** of 1 to 10 or "Any" may be selected as the length of the code.

- Check **Generate WBS code for new task** and each new task will be automatically coded when created. When left unchecked, no WBS code is assigned to new tasks.

- Check **Verifies uniqueness of new WBS codes** to prevent the creation of duplicate WBS codes.

By selecting **All** or Selected Tasks, you may renumber the WBS codes. Select **Project**, **WBS**, **Renumber…** from the menu.

WORKSHOP 14

Reorganization of the Schedule

Preamble

We want to issue another report for comment by management by grouping the activities without float and showing the WBS columns.

Assignment

1. Grouping – to group tasks without float:
    *   Apply the **Entry** table and ensure the **Total Slack** column is visible.
    *   Create a new Group titled **Total Float** and group the tasks by **Total Slack**.
    *   Check the **Show in menu** option.
    *   Apply this grouping.
2. Outline Codes
    *   Remove the above grouping by selecting **Project**, **Group by: No Group**.
    *   Copy the **Schedule** Table and rename it by **Outline Codes**.
    *   Insert the **Outline Level** column between the Task **ID** and Task **Name**, then
    *   Align the content of the inserted column to the left and apply the table.
    *   Select **Tools**, **Options…**, **View** tab and **Show outline number**.
3. Work Breakdown Structure – we wish to display the WBS Predecessors & Successors
    *   Hide the Outline Level column.
    *   Display the **WBS**, **WBS Predecessors** and **WBS Successors** columns to the left of the descriptions. Align the column data to the left as shown in the following page. Note the WBS Predecessor and Successor columns may not be edited.

ANSWERS TO WORKSHOP 14

Grouped by Total Float:

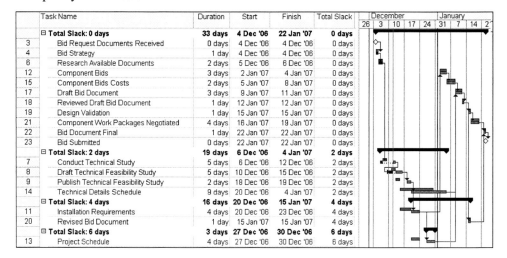

	Task Name	Duration	Start	Finish	Total Slack
	⊟ **Total Slack: 0 days**	**33 days**	**4 Dec '06**	**22 Jan '07**	**0 days**
3	Bid Request Documents Received	0 days	4 Dec '06	4 Dec '06	0 days
4	Bid Strategy	1 day	4 Dec '06	4 Dec '06	0 days
6	Research Available Documents	2 days	5 Dec '06	6 Dec '06	0 days
12	Component Bids	3 days	2 Jan '07	4 Jan '07	0 days
15	Component Bids Costs	2 days	5 Jan '07	8 Jan '07	0 days
17	Draft Bid Document	3 days	9 Jan '07	11 Jan '07	0 days
18	Reviewed Draft Bid Document	1 day	12 Jan '07	12 Jan '07	0 days
19	Design Validation	1 day	15 Jan '07	15 Jan '07	0 days
21	Component Work Packages Negotiated	4 days	16 Jan '07	19 Jan '07	0 days
22	Bid Document Final	1 day	22 Jan '07	22 Jan '07	0 days
23	Bid Submitted	0 days	22 Jan '07	22 Jan '07	0 days
	⊟ **Total Slack: 2 days**	**19 days**	**6 Dec '06**	**4 Jan '07**	**2 days**
7	Conduct Technical Study	5 days	6 Dec '06	12 Dec '06	2 days
8	Draft Technical Feasibility Study	5 days	10 Dec '06	15 Dec '06	2 days
9	Publish Technical Feasibility Study	2 days	18 Dec '06	19 Dec '06	2 days
14	Technical Details Schedule	9 days	20 Dec '06	4 Jan '07	2 days
	⊟ **Total Slack: 4 days**	**16 days**	**20 Dec '06**	**15 Jan '07**	**4 days**
11	Installation Requirements	4 days	20 Dec '06	23 Dec '06	4 days
20	Revised Bid Document	1 day	15 Jan '07	15 Jan '07	4 days
	⊟ **Total Slack: 6 days**	**3 days**	**27 Dec '06**	**30 Dec '06**	**6 days**
13	Project Schedule	4 days	27 Dec '06	30 Dec '06	6 days

Showing Outline Level in the Task Name:

	Outline Level	Task Name
1	1	⊟ **1 OzBuild Bid**
2	2	⊟ **1.1 Research**
3	3	1.1.1 Bid Request Documents Received
4	3	1.1.2 Bid Strategy
5	3	⊟ **1.1.3 Technical Feasibility Study**
6	4	1.1.3.1 Research Available Documents
7	4	1.1.3.2 Conduct Technical Study
8	4	1.1.3.3 Draft Technical Feasibility Study
9	4	1.1.3.4 Publish Technical Feasibility Study
10	2	⊟ **1.2 Estimation**
11	3	1.2.1 Installation Requirements

Showing WBS, WBS Predecessors and WBS Successors:

	WBS	WBS Predecessors	WBS Successors	Task Name
1	1			⊟ **1 OzBuild Bid**
2	1.1			⊟ **1.1 Research**
3	1.1.1		1.1.2	1.1.1 Bid Request Documents Received
4	1.1.2	1.1.1	1.1.3,1.1.3.1	1.1.2 Bid Strategy
5	1.1.3	1.1.2		⊟ **1.1.3 Technical Feasibility Study**
6	1.1.3.1	1.1.2	1.1.3.2	1.1.3.1 Research Available Documents
7	1.1.3.2	1.1.3.1	1.1.3.3	1.1.3.2 Conduct Technical Study
8	1.1.3.3	1.1.3.2	1.1.3.4	1.1.3.3 Draft Technical Feasibility Study
9	1.1.3.4	1.1.3.3	1.2.1,1.2.4	1.1.3.4 Publish Technical Feasibility Study
10	1.2			⊟ **1.2 Estimation**
11	1.2.1	1.1.3.4	1.2.2,1.2.3	1.2.1 Installation Requirements

17 OPTIONS

17.1 Options

The **Options** forms allow you to decide how Microsoft Project 2003 calculates and displays information. Most of the options are self-explanatory. Under **Tools**, **Options...**, there are ten tabs:

Interface	Security		
Schedule	Calculation	Spelling	Save
View	General	Edit	Calendar

There are many options which are not essential for scheduling. Unfortunately, it is often difficult for new users to determine which are important and which are not, which can lead to confusion. This chapter will explain most of the functions identified on each Options form tab and indicate the important options.

- **View**   Controls the display of data.

- **General**   Controls the display of software productivity tools and help, and default resource settings.

- **Edit**   Mainly controls edit and display functions.

- **Calendar**   These options **SHOULD** be understood especially if multiple **Task** calendars are used.

- **Schedule**   These options affect how your schedules calculate and **SHOULD** be understood.

- **Calculation**   These options **SHOULD** be understood if you are progressing your schedule.

- **Spelling**   Controls the spelling check options.

- **Security**   This is a new feature in Microsoft Project 2003 allowing file attributes to be removed on save and security options for the running of Macros.

- **Save**   Specifies where and how your files are saved and do not affect how your project calculates.

- **Interface**   This new form has options for the Indicator and Options button settings and the Project Guide, which are intended to assist the user but do not provide further scheduling options.

Some options apply to the current project only and some to all projects:

- Those that apply to the current project have a subheading **Calculation options for 'Project 1'**.

- Those that apply to all projects have a subheading of **Calculation options for Microsoft Office Project**.

It is important that you understand these options before you embark on developing and statusing some complex schedules.

17.2 View

The options in this form control the display of data and not the results of calculation.

- **Default view:** Selecting the View applied when a new project is created.

- **Date format:** A selection of date formats are available from the drop-down box for the display of data in columns. This format is applied to all projects and all views.

  ➢ The date format will be displayed according to a combination of your system default settings and the Microsoft Project 2003 Options settings. You may adjust your date format under the system Control Panel, Regional and Language Options. Changing the Control Panel setting will change the options available in the Microsoft Project 2003 **Options** form.

  ➢ The dates on the bars are formatted in the **Format**, **Layout...** option.

  ➢ Individual Tables may also have their dates formatted differently to the default format.

 On international projects there can be confusion between the numerical US date style (mmddyy) and the numerical European date style (ddmmyy). For example, in the United States 020705 is read as 07 Feb 05 and in many other countries as 02 Jul 05. You should consider adopting the ddmmmyy style, **30 Jan 00** or mmmddyy style, **Jan 30 00**.

- **Show** allows each of the display options to be hidden or displayed.

- **Cross project linking options for 'Project 1'** are options for displaying predecessor and successor task information from other projects. Inter-project relationships are not covered in this book.

- **Currency options for 'Project 1'** allows you to specify the:
  - ➢ Currency sign by inserting a sign into the box next to **Symbol:**,
  - ➢ How it is placed(before or after the value) as selected from the **Placement:** box, and
  - ➢ The number of decimal places displayed from the **Decimal digits:** box.

- **Outline options for 'Project 1':**

➢ **Indent name**	Indents the title for each Outline level to the right.
➢ **Show outline number**	Shows the Outline Number 1, 1.1, 1.1.1, etc.
➢ **Show outline symbol**	– Displays the – and + sign by the Task Name.
➢ **Show summary tasks**	Uncheck this to hide the summary tasks.
➢ **Show project summary task**	Displays the Project Title as Task – **OzBuild Bid** and a Summary bar that spans the duration of the project.

	Task Name
1	⊟ **1 OzBuild Bid**
2	⊟ **1.1 Research**
3	1.1.1 Bid Request Documents Received
4	1.1.2 Bid Strategy Meeting

17.3 General

These options control the display of software productivity tools, display of help, and default resource settings when resources are calculated.

- **General options for Microsoft Project** – These options are self-explanatory and apply to all projects.

- **Planning Wizard** – These options specify what advice the Planning Wizard will offer you and apply to all projects.

- **General options for 'Project 1'**
  - ➢ **Automatically add new resources and tasks** – This option confirms if a resource exists in the resource pool. If it does not, a form will ask you to confirm if you want the resource to be added.
  - ➢ **Default standard rate:** – The default standard hourly rate assigned to new resources.
  - ➢ **Default overtime rate**: – The default overtime rate assigned to new resources.

- **Set as Default** – Makes these rates the default rates for each new project.

17.4 Edit

This form mainly controls the edit and display functions.

- **Edit options for Microsoft Project** when checked:
  - ➢ **Allow cell drag and drop** – Allows you to select a cell and drag the contents to another location.
  - ➢ **Move selection after enter** – After completing an entry in a cell, pressing the **Enter Key** will result in the cursor moving down a line to the cell below.
  - ➢ **Ask to update automatic links** – On opening a file which has links to other programs such as Excel, you will be asked if you want to refresh the links to the most recent data. To create a link, copy the selected data from another program. Then, in Microsoft Project 2003, select **Edit**, **Paste Special…**, select the **Paste Link** option, and the data will be placed in the bar chart area.
  - ➢ **Edit directly in cell** – Allows you to edit the data directly in the cell. Otherwise data has to be edited in the **Edit Bar** near the top of the screen.

- **View options for time units in 'Project 1'**
  - ➢ **Minutes:, Hours:, Days:, Weeks:, Months:, Years:** – From the drop-down boxes, select your preferred designators for these units.
  - ➢ **Add space before label** – Places a space between the value and the label; this makes the data column wider.

- **Hyperlink appearance in 'Project 1'**
  - ➢ **Hyperlink color:** and **Followed hyperlink color:** – Select from the drop-down box the color you require for these data items.
  - ➢ **Underline hyperlinks** – Select if you want these data items to be underlined.
- Three phonetics options are available with some Asian operating systems that have IME (Input Method Editor) loaded: Katakana Half , Katakana, or Hiragana.

- **Add space before label** when checked allows a gap to be placed between the amount of days and the word 'day' in the Duration column.

17.5 Calendar

The title of these options does not clearly indicate their functionality. Options for **Hours per day:**, **Hours per week:** and **Days per month: SHOULD** be understood, especially if multiple Task calendars are used.

- **Calendar options for 'Project 1'**
  - ➤ **Week starts on:** – Sets the first day of the week. This is the day of the week that is displayed in the timescale. This setting affects the display of the calendar in the Change Working Time form.
  - ➤ **Fiscal year starts in:** – A month other than January may be selected as the first month of the fiscal year for companies that want to schedule projects using their financial years.
  - ➤ **Use starting year for FY numbering** – This option becomes available when a month other than January is selected as a **Fiscal year starts on:**. The year in the timescale may be assigned as the year that the fiscal starts or the year that the fiscal year finishes.

- **Default times**:
  - ➤ **Default start time:** – This is the time of day that tasks are scheduled to start when a start date constraint (without a time) is applied. It is also the default time for an Actual Start when an Actual Start (without a time) date is entered.
  - ➤ **Default end time:** – This is the time of day that tasks are scheduled to finish when a finish date constraint (without a time) is applied. It is also the default time for an Actual finish when an Actual finish date (without a time) is entered.

 It is best to match both of these times with your project calendar normal start and finish times. When the **Default start time:** is set later than the calendar normal start time, a task set with a constraint without a time will appear to finish one day later than scheduled. Therefore a one-day task will span two days and a two-day task, three days.

- The following options need to be understood as they affect how summary durations are displayed. **NOTE: THESE OPTIONS ARE IMPORTANT**. Microsoft Project 2003 effectively calculates in hours. Task durations may be displayed in days, weeks and months. These summarized durations are calculated based on the parameters set in **Options**, **Calendar**. These options work fine when all project calendars are based on the same number of work hours per day. When tasks are scheduled with calendars that do not conform to the **Options**, **Calendar** settings (e.g. when the **Options**, **Calendar** settings are set for 8 hours per day and there are tasks scheduled on a 24 hour/day calendar), the results often create confusion for new users. The examples below use the **Options**, **Calendar** settings from the previous page:

  ➢ **Hours per day:** – This setting is used to convert the calendar hours to days. For example, a task entered as a 3-day duration and assigned a 24 hour per day calendar will be displayed as 1-day elapsed duration. (This is 1/3 of the "normal" duration since each day is an 8-hour equivalent on a 24-hour calendar.) See Task 1, below:

  ➢ **Hours per week:** – This setting is used to convert the calendar hours to weeks. For example, a task entered as 2 weeks (10 working days) and assigned a 24 hour per day calendar is displayed with a 3-day and 6-hour duration in the bar chart. This is 1/3 of the "normal" duration. See Task 2, below:

  ➢ **Days per month:** – This option is used to convert the displayed task duration from days to months. For example, a 0.5-month task on a 24 hour per day calendar is displayed as 3-day and 6-hour duration in the bar chart. See Task 3, below:

	Task Calendar	Duration	Mon 29 Apr					Tue 30 Apr				Wed 1 May				Thu 2 May
			8	12	4	8	12	4	8	12	4	8	12	4	8	12	4	8
1	24 Hours	3 days														
2	24 Hours	2 wks														
3	24 Hours	0.5 mons														

  ➢ **Set as Default:** – Sets the current calendar settings as the default in the Global.mpt project and is used thereafter as the calendar settings in all new projects.

 Other scheduling software also exhibit this time conversion problem when using multi-calendars. This display can lead to a great deal of confusion. To avoid confusion when using multi-calendars, it is suggested that you only display durations in hours.

17.6 Schedule

The options below affect how your schedules calculate and **SHOULD** be understood. The Author prefers the options below for most projects.

- **Schedule options for Microsoft Project**
  - ➤ **Show scheduling messages** – Uncheck this box to prevent the software from displaying advice on scheduling.
  - ➤ **Show assignment unit as a:** – The options are **Percentage** or **Decimal**. You have the option of assigning and displaying resource assignments as either a percentage, such as 50%, or a decimal, such as 0.5. Both these values would assign a person to work half time on that task.

- **Scheduling options for 'Project 1'**
  - ➤ **New tasks:** – When adding new tasks, you have the option of the new task either:
    - o Scheduled to **Start On Project Start Date** and the task will be scheduled **As Soon As Possible**, or
    - o **Start on Current Date** and the task will be assigned (without any warning dialog box) a **Start No Earlier Constraint** equal to the current date.
  - ➤ **Duration entered in:** – You should select the units you will most frequently use for your task duration units. When "days" are selected, you will only need to type "**5**" in order to enter a 5-day task duration. Similarly, you will have to enter "**5w**" for a task that is 5 weeks long or "**5h**" for a task that is 5 hours long.
  - ➤ **Work entered in:** – This is similar to the **Durations entered in:** function, but applies to assigning work to a task. When hours are selected, you will only need to type "**48**" to enter 48 hours of work. If 5 days of work are to be assigned then "**5d**" needs to be entered.

The next two subjects, **Default task type:** and **Effort Driven**, are **EXTREMELY** important for understanding how resources are used and applied.

> **Default task type:** – There is a relationship between the **Duration** of a task, the **Work** (the number of hours required to complete a task) and the **Units per Time Period** (the rate of doing the work or the number of people working on the task). The relationship is:

   Duration x Units per time Period = Work

The three options for the **Default task type:** are:

   Fixed Duration – The **Duration** will stay constant if either **Units per time Period** or **Work** is changed. If you change the **Duration**, then **Work** changes.

   Fixed Units – The **Units** stay constant if either **Duration** or **Work** is changed. If you change the **Units per time Period**, then **Duration** changes.

   Fixed Work – The **Work** stays constant if either **Duration** or **Units per time Period** is changed. Your estimate will not change when you change **Duration** or **Units per time Period**. If you change the **Work**, then **Duration** changes.

- Check any of the six boxes at the bottom of the form:
  > **New tasks are effort driven:** – An **Effort Driven** task keeps the total work constant as resources are added and removed from a task. When a task is not **Effort Driven** then the addition of resources to a task will increase the total work assigned to a task. This option is not available with a **Fixed Work** task since, otherwise, it would not be fixed work.
  > **Autolink inserted or moved tasks:** – With this box checked, new or moved tasks are automatically linked to the tasks above and below in the new or inserted location. Moved tasks that had relationships to tasks immediately above and below in the old location are deleted and the original predecessors and successors are now joined with an FS relationship. This function may confuse you since the logic is changed automatically without warning when you add or move tasks.
  > **Split in-progress tasks:** – This option allows the splitting of in-progress tasks. This option must be checked for the following functions to operate:
  >> 1. **Tools, Tracking, Update Project…, Update work as completed through**,
  >> 2. **Tools, Tracking, Update Project…, Reschedule uncompleted work to start after**, and
  >> 3. **Tools, Options…, Calculation** tab, **Status Date Calculation Options** which are the found option found under **Calculation options for 'Project 1'** allowing incomplete or completed parts of tasks to be moved to the Status Date.

➤ **Tasks will honor their constraint dates:** – This option will make all constraints override relationships. For example, a task with a **Must Start On** constraint, which is prior to a predecessor's Finish Date, will have an Early Start on the constraint date and not the scheduled date. (This is similar to converting all P3 and SureTrak **Must Start On** constraints to **Mandatory** constraints.) When checked, the **Total Slack** may not calculate as the difference between Late Start and Early Start. Examine the following two examples with the option box checked and unchecked:

Tasks will honor their constraint dates: option box checked.

	Start	Finish	Late Start	Late Finish	Total Slack	Constraint Date	Constraint Type	16 Oct S M T W T F S	23 Oct S M T W T F S	30 Oct S M T W T F S
1	17 Oct '05	28 Oct '05	10 Oct '05	21 Oct '05	-5 days	NA	As Soon As Possible			
2	24 Oct '05	4 Nov '05	24 Oct '05	4 Nov '05	-5 days	24 Oct '05	Must Start On			

Note: the second task starts before the predecessor finishes and the total slack of the second task is calculated at –5 days, which is not the difference of the early and late dates.

Tasks will honor their constraint dates: option box NOT checked.

	Start	Finish	Late Start	Late Finish	Total Slack	Constraint Date	Constraint Type	16 Oct S M T W T F S	23 Oct S M T W T F S	30 Oct S M T W T F S	6 Nov S M T W T F S
1	17 Oct '05	28 Oct '05	10 Oct '05	21 Oct '05	-5 days	NA	As Soon As Possible				
2	31 Oct '05	11 Nov '05	24 Oct '05	4 Nov '05	-5 days	24 Oct '05	Must Start On				

- **Estimated Durations** – These two options do not affect the calculation of projects. A new task is assigned an estimated duration. Once a duration is entered, this assignment is removed. The **General** tab on the **Task** form has a check box which establishes when a task has an estimated duration.

  ➤ **Show that tasks have estimated durations:** – A task with an estimated duration is flagged with a "?" after the duration in the data columns when this option is checked.

  ➤ **New tasks have estimated durations:** – When a task is added, it will have the estimated check box checked.

17.7 Calculation

The following options **SHOULD** to be understood to confidently progress your schedule.

- **Calculation options for Microsoft Project**:– Select one of the following two options:
  - ➤ **Automatic** – This option recalculates the schedule every time a change is made to data.
  - ➤ **Manual** – This option requires you to press the **F9 Key** to recalculate the schedule.

- Also, select one of the two following options:
  - ➤ **Calculate all open projects** – Calculates all open projects when the recalculation takes place.
  - ➤ **Calculate the active project** – Calculates only the active project (the one that is displayed on your screen) when recalculation takes place.
  - ➤ **Calculate Now** – Recalculates the schedule(s) in accordance with the selected option above.

  To recalculate a project when calculation option is set to manual, press **F9**.

- **Calculate options for 'Project 1'**
  - ➤ **Updating task status updates resource status:** – This option links **% Complete** and **Actual Work**. Therefore:

    Actual Work = % Complete x Work and
    Remaining Work = Work – Actual Work

The example above shows the calculations with this option checked. If you uncheck this option, you may enter actual work and remaining work independently of the **% Complete**.

This option also determines the manner in which a % Complete that is assigned to a Parent Task gets spread to detailed tasks. See the following two examples where 60% is applied to the summary task entitled "Research":

  - ➤ With the **Updating task status updates resource status CHECKED**.

  - ➤ With the **Updating task status updates resource status UNCHECKED**.

- New functions have been introduced in Microsoft Project 2002, which are intended to assist schedulers to place new tasks in a logical position with respect to the **Status Date**. The following four options are new to Microsoft Project 2002 and are covered in detail in the **Status Date Calculation Options** section of the **TRACKING PROGRESS** chapter.
  - ➤ **Move end of completed task parts after status date back to status date**
  - ➤ **And move start of remaining parts back to status date**
  - ➤ **Move start of remaining parts before status date forward to status date**
  - ➤ **And move end of completed parts forward to status date**

  These functions do not work intuitively and the instructions in the Microsoft documentation do not outline clearly how these functions work. It is recommended that you review these options carefully before applying them.

> The ⌐Earned Value...⌐ button opens the **Earned Value** form:

- o The **Default task Earned Value method:** may be set to use the task **% Complete** or the new field in Microsoft Project 2002 – **Physical % Complete**. This is useful when the Earned Value is not progressing in proportion to the duration.
- o The **Baseline for Earned Value calculations:** allows the selection of any of the baselines for the calculation of the Earned Value.

> **Edits to total task % complete will be spread to the status date** – When this option is selected and a **Status Date** is set in the **Project Information** form, then the % Complete is spread from the Actual Start to the Status Date and may be viewed in the **Task** or **Resource Usage** forms. (Right-click to add a % Complete column.)

> **Inserted projects are calculated like summary tasks** – When checked, an inserted project task's Total Float is calculated to the end of all Projects like a group of related projects. When unchecked, each Project's Total Float is calculated to the end of that Project only.

> **Actual costs are always calculated by Microsoft Project** – With this option checked, the resource **Actual Cost** is calculated by Microsoft Project 2003 from the resource **Work** and **Rates**. When unchecked, you have to directly enter the **Actual Cost** and **Actual Work**.

> **Edits to total actual costs will be spread to the status date** – When this option is selected and a **Status Date** is set in the **Project Information** form, then Actual Costs are spread from the Actual Start to the Status Date. Actual Costs should not be entered in a time-phased form such as the Task or Resource Usage forms, but the results may be viewed in these forms.

> **Default fixed costs accrual:** – This option sets the default accrual method for **Fixed Costs** (covered in the **ASSIGNING RESOURCES AND COSTS TO TASKS** chapter). Fixed cost may be accrued at the **Start**, **End**, or **Prorated** over the duration of the task.

> **Calculate multiple critical paths** – When checked Tasks without successors have their Late Dates set to equal their Early Dates, and are calculated with zero Total Slack, and are on the critical path. (This is the same function as the Primavera SureTrak and P3 **Open Ends** options.)

> **Tasks are critical if slack is less than or equal to ? days** – This option will flag tasks as being critical that have **Total Slack** (Total Float) less than or equal to the value as established in this form. Critical tasks may be displayed in the **Critical** column and on bars when the "critical bar" is displayed. This is useful for flagging "near critical" tasks.

17.8 Spelling

The spell check options are self explanatory and are applied to all projects:

17.9 Security

This is a new feature in Microsoft Project 2003 allowing:

- The properties of Author, Manager, Company and Last Saved by are removed from a file when it is saved, and

- There are security options that may be set to nominate which Macros may be used or not used. This is aimed at preventing Macros with a virus being activated.

17.10 Save

This Options tab specifies where and how your files are saved. It does not affect how your project calculates.

- **Save Microsoft Project files as:** – There are several formats that your project may be saved in. The default file type may be defined here but the file type may be changed at the time a project file is saved. This book only covers **Project (*.mpp)** and **Template (*.mpt)** formats in detail:
  - ➢ **Project (*.mpp)** – The normal format to save Microsoft Project 2003 files.
  - ➢ **Template (*.mpt)** – Use this format to save projects that you want to use as project templates. Save them in the **User templates** directory that is specified in the **Tools**, **Options…**, **Save** tab.
  - ➢ **Microsoft Project 98 (*.mpp)** – This format will allow users of Microsoft Project 98 to read your files. If you have Microsoft Project 98, you may save the file in MPX format for transfer to other scheduling programs.
  - ➢ **Project Database (*.mpd)** – This is a database format, which allows multiple projects to be saved in one database. It may be used for exporting data to other programs.
  - ➢ **Microsoft Access Database (*.mdb)** – A part or all of a project may be saved in Microsoft Assess format and may be read and modified by Access.
  - ➢ **ODBC Database** – your project may be saved as an ODBC compliant database.
- **File Locations** – This is where you set the default locations for your project data files, template files, workgroup templates, and ODBC database files.
- **Auto Save** – These options are self-explanatory.
- **Database save options for 'Project 1'**
  - ➢ **Expand time-phased data in the database** – This function creates time phased data in external databases.

17.11 Interface

This form, new to Microsoft Project 2002, has options for:

- The **Show indicator and Options buttons for:** settings, and

- The Project Guide, which are intended to assist the user but do not provide further scheduling options.

17.11.1 Graphical Indicators

The Indicator buttons give advice to the scheduler when certain functions are used which have more than one potential outcome.

- Below is an example of how the **Show indicators and buttons for:** options work when a task description is deleted:

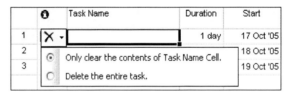

and when a date is edited:

17.11.2 Project Guide

The **Project Guide** is a wizard type function that assists the user to create a new schedule. It is self explanatory and not covered in this book.

18 CREATING RESOURCES

A resource may be defined as something or someone that is assigned to a task and is required to complete the task. This includes people or groups of people, materials, equipment and money. There are a large number of resource functions available in Microsoft Project. Without getting into too much detail, this book will outline the important resource-related functions to enable you to create and assign resources to your schedules.

It is recommended that you assign the minimum number of resources to tasks. Avoid cluttering the schedule with resources that are in plentiful supply or are of little importance. Every resource added to the schedule will need to be statused. In this way, the workload will go up as more resources are allocated to schedule.

Depending on the decision to assign or not to assign costs to resources, resources may be used to assist in the following *PMBOK® Guide* processes:

- **6.3 Activity Resource Estimating** and **6.4 Activity Duration Estimating** without costs, and

- **7.1 Cost Estimating** and **7.2 Cost Budgeting** with costs.

When you create your resources, you should consider them within the context of the following headings:

- **Input Resources** – Those that are required to complete the work:
  - ➢ Individual people by name.
  - ➢ Groups of people by trade or skill.
  - ➢ Individual equipment or machinery by name.
  - ➢ Groups of equipment or machinery by type.
  - ➢ Groups of resources such as Crews or Teams made up of equipment and machinery.
  - ➢ Materials.
  - ➢ Money.

- **Output Resources** – Things that are being delivered or produced:
  - ➢ Specifications completed.
  - ➢ Bricks laid.
  - ➢ Lines of code written.
  - ➢ Tests completed.

The following steps should be followed to create and use resources in a Microsoft Project 2003 schedule:

- Create your resources in the **Resource Sheet**.

- Assign the resources to tasks.

- Manipulate the resource calendar if resources have special timing requirements.

This chapter will concentrate on:

- The creation of Resources in the **Resource Sheet**,

- Understanding **Task Type** and **Effort-Driven Tasks**,

- Assign the Resources to Tasks, and

- Editing **Resource Calendars**.

Resources may be shared between projects using the **Tools**, **Resource Sharing** function.

18.1 Creating Resources in the Resource Sheet

Select **View**, **Resource Sheet** to add resources to the Resource Sheet.

- To add a new resource:
  - ➢ Click on the first blank line, or
  - ➢ Highlight the line where you would like to insert your resource and select **Insert**, **New Resources**, or
  - ➢ Use the **Ins Key**.

- The first column, with a 🛈 in the header, is the indicator column; 📝 is the Notes indicator; and ⬦ is the resource over-allocation indicator.

- Enter the **Resource Name**. Microsoft Project 2003 allows duplicate Resource Names to be entered into the Resource Table, but this situation should be avoided by visually checking all your Resource Names.

- Enter one of the two Resource **Types**: **Work** or **Materials**. They function differently:
  - ➢ **Work** resources, such as people, often have a limit to the number that are available. This type of resource may have a maximum number assigned, an overtime rate and a calendar. It is not available with a **Materials** resource.
  - ➢ **Materials** resources have a **Material Label** which is not available with a **Work** resource.

- A **Material** resource may be assigned a **Material Label**, which may be the unit of measurement, such as m^3 or feet.

- The **Initials** are filled out by Microsoft Project 2003 with the first character of the **Resource Name**. This Initial field should be unique and is displayed in some Views and should be edited so it makes sense to you. For example, you could make this a person's initials, log-in name or payroll number.

- You may enter any text in the **Group** field if you want to group, filter or sort your resources by this field. This could be used for Department, Branch or Skill.

- Enter the **Max Units**. 100% (or 1.00) would represent one person and 400% (or 4.00) would represent four people. The method of entering the **Resource Units** may be formatted as a percentage or as a decimal. Select the **Tools**, **Options...**, **Schedule** tab to set your option:

- Edit the **Standard Rate**, if required, for the resource. The default units are "hours" (hr), but this may be edited to be the cost per:
  - ➢ minute – min
  - ➢ hour – hr
  - ➢ day – day
  - ➢ week – wk
  - ➢ month – mon

- Enter the **Overtime Rate** for the resource. A salaried person may not be paid overtime and would have a zero rate for overtime.

- Enter the **Cost per Use**. This could represent a mobilization cost and is applied each time a resource is assigned to a task. The **Cost per Use** is accrued when an actual start date is entered.

- **Accrue At**:
  - ➢ **Start** – The costs for this resource are incurred when the task commences.
  - ➢ **Prorated** – The costs for this resource are spread over the duration of the task.
  - ➢ **End** – The costs for this resource are incurred when the task is complete.

- **Base Calendar** – This is the calendar assigned to the resource and may be edited to suit each individual resource.

18.2 Grouping Resources in the Resource Sheet

Resources may be Grouped using the **Project**, **Group by:** function. The example below shows resources grouped by **Resource Group**:

Resource Name	Type	Material Label	Initials	Group	Max. Units	Std. Rate	Ovt. Rate	Cost/Use	Accrue At	Base Calendar
⊟ **Group: Equipment**				**Equipment**	**7**			**$1,700.00**		
Dozer	Work		DOZER	Equipment	6	$2,500.00/wk	$0.00/hr	$1,000.00	Prorated	Standard
Excavator	Work		EXCAV	Equipment	1	$400.00/day	$0.00/hr	$700.00	Prorated	Standard
⊟ **Group: Material**				**Material**				**$50.00**		
Concrete	Material	m3	CONC	Material		$120.00		$50.00	Prorated	
Crushed Rock	Material	ton	CRCK	Material		$80.00		$0.00	Prorated	
⊟ **Group: Office**				**Office**	**7**			**$0.00**		
Clerical Support	Work		CS	Office	2	$25.00/hr	$30.00/hr	$0.00	Prorated	Standard
Sales Engineer	Work		SALESENGI	Office	1	$40.00/hr	$0.00/hr	$0.00	Prorated	Standard
Scheduler	Work		SC	Office	1	$27.00/hr	$0.00/hr	$0.00	Prorated	Standard
System Engineer	Work		SYSENG	Office	2	$40.00/hr	$0.00/hr	$0.00	Prorated	Standard
Tender Manager	Work		TM	Office	1	$50.00/hr	$0.00/hr	$0.00	Prorated	Standard

18.3 Resources Information Form

The **Resource Information** form is opened by double-clicking on a specific row with in the **Resource Sheet** view. There five four tabs in this form. These will not be described in detail:

18.3.1 General

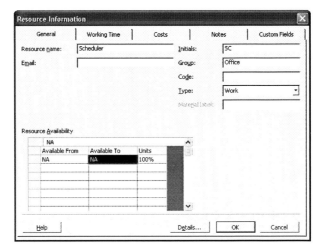

- The **Resource Availability** section in this form allows you to decide the availability of all resources.

- The **Email** field is used in email communication and not covered in this book.

18.3.2 Working Time

- This is where you may select each resource's **Base calendar** and edit the calendar to suit the resource's availability.

18.3.3 Costs

The **Cost rate** table allows you to adjust the resource rate over time and assign up to five different rates to a resource. The rate is assigned in the **Resource Information** form. This form is opened by double-clicking on the **Resource Name** for any assigned resource in either the **Resource Sheet**, **Task Usage** view and the **Resource Usage** view.

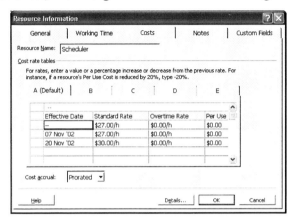

18.3.4 Notes

This is where notes are made about the resource.

18.3.5 Custom Fields

Custom Fields are for assigning user defined costs to resources and not covered in detail in this book.

- Custom Resources fields may be created in the **Customize Fields** form by selecting **Tools**, **Customize**, **Fields…**.

- After the fields have been defined in the **Customize Fields** form then these fields may be used to assign custom defined costs to resources from the **Custom Fields** tab of the **Resource Information** form.

18.4 Editing and Using Resource Calendars

Base Calendars are applied to tasks but they may not accommodate specific resource requirements. For example, a base calendar would not reflect when a person goes on vacation or is occupied on another project. Resource Calendars, on the other hand, can be used to schedule this resource-specific non-work time. Resource Calendars should be used when specific resources have a unique availability.

When a resource is created, a unique resource calendar is created automatically and is a copy of the **Base Calendar** selected when the resource is created. This Resource Calendar may be modified, if required.

The Resource Calendar may be edited by either:

- Clicking on **Resource Calendar** in the **Resources Sheet**, or

- Opening the **Resource Information** form by double-clicking on a **Resource Name** in most forms and selecting the **Working Time** tab.

All edits to the calendars are performed in the same manner as the Base Calendars.

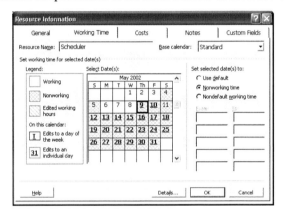

A task will always be calculated using a **Resource Calendar** except when a **Task Calendar** has been assigned. In this case, the **Scheduling ignores resource calendars** option in the **Task Information** form becomes available.

WORKSHOP 15

Defining Resources

Preamble

The resources must now be added to this schedule. Since we have statused our project, we need to revert to the un-statused schedule that we saved in Workshop 9 prior to statusing the current schedule titled **OzBuild No Resources**.

Assignment

1. Save and close your current project.
2. Open the **OzBuild No Resources** project and save it as **OzBuild With Resources**.
3. Select **Tools, Options…** from the menu. From the **Schedule** tab, set **Show assignment Units as a: Decimal**.
4. Open the **Resource Sheet** view and add the following resources to the project:

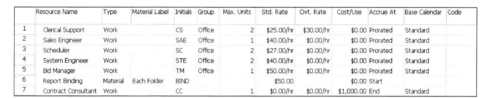

	Resource Name	Type	Material Label	Initials	Group	Max. Units	Std. Rate	Ovt. Rate	Cost/Use	Accrue At	Base Calendar	Code
1	Clerical Support	Work		CS	Office	2	$25.00/hr	$30.00/hr	$0.00	Prorated	Standard	
2	Sales Engineer	Work		SAE	Office	1	$40.00/hr	$0.00/hr	$0.00	Prorated	Standard	
3	Scheduler	Work		SC	Office	2	$27.00/hr	$0.00/hr	$0.00	Prorated	Standard	
4	System Engineer	Work		STE	Office	2	$40.00/hr	$0.00/hr	$0.00	Prorated	Standard	
5	Bid Manager	Work		TM	Office	1	$50.00/hr	$0.00/hr	$0.00	Prorated	Standard	
6	Report Binding	Material	Each Folder	BIND			$50.00		$0.00	Start		
7	Contract Consultant	Work		CC		1	$0.00/hr	$0.00/hr	$1,000.00	End	Standard	

5. Save your project file.

19 ASSIGNING RESOURCES AND COSTS TO TASKS

When a resource is assigned to a task it has the following principal components:

- **Quantity**, in terms of **Work** or **Material** required to complete the task,

- **Units** which represents the number of people working on a task and

- **Cost**, calculated from the **Standard Rate**, **Overtime Rate** and **Cost per Use**.

Microsoft Project 2003 also has a function titled **Fixed Costs**, which are costs assigned to tasks without resources.

The resource data may be assigned and displayed in a number of Microsoft Project 2003 forms. You may either enter the **Units** and then the **Work** will be calculated, or enter the **Work** and then the **Units** will be calculated.

Some forms allow the **Units** only, some allow the **Work** only, and some allow both **Units** and **Work** to be entered and displayed in the one form.

Resources may be assigned to tasks using a number of methods including:

Method	Menu Command
• **Fixed Costs** assignment	Display the **Fixed Costs** and **Fixed Costs Accrual** columns.
• **Resource Assignment** form	Click on the **Assign Resource** icon 🖁. You may assign **Units** only.
• **Task Information** form	Double-click on a **Task** name or click on the **Task Information** icon 📧 You may assign **Units** only.
• The **Resource Task Details** forms	In the bottom window, select the **Task Details Form**, **Task Form** or **Task Name Form**, and then select the appropriate option from the **Format**, **Details** option. Each form has different options.
• The **Resources Names** and **Resource Initials** columns	Insert appropriate columns by right-clicking on the column heading where you want to insert a column and then assign a Resource.
• **Contoured** Resource assignment	Open the **Assignment Information** form by: • Double-clicking on a resource in the **Task Usage** or **Resource Usage** view, or • Right-clicking on a resource and selecting **Assignment Information** from the menu.
• **Shared Resources**	Select **Tools**, **Resource**, **Share Resources…** to share resources with other projects.

It is important that you fully understand these functions before you embark on developing and statusing some complex schedules.

19.1 Task Type and Effort-Driven

These **Task type** and **Effort-driven** options operate after the first **Work** resource has been assigned to a task. The relationship amongst the following four variables are controlled by these functions:

- The number of **Resources**,

- The **Task duration**,

- The resource **Units per time Period**, and

- The amount of **Work** to be performed.

The **Task type** and **Effort-driven** functions control which variable changes when one of these four parameters is changed or when **Work** resources are added or removed from a task. These options may be set in a number of forms including the **Task** and the **Task Details** form. **Material** resources do not change values after they have been assigned.

19.1.1 Task Type – Fixed Duration, Fixed Units, Fixed Work

There is a relationship between the **Duration** of a task, the **Work** (the number of hours required to complete a task) and the **Units per Time Period** (the rate of doing the work or number of people working on the task). The relationship is:

Duration x Units per time Period = Work

There are three options for the **Default task type:** which decide how this relationship operates. They are:

- **Fixed Duration**   The **Duration** stays constant if either **Units per time Period** or **Work** are changed. If you change the **Duration**, then the **Work** changes.

- **Fixed Units**   The **Units per time Period** stay constant if either **Duration** or **Work** is changed. If you change the **Units per time Period**, then the **Duration** changes.

- **Fixed Work**   The **Work** stays constant if either **Duration** or **Units per time Period** are changed. Your estimate will not change when you change **Duration** or **Units per time Period**. If you change the **Work**, then the **Duration** changes.

19.1.2 Effort-Driven

Once a resource has been assigned to a task, the **Effort** is the number of Resource hours assigned to a task. The **Effort-driven** option decides how the effort is calculated when a resource is added or when a resource removed to a **Fixed Units** or **Fixed Work** task. There are two options:

- **Effort-driven**   When a resource is added or removed from a task, the total effort assigned against a task remains constant. Adding or removing resources leaves the total effort assigned to a task as a constant unless all resources are removed.

- **Non Effort-driven**   When a resource is added or removed from a task, the total effort against the other resources remains constant. Adding or deleting resources increases or decreases the total task effort.

It is recommended that you consider setting your default options to:

- The **Default task type:** as **Fixed Work** in the **Tools**, **Options…**, **Schedule** tab.

- This will make new tasks as **NOT** effort driven. The **New tasks are effort driven** box in the **Tools**, **Options…**, **Schedule** tab appears gray.

Then set these as your default options by clicking on the ⌊ Set as Default ⌋ icon and all new projects will have these options set. With this scenario:

- When you change the durations of your tasks your estimate of hours and cost will not change, and

- You will be able to enter resources against a task and you will be able to assign the hours against each resource as you assign the resource.

- You may then change tasks to different options as required by exception.

19.2 Fixed Costs

Fixed costs are a function where you may assign costs to a task without creating resources. It is a useful function if you require a cash flow only.

A fixed cost may be assigned directly to a task without a Resource Assignment.

- A fixed cost is assigned using the **Fixed Cost** column.

- The fixed cost may be accrued at the **Start**, **End** or **Prorated** over the duration of the task. This option is selected from the **Fixed Cost Accrual** column. The default for the **Fixed Cost Accrual** is set in the **Tools**, **Options…**, **Calculation** tab:

	Task Name	Duration	Fixed Cost	Fixed Cost Accrual	24 Oct '05				
					M	T	W	T	F
1	⊟ **Summary**	**5 days**	**$0.00**	**Prorated**	$240.00	$40.00	$40.00	$40.00	$240.00
2	$200.00 Fixed cost accrued at Start	5 days	$200.00	Start	$200.00				
3	$200.00 Fixed cost Prorated	5 days	$200.00	Prorated	$40.00	$40.00	$40.00	$40.00	$40.00
4	$200.00 Fixed cost accrued at End	5 days	$200.00	End					$200.00

- Fixed Costs will not be displayed in the **Resource Sheet** or **Resource Usage** views but are available in the **Task Usage** view and in a **Report**. The **Cash Flow** report will only give you the cash flow in weeks.

- Fixed costs are added to resource costs and the total of the two is shown in the **Cost** column.

Task Name	Fixed Cost	Fixed Cost Accrual	Resource Initials	Cost
⊟ **Summary**	**$0.00**	**Prorated**		**$8,800.00**
$200.00 Fixed cost accrued at Start	$200.00	Start		$200.00
$200.00 Fixed cost Prorated	$200.00	Prorated		$200.00
$200.00 Fixed cost accrued at End	$200.00	End		$200.00
Activity With Resources Only	$0.00	Prorated	PEH	$4,000.00
Activity With Costs & Resources	$200.00	Prorated	PEH	$4,200.00

When there are both **Fixed Costs** and **Resource Costs** assigned to a task, there is no column to display **Resource Costs** only.

When a Baseline is set, the Fixed costs and the Resource costs are added together in the Baseline costs value.

19.3 Assigning Resources Using the Resource Assignment Form

Highlight one or more tasks that you want to assign resources. Click the **Assign Resource** icon 🔲 on the **Standard** toolbar to display the **Assign Resource** form.

The **Units** may be the number of people working on a task and may be displayed as Units shown in the left picture below, or as a Percentage shown in the right picture below. This option is changed in the **Schedule** tab of the **Options** form.

 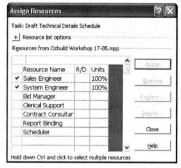

- Select the **Resource** from the form.
  - ➤ Type in the number of resources you want to assign under **Units**. This may be displayed in % or whole numbers depending on how your options are set. 1.00 is the same value as 100%.
  - ➤ Click on the ⬚ Assign button to assign a resource to a task.
- You may then assign another resource to a task.

- Select a resource and click on the ⬚ Remove button to remove a resource.

- Select a resource and click on the ⬚ Replace... button to open the **Replace Resource** form to replace a resource.

19.4 Assigning Resources using the Task Details Form

In the bottom window select the **Task Detail Form**, **Task Form** or **Task Name Form**. Then select the appropriate option from the **Format**, **Details** option. See below:

Form	Assignment Option
• **Resource & Predecessors**	**Units** and **Work**
• **Resource & Successors**	**Units** and **Work**
• **Resource Schedule**	**Work** only
• **Resource Work**	**Units** and **Work**
• **Resource Cost**	**Units** only with calculated costs

The **Task Entry** form with the **Resource Work** details form is displayed below.

- Select the required resource in the drop-down box under the **Resource Name** heading.

- Enter the number of resources under **Units**, or

- Enter the amount of **Work** – The number of hours may be entered under this heading.

- **Ovt. Work** – Overtime Work may be assigned to reduce the duration of the task. The **Work** remains the same, but the **Overtime** value represents the amount of work being done on overtime.

- **Baseline Work** is copied from **Work** when a **Baseline** is set.

- **Act. Work** – **Actual Work** is entered when work is in-progress.

- **Rem. Work** – **Remaining Work** is calculated by subtracting **Actual Work** from **Work**.

19.5 Assigning Task Information Form

Double-click on a **Task** name or click on the **Task Information** icon to open the **Task Information** form.

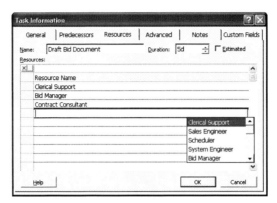

- Select the required resource from the drop-down box.
- Type in the number of required resources in the **Units** box.

19.6 Assignment of Resources to Summary Tasks

Summary tasks may be assigned **Fixed Costs**, **Work Resources** and **Material Resources**.

You must also be aware that when a Work resource is assigned to a summary task the task type is set to **Fixed Duration** and that setting may not be changed. Thus, any change in duration of a summary task due to rescheduling of associated detailed tasks will result in a change to the work assignment and the calculated costs of a Summary task.

It is recommended that unless a Summary task Work resource is required to vary in proportion to the Summary task duration, then Work Resources should not be assigned to a Summary task. You should consider using Fixed Costs or a Material resource if appropriate.

19.7 Sharing Resources From With Other Projects

Microsoft Project allows resources to be shared with multiple projects. This feature is not covered in detail in this book. Select **Tools**, **Resource**, **Share Resources...** to open the **Share Resources** form where the project that it is wished to share resources from may be nominated and calculations options for leveling may be set.

19.8 Rollup of Costs and Hours to Summary Tasks

The task **Cost** and **Work** fields are calculated from the sum of the costs and work assigned to the related detailed tasks and those of the summary task.

> It becomes difficult for a scheduler to check the total cost of a Summary task after costs and work have been assigned to both the Summary task and associated Detailed tasks. It is recommended that you consider only assigning costs and work to Detailed tasks.

Summary Tasks have the costs and work rolled up to give you a cost at any Outline level.

	Task Name	Duration	Start	Finish	Cost	Work
1	⊟ OzBuild Bid	33 days	5 Dec '05	23 Jan '06	$26,046.00	656 hrs
2	⊟ Research	13 days	5 Dec '05	21 Dec '05	$8,720.00	216 hrs
3	Bid Request Documents Received	0 days	5 Dec '05	5 Dec '05	$0.00	0 hrs
4	Bid Strategy Meeting	1 day	5 Dec '05	5 Dec '05	$1,040.00	24 hrs
5	Investigate Technical Feasibility	8 days	6 Dec '05	15 Dec '05	$5,120.00	128 hrs
6	Document Installation Requirements	4 days	16 Dec '05	21 Dec '05	$2,560.00	64 hrs
7	⊟ Estimation	15 days	15 Dec '05	9 Jan '06	$8,416.00	232 hrs
8	Request Component Tenders	3 days	3 Jan '06	5 Jan '06	$960.00	24 hrs
9	Develop Project Schedule	4 days	22 Dec '05	29 Dec '05	$864.00	32 hrs
10	Draft Technical Details Schedule	11.25 days	15 Dec '05	4 Jan '06	$5,952.00	160 hrs
11	Compile Cost from Component Bids	2 days	6 Jan '06	9 Jan '06	$640.00	16 hrs
12	⊟ Proposal	10 days	10 Jan '06	23 Jan '06	$8,910.00	208 hrs
13	Draft the Bid Document	3 days	10 Jan '06	12 Jan '06	$2,800.00	72 hrs
14	Meeting to Review the Draft Bid Document	1 day	13 Jan '06	13 Jan '06	$1,040.00	24 hrs
15	Design Presentation	1 day	16 Jan '06	16 Jan '06	$720.00	16 hrs
16	Edit Proposal Draft Bid Document	1 day	16 Jan '06	16 Jan '06	$600.00	16 hrs
17	Negotiate Component Work Packages	4 days	17 Jan '06	20 Jan '06	$3,030.00	64 hrs
18	Final Review of Bid Document	1 day	23 Jan '06	23 Jan '06	$720.00	16 hrs
19	Submit Bid	0 days	23 Jan '06	23 Jan '06	$0.00	0 hrs

The Baseline Costs and Work are copied from the Cost and Work fields at the time that the Baseline is set and are not calculated from their child tasks. Thus, when tasks are added, deleted or moved to different Summary tasks then the Baseline Costs and Work are no longer the sum of their child tasks.

There is a function titled **Summary Task Interim Baseline Calculation**, which is covered in the **STATUSING PROJECTS WITH RESOURCES** chapter. This will allow the Summary Tasks Baseline Dates and Costs to be recalculated.

19.9 Contour the Resource Assignment

A Resource Assignment may be assigned to a task with a non-linear profile. This function is titled **Work Contour** and is similar to the Resource Curve function in Primavera P3 and SureTrak software. To assign a contour to a resource assignment:

- Open the **Assignment Information** form by:
  - ➢ Double-clicking on a resource in the **Task Usage** or **Resource Usage** view, or
  - ➢ Right-clicking on a resource and selecting **Assignment Information** from the menu.

- The picture below shows the Sales Engineer being assigned as **Back Loaded**.

- From the **Work contour:** drop-down box, select the **Work Contour** type.

- The picture below is the **Resource Usage** form. It shows one task titled **Example Task** with six resources. Each resource name is the same as the assigned **Work** contour. The picture shows the effect of:
  - ➢ The assignment for each of the **Work Contour** types, and
  - ➢ The icon displayed in the **Task Information** column is a graphical representation of the contour.

		Task Name	Work	Details	10 June				
	❶				M	T	W	T	F
1		Example Task	320 hrs	Work	39.68h	95.27h	68.1h	78.27h	38.68h
	↗	Flat	40 hrs	Work	4h	25h	0h	8h	3h
	ꛥ	Back Loaded	40 hrs	Work	1.67h	5h	8.33h	11.67h	13.33h
	ꛦ	Front Loaded	40 hrs	Work	13.33h	11.67h	8.33h	5h	1.67h
	ꛧ	Double Peak	40 hrs	Work	6h	12h	4h	12h	6h
	ꛨ	Early Peak	40 hrs	Work	6h	16h	10h	6h	2h
	ꛩ	Late Paek	40 hrs	Work	2h	6h	10h	16h	6h
	ꛪ	Bell	40 hrs	Work	2.4h	9.6h	16h	9.6h	2.4h
	ꛫ	Turtle	40 hrs	Work	4.28h	10h	11.43h	10h	4.28h

The **Flat** option allows you to type in any value into each on the cells. A resource assignment is automatically set to **Flat** when one entry is made in the table.

WORKSHOP 16

Assigning Resources to Tasks

Preamble
The resources must now be assigned to their specific tasks.

Assignment
Open the **OzBuild With Resources** project and complete the following steps:

1. Select the **Gantt Chart** view.
2. Split the pane by selecting **Window, Split**.
3. Display the **Task Details Form** in the lower pane window, select **Format, Details**, and choose **Resource Work**.
4. Using the **Resources Work** and the **Assign Resources** form assign the following resources:

   Note: Once you have entered the **Resource Name** in the **Resources Work** form and assigned the **Units**, Microsoft Project will calculate the worked hours automatically after you click out of the form. Ensure the tasks are **NOT Effort Driven** as you enter resources, otherwise the Total Work may stay constant as you add additional resources.

   * Task 7 & 9 have Task calendars of 6 Day per week. All the Resource Calendars are 5 Day per week. When a task is assigned a resource the assignment is calculated on the resource calendar unless the **Scheduling ignores resource calendars** option in the task form is selected for each task. If these tasks increase by the incorrect duration, check the resources have were not set to **Contoured** (when the resource was assigned) by clicking on the resource in the Task Usage form.

Task	Task Name	Resource	Units	Work
4	Bid Strategy	Sales Engineer	1	8 hrs
		System Engineer	1	8 hrs
		Bid Manager	1	8 hrs
5	Technical Feasibility Study *Check the duration has not decreased from 8 to 4 days after assigning the resource.*	System Engineer	2	128 hrs
7*	Installation Requirements *Check **Scheduling ignores resource calendars** before assigning the resource.*	Sales Engineer	1	32 hrs
		System Engineer	1	32 hrs
8	Component Bids	Sales Engineer	1	24 hrs
9*	Project Schedule *Check **Scheduling ignores resource calendars** before assigning the resource.*	Scheduler	1	32 hrs
10	Technical Details Schedule	Sales Engineer	1	72 hrs
		System Engineer	1	72 hrs
11	Component Bids Costs	Sales Engineer	1	16 hrs

continued over…

WORKSHOP 16 CONTINUED

5. Use the **Task Information** form and the **Assign Resources** form to assign the remaining resource to each task. You may display the **Task Information** form by double-clicking the Task Name item on your Gantt Chart.

Task	Task Name	Resource	Units	Work
13	Draft Bid Document	Clerical Support	1	24 hrs
		Bid Manager	1	24 hrs
		Contract Consultant	1	24 hrs
14	Reviewed Draft Bid Document	Sales Engineer	1	8 hrs
		System Engineer	1	8 hrs
		Bid Manager	1	8 hrs
15	Design Validation	System Engineer	1	8 hrs
		Bid Manager	1	8 hrs
16	Revise Bid Document	Clerical Support	1	8 hrs
		Bid Manager	1	8 hrs
17	Component Work Packages` Negotiated	Sales Engineer	1	32 hrs
		Bid Manager	1	32 hrs
		Report Binding	3 Folders	
18	Bid Document Final	System Engineer	1	8 hrs
		Bid Manager	1	8 hrs

6. Insert the **Resource Names** and **Resources Initials** columns to the right of the Task Name. Align the data in the columns to the left.

7. Now display the **Task Usage** view in the top pane, insert the **Assignment Units** and **Cost** columns and check that your Assignment Units, Work and Costs are correct.

20 STATUSING PROJECTS WITH RESOURCES

The following *PMBOK® Guide* processes may be directly supported with by use of Microsoft Project when statusing a project with resources:

- **4.4 Direct and Manage Project Execution**
- **4.5 Monitor and Project Work**
- **4.6 Integrated Change Control**
- **6.6 Schedule Control**
- **7.3 Cost Control**

Statusing a project with resources uses a number of features which are very interactive. It is suggested that after you have read this chapter and before you work on a live project that you create a simple schedule with a couple of tasks and assign two or three resources against each task. Set the **Options** to reflect the information that you want to enter and what you want Microsoft Project 2003 to calculate. Go through the statusing process with dummy data representing all the data you want to collect. Then enter and check that the results are as you expected. The options to consider are:

- Have you linked **% Complete** and **Actual Work** with the **Updating task status updates resource status:** option?

- Are the resource **Actual Costs** calculated by Microsoft Project 2003 with setting the **Actual costs are always calculated by Microsoft Project** option checked?

- Are your tasks scheduled to start after a date using the **Reschedule uncompleted tasks to start after:** in conjunction with the **Split** task option?

Statusing a project with resources takes place in two distinct steps:

- The dates are statused using the methods outlined in the **TRACKING PROGRESS** chapter, and

- The resources' hours and costs are updated.

This chapter covers the following topics:

- Understanding **Baseline Dates** (Target Dates), **Baseline Costs** (Budget) and **Baseline Work**.

- Understanding the **Status Date**, **Work After Date** and **Current Date** with respect to resources.

- Information Required to Update a Resourced Schedule.

- Updating Resources.

- Splitting Tasks.

- Summary Task Interim Baseline Calculation.

- How to **Contour the Resource Assignment**.

Microsoft Project 2003 does not provide the capability for producing S-Curves. The data may be exported or copied and pasted to products such as Excel where the S-Curves may be created.

20.1 Understanding Baseline Dates, Duration, Costs and Hours

Baseline Dates are also known as Target Dates and are normally the original Project Early Start and Early Finish dates. These are the dates against which project progress is measured.

Baseline Duration is the original planned duration of a task.

Baseline Costs are also known as Budgets and represent the original project cost estimate. These are the figures against which the expenditures and Cost at Completion (or Estimate at Completion) are measured.

Baseline Work is also known as Budgeted Quantity and represents the original estimate of the project quantities. These are the quantities against which the consumption of resources are measured.

The **Baseline Costs** and **Work** of resources are **NOT** automatically recorded in the Baseline fields of each resource as the resource is assigned to a task. All **Baseline** information (**Dates**, **Costs** and **Work**) are saved when the project or selected Tasks have the Baseline set.

If resources have been assigned then the Baseline Costs and Work are recorded at the same time as the Baseline dates.

Setting the **Baseline Dates** is covered in the **TRACKING PROGRESS** chapter.

Baseline Dates may be displayed by using the following methods:

- Baseline Date Start and Finish columns, or

- Bar Chart Bars, or

- Dates on the Bars.

20.2 *Understanding the Data Date*

The **Data Date** is a standard scheduling term. It is also known as the **Review Date**, **Status Date**, **As of Date** and **Update Date**.

- The **Data Date** is the date that divides the past from the future in the schedule. The **Data Date** is not normally in the future but is often in the recent past due to the time it may take to collect the information to status the schedule.

- **Actual Costs** and **Quantities/Hours** or **Actual work** occur before the data date.

- **Costs** and **Quantities/Hours To Complete** or **Work to Complete** occur after the Data Date.

- **Remaining duration** is the duration required to complete a task. It is calculated forward from the **Data Date**.

Microsoft Project 2003 has four dates associated with updating a schedule. These are covered in the **TRACKING PROGRESS** chapter. In summary, these date fields are:

- **Current Date** – This date is set to the computer's system date each time a project file is opened. It is used to calculate **Earned Value** data when a **Status Date** has not been set.

- **Status Date** – By default this is blank. After assigning this date it will not change (as the **Current Date** does) when the project is saved or reopened at a later date. When set, this date overrides the **Current Date** for calculating **Earned Value** data.

- <u>U</u>**pdate work as completed through:** – When a project is updated using the **Update Project** form (the project is statused as if it were progressed exactly according to plan), the **Status Date** is set to the same date as **Project Update Date**.

- **Reschedule uncompleted work to start after:** date – This function is used to move the **Incomplete Work** of **In-Progress** tasks into the future.
  - ➢ **In-Progress** tasks must be able to **Split** for this function to operate. The option to split tasks is found on the **Tools**, **Options…**, **Schedule** tab.
  - ➢ The **Status Date** is **NOT** set to the <u>R</u>**eschedule uncompleted work to start after:** date when this function is invoked.
  - ➢ This function will not move the incomplete portions of tasks back in time when a task is completed ahead of schedule. This causes the task's **Remaining Duration** to occur sometime in the future and not immediately after the selected date. The example below shows a schedule with the **Reschedule uncompleted work to start after:** date set to 10 June. The top task's Remaining Duration commences on 11 June, the task is split and the Remaining Duration occurs immediately after 10 June. The lower task's Remaining Duration does not commence until 18 June. This is not realistic and manual intervention is required to correct this.

NEITHER the **Current Date** nor the **Status Date** is used to calculate the **Early Finish** of an **In-Progress** task when a schedule is calculated using **F9**, or when the **Calculation options for Microsoft Project**'s option of **Automatic Scheduling** is enabled. The end date of an in-progress task in Microsoft Project 2003 is normally calculated from the **Actual Start Date** plus the **Duration**. This is a different method of calculation than employed by some other scheduling software, which calculate the end date of a task from a single **Data Date** plus the **Remaining Duration**.

20.3 Formatting the Current Date and Status Date Lines

To format the display of the **Current Date** and **Status Date** lines on the Bar Chart, select **Format**, **Gridlines…** to display the **Gridlines** form:

- These **Options** allow the selection of colors and line types for all sight lines as shown in the Lines to Change box on the left of the example above.

- All other sight lines may also be formatted in this form.

20.4 Information Required to Update a Resourced Schedule

A project schedule is usually updated at the end of a period, such as each day, week or month. One purpose of updating a schedule is to establish differences between the plan and the current schedule.

Microsoft Project 2003 may calculate task Actual Costs from the rates entered in the Resource Table or the Costs may be entered manually. If the Actual Costs are to be calculated by Microsoft Project 2003 then the Actual Costs do not need to be collected.

The following information is required to status a resourced schedule:

Tasks completed in the update period:
- **Actual Start** date of the task.

- **Actual Finish** date of the task.

- **Actual Costs** spent, **Actual Resource Hours** spent, and/or **Actual Material Quantities**.

Tasks commenced in the update period:
- **Actual Start** date of the task.

- **Remaining Duration** or **Expected Finish** date.

- **Actual Costs** and **Actual Resource Hours** and/or **Actual Material Quantities**.

- **Hours** or **Quantities** to complete. Costs to complete are always calculated using the resource rates in the Resource Table.

- **Suspend** and **Resume** dates for tasks that have had their work suspended. These are used for splitting tasks.

Tasks Not Commenced:
- Changes in Logic or date constraints.

- Changes in estimated **Costs**, **Hours** or **Quantities**.

The schedule may be updated once this information is collected.

You have the option of allowing Microsoft Project 2003 to calculate many of these fields from the **% Complete** by selecting the appropriate option found in the **Tools**, **Options...**, **Calculation** tab.

20.5 Updating Dates and Percentage Complete

The schedule should be first updated as outlined in the **TRACKING PROGRESS** chapter. In summary, this is completed by entering:

- The **Actual Start** and **Actual Finish** dates of **Complete** tasks.

- The **Actual Start**, **% Complete** and **Remaining Duration** or **Expected Finish** of **In-Progress** tasks.

- Adjust Logic and **Durations** of **Unstarted** tasks.

Before you do this, you should set the **Tools**, **Options…**, **Calculation** tab to ensure that the actual costs and hours calculate the way you want.

A simple process to update a project is to:

- Use the **Tools**, **Tracking**, **Update Project…** and select **Update work as complete through:** to update the project through to the data date.

- Adjust the **Actual Start** and **Actual Finish** dates for **Complete** tasks.

- Drag the finish date of **In-Progress** tasks to the required date.

- Adjust the **Actual Start** dates of **In-Progress** tasks and drag the **% Complete** to the required value.

The option of **Tools**, **Tracking**, **Update Project…** will only work when the following Project Options are enabled. Then, **Work** and **Costs** are calculated by Microsoft Project 2003.

- **Updating task status updates resource status**, and

- **Actual costs are always calculated by Microsoft Project.**

20.6 Entering a % Complete Against Summary Tasks

A **% Complete** may be entered against a summary task and all the child tasks and their resources will be updated automatically to reflect the Summary % Complete. Full details of this function are outlined in the **TRACKING PROGRESS** chapter. In the picture below 75% was entered against the **Research** task:

20.7 Updating Resources

There are many permutations available in the **Tools**, **Options…** form for calculating resource data. Due to the number of resource options and numerous forms available in Microsoft Project 2003, it is not feasible to document all the combinations available for resource calculation.

This book, therefore, outlines some typical scenarios and examples of entering the status data that you may want to try on your projects.

Material resources are updated in the same way as **Work** resources and are not covered separately.

20.7.1 Updating Tasks with Fixed Costs Only

A project with fixed costs only is the simplest option for managing costs. The example below displays:

- A 10-day **Duration** task which is 40% Complete.

- A **Baseline Cost** of $100.00 which was created by an original **Fixed Cost** of $100.00 when the **Baseline** was set.

- A **Fixed Cost** of $80.00 representing a revised estimate which has reduced the original estimate by $20.00 to $80.00.

- An **Actual Cost** of $32.00 and **Remaining Cost** of $48.00, which are calculated from the 40 **% Complete**.

- The **Current Bar** (the upper bar in the picture below) shows that the task started two days late and is scheduled to end two days late as compared to the **Baseline Bar** (the black lower bar).

You will notice that the **Task Details** view with the **Resource Cost** details form does not show any resources or costs when **Fixed Costs** are used.

20.7.2 Forecasting Resource Hours

The next level of complexity usually occurs when a schedule is used for the management of resource hours but not costs.

One or more resources may be applied to a task and you may want to enter both the **Actual Work** and the **Remaining Work** independently. In this situation you will need to unlink **% Complete** and **Actual Work** with the **Updating task status updates resource status:** option in the **Tools**, **Options…**, **Calculation** tab. Now the field **% Work** field will be linked to the **Work**, **Actual Work** and **Remaining Work** fields and will now operate independently of the **% Complete** field..

The example below uses the **Task Details** form.

- A 10-day **Duration** task which is 40% Complete.

- The task's **Baseline Work** of 240hrs is from the addition of the two resource allocations when the **Baseline** was set.
  - ➢ The **Bid Manager** was originally assigned at 100%, or full-time, giving a **Baseline Work** of 80 hours.
  - ➢ The **Clerical Support** was originally assigned at 200%, or 2 full-time people, giving a **Baseline Work** of 160 hours.

- The task's **Actual Work** of 90 hours is the addition of the two resources' **Actual Work** of 20 hours and 70 hours.

- The task's **Remaining Work** of 220 hours is the addition of the **Remaining Work** of 70 hours and 150 hours.

- The **% Work** of 29% is calculated by dividing the **Actual Work** by the **Work.** This is different than the **% Complete**, which represents the elapsed time.

- Again, the **Current Bar** shows the task started two days late and is scheduled to end two days late.

- The **Actual Work** and **Remaining Work** were entered manually and have not been calculated by Microsoft Project 2003 from the **% Complete**.

- The duration of the task is still 10 days long because it is a **Fixed Duration** task. The **Units** have increased from 1 to 1.17 and 2 to 3.33 for the Bid Manager and Clerical Support, respectively, as the **Work** is now greater than the **Baseline Work** due to the increase in the number of hours required to complete the task.

20.7.3 Forecasting Resource Hours and Costs Form

The example below is similar to the previous example, but it now displays the **Resource Costs** (not the **Work**) calculated by Microsoft Project 2003 with **% Complete** and **Actual Work** unlinked.

The next level of complexity occurs usually when a schedule is used for the management of resource hours and costs.

You may want to enter both the **Actual Work** and **Actual Costs** separately. For example, you may want to take the costs and hours from a timesheet and/or an accounting system that may have a different resource rate than your schedule. Input your data in the lower pane of the window, which is known as the **Resource Details** form.

In this situation you will need to:

- Unlink **% Complete** and **Actual Work** with the **Updating task status updates resource status:** option in the **Tools**, **Options…**, **Calculation** tab, and

- Unlink the **Actual Work** and **Actual Costs** by disabling the **Actual costs are always calculated by Microsoft Project** option in the **Tools**, **Options…**, **Calculation** tab.

The example below shows how the costs are calculated with:

- **Work** and **Costs** unlinked, and

- Updated hours as per the previous example.

The **Actual Costs** have not been calculated by Microsoft Project 2003 and remain at zero. The **Remaining Costs** are based on the resources' **Standard Rate**.

Now that the Actual Costs and Actual Work are unlinked, you may type in the **Actual Costs** per resource in the lower pane of the window (i.e. the **Resource Details** form) without affecting the **Actual Work**.

20.7.4 Using the Task Usage and Resource Usage Views

The Task Usage and Resource usage forms allow the most flexibility when entering resource quantities to-date and to go. The picture below is the **Task Usage** form from the OzBuild workshops showing the **Work**, **Actual Work** and **Baseline Work** rows. Additional rows of information may be obtained by right-clicking to display a menu or selecting **Format**, **Details**.

A timesheet style view may be created with the **Resource Usage** view. This view may be printed or used by team members to directly update their hours to date in the **Act. Work** (Actual Work) rows and their estimate hours in the **Work** rows. The advantage of this view is that all activities are grouped together in one band under each name.

Calculated cost fields that may not have data entered into are shown as gray.

20.8 Splitting Tasks

When the **Split in-progress tasks** option is enabled, a task may be **Split** by:

- Dragging the incomplete portion of a task in the bar chart, or

- Clicking on the [icon] icon and then moving your cursor over the point on the task bar where you want a split and drag the task, or

- Using the **Tools**, **Tracking**, **Update Project...**, **Reschedule uncompleted work to start after:** function, or

- Commencing a task before its predecessor finishes.

In the picture below the upper task was split using the [icon] icon and the lower task was split because it commenced before its predecessor.

A **Split** may be reversed by dragging the split portion back in the bar chart if there is no predecessor pushing the split out. The first task in the example below has been dragged back. The second task may not be dragged back due to the FS relationship.

Once a task is **Split**, then the resources are not scheduled to work during the split period. This concept is demonstrated in the **RESOURCE HISTOGRAMS S-CURVES AND TABLES** chapter.

20.9 Summary Task Interim Baseline Calculation

Microsoft Project 2002 introduced a new function titled **Summary Task Interim Baseline Calculation** that enables the Baseline dates and costs of summary activities to be recalculated when tasks are added, deleted or moved. The date aspect of this function is covered in the **TRACKING PROGRESS** chapter.

There are a number of permutations that may be used with this option and a little experimentation with a simple schedule, such as the one below, will enable you to understand this function.

Often it is required to recalculate the Baseline Costs Summary Tasks based on the Original Baseline Costs after activities have been moved to different Summary Tasks. This function may recalculate the Summary Task Baseline Costs from the detailed tasks Baseline Costs when the costs for a project have been revised and are showing a forecast with a deviation from the Baseline. The example below demonstrates this process:

- Original schedule with Baseline Costs and Dates:

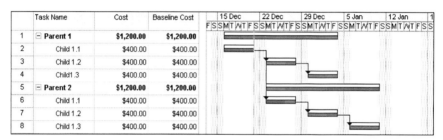

- After the project has been delayed and the task Child 1.3 moved under Parent 1:

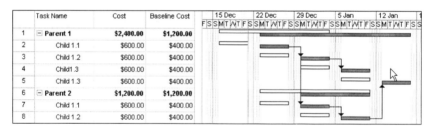

You will observe that neither the summary bars nor the Baseline Costs of Parent 1 or Parent 2 are now correct.

- Now highlight the parent tasks only and then select **Tools Tracking**, **Save Baseline….** and select the options shown in the Save Baseline form below:

You will see from the picture below that now both the Baseline Dates displayed as the upper bar and the Baseline Costs are recalculated from the original baseline data.

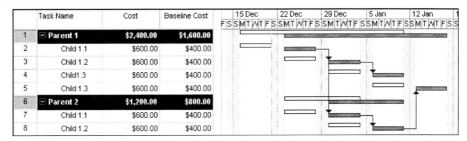

20.10 Summary Tasks and Earned Value

Actual Costs and **Work** may be summarized at any level in the same way as **Work** and **Costs**. The picture below is showing the **Earned Value** table and the costs have been summarized up to the Project Level:

	Task Name	BCWS	BCWP	ACWP	SV	CV	EAC	BAC	VAC
1	⊟ Ozbuild Bid	**$15,664.00**	**$12,608.00**	**$9,574.13**	**($3,056.00)**	**$3,033.87**	**$17,860.13**	**$25,134.00**	**$6,048.00**
2	⊞ **Research**	**$8,720.00**	**$8,720.00**	**$6,640.13**	**$0.00**	**$2,079.87**	**$6,640.13**	**$8,720.00**	**$2,079.87**
7	⊟ **Estimation**	**$6,944.00**	**$3,888.00**	**$2,934.00**	**($3,056.00)**	**$954.00**	**$3,030.00**	**$8,224.00**	**$2,017.93**
8	Request Componei	$320.00	$0.00	$320.00	($320.00)	($320.00)	$640.00	$960.00	$320.00
9	Develop Project Sc	$864.00	$432.00	$864.00	($432.00)	($432.00)	$0.00	$864.00	($864.00)
10	Draft Technical De	$5,760.00	$3,456.00	$1,750.00	($2,304.00)	$1,706.00	$1,750.00	$5,760.00	$2,843.33
11	Compile Costs fron	$0.00	$0.00	$0.00	$0.00	$0.00	$640.00	$640.00	$0.00
12	⊟ **Proposal**	**$0.00**	**$0.00**	**$0.00**	**$0.00**	**$0.00**	**$8,190.00**	**$8,190.00**	**$0.00**
13	Draft Bid Documen	$0.00	$0.00	$0.00	$0.00	$0.00	$2,800.00	$2,800.00	$0.00
14	Meeting to Review	$0.00	$0.00	$0.00	$0.00	$0.00	$1,040.00	$1,040.00	$0.00
15	Design Presentatio	$0.00	$0.00	$0.00	$0.00	$0.00	$720.00	$720.00	$0.00
16	Edit Proposal Draft	$0.00	$0.00	$0.00	$0.00	$0.00	$600.00	$600.00	$0.00
17	Negotiate Compon(	$0.00	$0.00	$0.00	$0.00	$0.00	$2,310.00	$2,310.00	$0.00
18	Final Review of Bi(	$0.00	$0.00	$0.00	$0.00	$0.00	$720.00	$720.00	$0.00
19	Submit Bid	$0.00	$0.00	$0.00	$0.00	$0.00	$0.00	$0.00	$0.00

The **Earned Value Technique (EVT)** is outlined in the *PMBOK® Guide* section **7.3 Cost Control**. The terminology below is used by a large number of companies and organizations. It provides standard terms to describe Earned Value calculations, which many people understand. The method that Microsoft Project calculates the Earned Value Fields is documented in the help file. Below are some of the terms that are in common use:

- AC or ACWP   Actual Cost or Actual Cost of Work Performed
- EV or BCWP   Earned Value or Budget Cost of Work Performed
- PV or BCWS   Planned Value or Budget Cost of Work Scheduled
- BAC   Budget At Completion
- C/SCSC   Cost/Schedule Control Systems Criteria (CS^2)
- CV   Cost Variance to date, BCWP – ACWP
- EAC   Estimate at Completion
- ETC Time   Estimate To Complete expressed in Time
- ETC   Estimate To Complete
- FAC $ Forecast at Completion
- FC CV   Forecast Cost Variance at Completion
                  (Budget – Forecast)
- FC SV   Forecast Schedule Variance at Completion
                  (Baseline End Date – Scheduled End Date)
- FTC CT   Forecast To Complete Calendar Time
- SV   Schedule Variance to date, BCWP – BCWS

The **Physical % Complete** field may be used to calculate the Earned Value (Budget Cost of Work Performed) independently from the value in the task **% Complete** field. This function is useful for measuring the progress of work that is not progressing linearly. This may be set for each individual task in the **General** tab of the **Task Information** form and the default for new tasks may be set with the Earned Value... button in the **General** tab of the Options form, where also the Baseline to be used for the Earned Value calculations may be selected

WORKSHOP 17

Updating Costs

Preamble

We need to status the tasks and resources.

Assignment

Note: If your settings are not exactly the same as the computer on which this exercise was undertaken you may end up with different results.

Open your project file and complete the following steps:

1. We will initially allow Microsoft Project to calculate costs and hours from the % Complete. Adjust the options using **Tools**, **Options…**, **Calculation** tabs to:
   - ➤ **CHECK** the **Updating task status updates resource status** option. This will link % Complete and Actual Work. (This option also needs to be checked to allow Summary % Completes to be spread correctly to detailed tasks.)
   - ➤ **UNCHECK** both **Move end of completed task parts after status date back to status date** and **Move start of remaining parts before status date forward to status date** options.
   - ➤ **CHECK** the **Actual costs are always calculated by Microsoft Project** option. With this option checked the resource Actual Cost is calculated by Microsoft Project 2002 from the resource Work and Rates.
   - ➤ Select the **Schedule** tab and **UNCHECK** the **Split in-progress tasks** option. This will prevent the splitting of tasks.

2. Split the screen. Display the **Gantt Chart** with **Tracking** table in the upper screen and the **Task Details Form** with **Resource Work** details form in the lower screen.

3. Hide the Physical % Complete column.

4. Run the **Format**, **Gantt Chart Wizard…** to format the bars. Display the **Baseline** without text and display logic links lines and adjust the timescale to months and weeks so you may see the whole schedule on half the screen.

5. Save the Baseline using the **Tools**, **Tracking**, **Save Baseline…**.

6. Use the **Format**, **Gridlines…** command to format the **Status Date** as a solid RED line. This will not be displayed until the Status Date is set.

Continued Over…

WORKSHOP 17 CONTINUED

7. The **Data Date** is 18 Dec 06:

> Update the project using **Tools**, **Tracking**, **Update Project…**, as per the picture below:

> Enter 50% Complete, then 10% against the summary task **Research**. Observe how the % Complete fields of the Detailed Tasks of Research are calculated based on the proportion of total of durations.

> Change the % Complete back to 100%

> Open the **Resource Cost** form in the lower pane. Observe how the resource costs have been updated in the **Installation Requirements** task.

> Enter a 20% Complete against task **Technical Details Schedule** and enter an actual Start Date of 14 Dec 06.

> Check the **Status Date** in the **Project Information** form it should be 18 Dec 06.

Your schedule should look like this:

8. We will now enter our hours and costs to date and hours to go. To prevent Microsoft Project from calculating the costs, open the **Options** form, **Calculation** tab and:

> **UNCHECK** the **Updating task status updates resource status**. This option is to prevent the updated % Complete from calculating **Actual Work** and **Remaining Work**.

> **UNCHECK** the **Actual costs are always calculated by Microsoft Project**. This option is to prevent Microsoft Project from calculating the **Actual Costs** from the **Actual Work**.

WORKSHOP 17 CONTINUED

> Display the Resource Work form in the bottom pane and update the **Technical Details Schedule** with the following information:
> 20 hours of **Actual Work** and 50 hours of **Remaining Work** against the **Sales Engineer**, and
> 20 hours of **Actual Work** and 70 hours of **Remaining Work** against the **System Engineer**.

Click the **OK** button to accept the changes.

> You will notice that the **Units** change to 1.35, therefore an over time of 35% is required, the task duration will remain the same due to **Fixed Duration** being used.

9. Apply the **Resource Cost** details form in the bottom pane:

> Update the **Technical Details Schedule** with the following information:
> **Actual Cost** of $1,000.00 against the **Sales Engineer**, and
> **Actual Cost** of $750.00 against the **System Engineer**.
> Click the **OK** button to accept the changes.
> Note: The **Remaining Costs** have been calculated by Microsoft Project.
> You schedule should look like this:

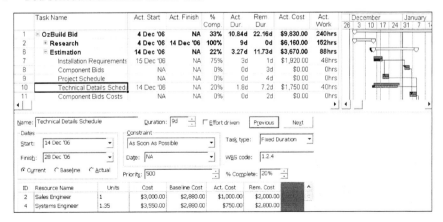

Note: There is some work on Task 10 – Technical Details Schedule that is in the past, which is not logical, and this work could be moved to the future either by splitting the task or using the **Tools**, **Tracking**, **Update Project…**, **Reschedule uncompleted work to start** function.

WORKSHOP 17 CONTINUED

10. Now apply the **Earned Value** table to review how your project is progressing:

	Task Name	BCWS	BCWP	ACWP	SV	CV	EAC	BAC	VAC
1	⊟ OzBuild Bid	$9,360.00	$9,232.00	$9,830.00	-$128.00	-$598.00	$27,528.69	$25,854.00	-$1,674.69
2	⊟ Research	$6,160.00	$6,160.00	$6,160.00	$0.00	$0.00	$6,160.00	$6,160.00	$0.00
3	Bid Request Docume	$0.00	$0.00	$0.00	$0.00	$0.00	$0.00	$0.00	$0.00
4	Bid Strategy	$1,040.00	$1,040.00	$1,040.00	$0.00	$0.00	$1,040.00	$1,040.00	$0.00
5	Technical Feasibility :	$5,120.00	$5,120.00	$5,120.00	$0.00	$0.00	$5,120.00	$5,120.00	$0.00
6	⊟ Estimation	$3,200.00	$3,072.00	$3,670.00	-$128.00	-$598.00	$12,883.23	$10,784.00	-$2,099.23
7	Installation Requirem	$1,920.00	$1,920.00	$1,920.00	$0.00	$0.00	$2,560.00	$2,560.00	$0.00
8	Component Bids	$0.00	$0.00	$0.00	$0.00	$0.00	$960.00	$960.00	$0.00
9	Project Schedule	$0.00	$0.00	$0.00	$0.00	$0.00	$864.00	$864.00	$0.00
10	Technical Details Sch	$1,280.00	$1,152.00	$1,750.00	-$128.00	-$598.00	$8,750.00	$5,760.00	-$2,990.00
11	Component Bids Cos	$0.00	$0.00	$0.00	$0.00	$0.00	$640.00	$640.00	$0.00
12	⊟ Proposal	$0.00	$0.00	$0.00	$0.00	$0.00	$8,910.00	$8,910.00	$0.00

11. You will notice that the project is scheduled to be $1,674.69 over cost. See the **VAC** (Variance at Completion) column.

12. To demonstrate the splitting of tasks, assume that the data date is 22 Dec 06 and no more work will continue until after the New Year. Apply the **Tracking** table and update the **% Complete** column as follows:
➢ **Installation Requirements** as 100%,
➢ **Project Schedule** as 50%, and
➢ **Technical Details Schedule** as 60%.

13. We will not update the Work and Costs, but ensure that **Split in-progress tasks** is checked in the **Tools**, **Options…**, **Schedule** tab.

14. Use the **Tools**, **Tracking**, **Update Project…** to reschedule all incomplete work after 02 Jan 07, allow scheduling conflict. There may be a warning sign, observe and click ok. The duration of Technical Details Schedule will be extended.

15. After rescheduling all incomplete work after 02 Jan 07, your schedule should look like the following:

16. You will notice there will be negative float on Submit Bid which is generated by the Must Finish By constraint and the Status Date needs to be adjusted manually.

21 RESOURCE/COST TABLES, HISTOGRAMS AND S-CURVES

Tables, Histograms and S-Curves are used to display resource and cost data over time during both the planning and execution of a project. The results are either displayed cumulatively or by period. This data is used in a number of PMBOK® Guide processes including:

- **4.4 Direct and Manage Project Execution**

- **4.5 Monitor and Project Work**

- **4.5 Monitoring and Control Project Work**

- **6.6 Schedule Control**

- **7.1 Cost Estimating**

- **7.2 Cost Budgeting**

- **7.3 Cost Control**

- **10.2 Information Distribution**

- **10.3 Performance Reporting**

S-Curves are often used to display data created using the **Earned Value Technique (EVT)** which is outlined in the *PMBOK® Guide* section **7.3 Cost Control**.

This chapter will briefly cover the following topics:

- **Resource Tables** – Allow the display of one or more resource requirements in a table on a time-phased basis. This information is displayed by the **Task Usage** and **Resource Usage** views.

- **Resource Histograms** – Allow the display of each resource on a time-phased vertical bar graph. These are termed **Resource Graphs** in Microsoft Project 2003.

- **S-Curves** – Allow the display of the **Planned**, **Earned**, **Actual** and **ETC** of resource quantity (in hours or material quantity) or costs as a line chart. A single S-Curve may be produced for one or selected resource costs or hours using the Resource Graph View. The display of multiple S-Curves showing the Planned, Actual, Earned and ETC cost or hours of resources is not possible in Microsoft Project. It is also not possible to display Fixed Costs on the S-Curves, but the source data for resources may be exported to a spreadsheet where charts may be readily created for multiple S-Curves which are typically used for **Earned Value Technique**.

Function	Command Menu
• To display a **Resource Graph**	Select the **Resource Graph** View.
• To display a **Resource Tables**	Select the **Task Usage** or **Resource Usage** Views.
• To print a **Resource Profile** or **Resource Table**	Select the appropriate **View**, make the view active and use the normal print commands.

21.1 Resource Graph

A **Resource Graph** may be displayed with the **Resource Graph** view:

- The **Resource Graph** may be viewed in the top or bottom pane. The view below displays the Gantt Chart in the top pane and Resource Graph in the bottom pane and shows the Sales Engineer is overloaded:

- Only one resource is displayed at a time. You may scroll through the resources by:
  - ➢ Striking the **Page Up** and **Page Down Keys**, or
  - ➢ Clicking on the scroll bar in the lower left-hand side of the **Resource Graph** view.

- The **Resource Graph Units** options may display the vertical scale by using any of the units shown in the gray box on the right. The **Units** to be displayed may be selected by:
  - ➢ Selecting **Format**, **Details**, or
  - ➢ Right-clicking in the graph area of the screen.

- The **Resource Graph** gridlines and colors may be formatted by opening the **Bar Styles** form and:
  - ➢ Selecting **Format**, **Bar Styles...** when the **Resource Graph** is the active pane, or
  - ➢ Right-clicking in the graph area of the screen and selecting the **Bar Styles** option.
- The **Timescale** of the graph is adopted from the timescale setting. You will find the **Zoom** icons useful for changing the timescale.

21.2 Resource Tables

Resource tables are displayed using the **Task Usage** or **Resource Usage** views.

- The **Task Usage View** organizes the schedule by **Task** and then by **Resource**:

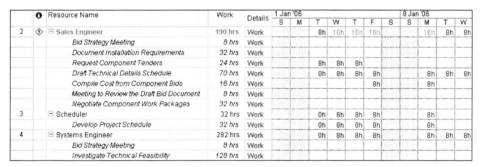

- The **Resource Usage** view organizes the schedule by **Resource** and then by **Task**. Note the Sales Engineer is overloaded as indicated by the icon in the indicators column:

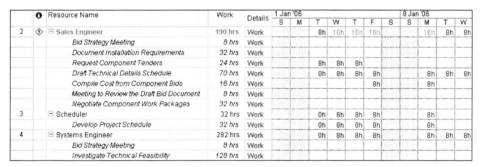

- When these views are displayed in the top **Pane** they display all resources and all tasks.

- When these views are displayed in the bottom **Pane** they display values for resources or tasks that have been selected in the top **Pane**.

The resource Usage options may be displayed by right clicking in the table area:

21.3 Creating an S-Curve from Microsoft Project

A single S-Curve may be created graphically and displayed by Microsoft Project, the example below is produced by:

- Displaying the **Resource Sheet** in the top pane and selecting all the resources,

- Displaying the **Resource Graph** in the bottom pane,

- Displaying the **Cumulative Costs** and

- Selecting the **Show as:** option as **Line**.

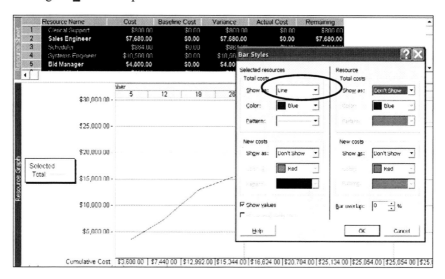

21.4 Printing Resource Profiles and Tables

To **Print** a **Task Usage**, **Resource Usage**, or **Resource Graph**, make the appropriate **Pane** active and use the print functions as described in the **PRINTING AND REPORTS** chapter.

21.5 Creating Table, S-Curves and Histograms in a Spreadsheet

Tables, S-Curves and histograms may be created for displaying:

- Planning information, such as the required number of people on a project,

- Measuring progress, and

- Evaluating performance.

Earned Value Technique (EVT) also know as **Earned Value Performance Measurement (EVPM)** is a well document technique used for the management of projects. This technique requires the results output in a number of formats which Microsoft Project is not able to reproduce, but spreadsheets or specialists software will produce from data exported from Microsoft Project. There are many good Earned Value reference documents that may be used to assist in the establishment of an Earned Value Performance Measurement system including:

- The Australian Standard "AS 4817-2005 Project performance measurement using Earned Value", and

- The Project Management Institute Practice "Standard For Earned Value Management"

Excel is often used to create S-Curves and Histograms for the following reasons:

- The ability to easily record and display period information, this may be hours consumed or dollars spent per week or per month.

- The ability to simply record actuals at a summary level. It is simpler to record cost and hours at project or at WBS component than at multiple task level.

- The superior graphical output of Excel and flexibility compared to Microsoft Project, including the ability to display both tabular and graphical information on a single printout.

Many people are familiar with copying and pasting tabular data from one software program to another and are also comfortable with creating S-Curves and Histograms in spreadsheets which are titled charts in Excel. This section of this book will cover the basics of transferring the data from Microsoft Project 2003 to a spreadsheet for the creation of S-Curves and Histograms.

21.5.1 Export Using Analysis Toolbar

The **Analysis** toolbar is designed to allow you to export time-phased data to Excel. Excel may be used to export data and create graphs. This is a Wizard-style function and the instructions will step you through the process which results is the data being available in tabular format in Excel.

21.5.2 Export Using Copy and Paste

A data table may be highlighted, copied, and then pasted into spreadsheets to create S-Curves. The headings are not copied, and the data on the left-hand side of the **Pane** and the data on the right-hand side of the **Pane** have to be copied separately and aligned with the headings in Excel.

This process is not as simple as using the Analysis Toolbar but the precise data may be copied and pasted directing into an existing spread sheet.

To transfer the data into Excel by copy & paste:

- Organize the **Task Usage** or **Resource Usage** view and **Details** so it displays the rows, columns, units and timescale you require in your graph.

- Type the column headings from both sides of the pane into the top row of your spreadsheet.

- Highlight the rows on the left-hand side of your Pane that you want to copy to the spreadsheet. Position the cursor under the spreadsheet heading and paste. If your headings do not line up, move either the data or the headings so that they do line up.

- Follow the same process with the data on the right-hand side of the Pane.

You may now create your S-Curves in the spreadsheet using its built-in graphing function.

21.5.3 Creating S-Curves and Histograms in Excel

There are no set rules for calculating EVPM data and the information may be calculated in Microsoft Project or in Excel. The table below is a simple example of EVPM data which could be displaying data at Project or WBS Element level:

- The **Planned Value** may have been exported from Microsoft Project when the schedule was Baselined.

- The **Earned Value** could be calculated either:
  - ➢ In Microsoft Project after the % Complete has been entered and exported each month to Excel, or
  - ➢ Calculated in Excel from the original Baseline Costs multiplied by the % Complete.

- The **Actual Costs** could be calculated either:
  - ➢ Outside Microsoft Project and entered at summary level in Excel, or
  - ➢ Calculated in Microsoft Project by entering the detail cost information against each task in Microsoft Project and exporting the rolled up cost into Excel each month.

- The **Estimate To Complete** is often not displayed in an EVPM graph but may be generated in Microsoft Project after the schedule and resources have been revised and the rolled up Estimate To Complete exported to Excel.

	Jan	Feb	Mar	Apr	May	Jun	Jul	Aug
Planned or BCWS	$ -	$ 6,000	$15,000	$30,000	$43,000	$50,000	$ -	$ -
Earned or BCWP	$ -	$ 4,000	$10,000	$20,000	$ -	$ -	$ -	$ -
Actual or ACWP	$ -	$ 8,000	$20,000	$40,000	$ -	$ -	$ -	$ -
Estimate At Completion	$ -	$ -	$ -	$40,000	$55,000	$65,000	$70,000	$75,000

The Excel S-Curve Chart below may be created by highlighting the data in Excel, selecting **Insert, Chart...**, selecting a **Line** Chart Type and following the Wizard instructions. Histograms are created in a similar way by selecting a different Chart Type.

22 TOOLS AND TECHNIQUES FOR SCHEDULING

22.1 Understanding Menu Options

You will find that the menu options change as you select rows, cells, all rows and cells, or views. Therefore, not all menu options are always available. The following topics will be covered in this chapter:

- Menu items sometimes found under **Edit**:
  - ➢ **Cut**, **Copy** and **Paste Task**
  - ➢ **Cut**, **Copy** and **Paste Cell**
  - ➢ **Copy Picture**
  - ➢ **Fill**
  - ➢ **Clear**
  - ➢ **Find…** and **Replace…**
  - ➢ **Go To…**
- **Insert**, **Recurring tasks…**
- **Splitting** a Task
- **Copy**, **Cut** and **Paste** from Spread Sheets
- **Unique Task**, **Resource** and **Assignment ID**
- **Organizer**

22.2 Cut, Copy and Paste Row

This function allows you to select one or more consecutive or non-consecutive tasks (using Ctrl-Click) and either copy them, or cut them and paste as a group to a new location that you select with your mouse.

22.3 Cut, Copy and Paste Cell

You may cut or copy information and then paste into one or more cells from:

- One cell, or
- Adjacent cells by dragging in rows and/or columns, or
- A non-contiguous group of cells by Ctrl-clicking.

This function operates in a similar way to Excel's cut-and-paste operation:

- Highlight the cell(s) you want to copy or cut.
- Select **Edit**, **Copy Cell** or **Ctrl+C** to copy a cell or **Edit**, **Cut Cell** or **Ctrl+X** to cut a cell.
- Position the mouse where you want to paste the data and select **Edit**, **Paste** or **Ctrl+V**.

This is an interesting function since it allows you to copy from one column to another when the format is compatible. This function may also be used for transferring and/or updating your schedule from other software such as Excel and is covered later in this chapter.

22.4 Copy Picture

This allows a section or total screen to be copied to the clipboard and then either pasted into a document or saved as a **gif** file. Select **Edit**, **Copy Picture...** to open the **Copy Picture** form:

The options are self-explanatory and when pasted into a document the picture looks like the example below.

22.5 Fill

The **Edit**, **Fill** command allows you to select one cell or a range of cells and then copy them up, down, left, or right without the need to copy and paste.

22.6 Clear

The **Edit**, **Clear** command allows you to clear the following data from a task:

- **All** – This clears all information from the cell you have highlighted.

- **Format** – This sets the formats back to the default.

- **Notes** – Clears the Notes contents on a task.

- **Contents** – This clears the contents of the highlighted cells but leaves the formatting.

- **Entire task** – This deletes the entire task but leaves blank rows.

22.7 Find and Replace

The **Edit**, **Find…** and **Edit**, **Replace…** functions allow you to find any task by matching data with your defined criteria. This will also allow you to find the data and then replace it with another piece of information.

22.8 Go To

The **Edit**, **Go To…** function allow you to quickly find a date and move the timescale horizontally to that date or a task if you know the task ID number:

22.9 Insert Recurring Task

The **Insert**, **Recurring tasks…** function allows the insertion of more than one task that occurs on a regular basis. Select **Insert**, **Recurring Task…** to display the **Recurring Task Information** form. The options are self-explanatory.

22.10 Splitting a Task

A task may be manually split by clicking on the icon, moving your cursor over the point on the task bar where you want a split, and dragging the task. Splitting a task effectively increases the duration of the task but work associated with a split task is scheduled intermittently.

The Tools, Options, Schedule **Split in-progress tasks** option must be checked to allow the splitting of a task.

An in-progress task may also be split by:

- Dragging the incomplete portion of a task in the bar chart, or

- Using the **Tools, Tracking, Update Project…, Reschedule uncompleted work to start after:** function, or

- Commencing a task before its predecessor finishes as shown by the second task in the diagram below:

22.11 Copy or Cut-and-Paste to and from Spreadsheets

Microsoft Project 2003 will allow **Copy** or **Cut**-and-**Paste** to and from spreadsheets and other software packages. This may be useful for a number of purposes:

- Importing Tasks from other applications,

- Assigning Codes and Resources to Tasks,

- Statusing a schedule, and

- Exporting Data to other packages.

The **Copy** or **Cut** function copies the task data from highlighted columns and rows in the schedule to the Windows clipboard. These may then be pasted into another software package:

- Highlight the data in your schedule that you want to transfer to another software package and cut or copy the data.

- Move to the spreadsheet application and paste the task information. You will find the column headers are **NOT** pasted into the application; only data from the schedule is pasted.

- The data may be edited or updated in the application, as required.

- The tasks may be selected and pasted back into the schedule to update it with the normal copy and paste functions.

22.12 Unique Task, Resource and Assignment ID

The Task IDs change for all tasks below an inserted task. There are many contractual and management reasons to be able to identify each task by a unique task number.

22.12.1 Task Unique ID

When a new task is added to a blank schedule, it is assigned a **Unique ID** commencing with 1. When tasks are deleted these numbers are not reused and any new task is assigned a new sequential number. This **Unique ID** number may be displayed in a column titled **Unique ID**. It is also possible to display the **Unique Predecessor** and **Unique Successor** columns:

	Unique ID	Task Name	Unique ID Predecessors	Unique ID Successors
1	18	⊟ OzBuild Bid		
2	17	⊟ Research		
3	2	Bid Document Received		3
4	3	Bid Strategy Meeting	2	4
5	4	Investigate Technical Feasibility	3	5,6,8
6	5	Document Installation Requirements	4	7,9
7	19	⊟ Estimation		
8	6	Request Component Bids	4	9

22.12.2 Resource Unique ID

A resource **Unique ID** is created for each resource. Again, when a resource is deleted, the resource **Unique ID** is not re-used. This number may be displayed in the **Resource Sheet** or **Resources Usage** view column titled, **Unique ID**.

22.12.3 Resource Assignment Unique ID

When a resource is assigned to a task, the assignment is given a unique **Assignment ID**. This number may be displayed in the **Resource Sheet** or **Resources Usage** view column titled, **Unique ID**:

	ⓘ	Task Name	Unique ID
1		⊟ **OzBuild Bid**	**18**
2		⊟ **Research**	**17**
3		Bid Document Received	2
4		⊟ Bid Strategy Meeting	3
		Sales Engineer	*2097170*
		System Engineer	*2097181*
		Tender Manager	*2097169*
5		⊟ Investigate Technical Feasibility	4
		System Engineer	*2097171*
6	📝	⊟ Document Installation Requirements	5

22.13 Organizer

The **Global.mpt** file holds the schedule's default settings such as **Tables** and **Views**, which are inherited by new projects and not created from a template. The **Organizer** function is also used to copy information between projects or to update the **Global.mpt**.

Select **Tools**, **Organizer…**to open the **Organizer** form:

Except for the **Global.mpt** project, the projects you want to copy settings to and from will have to be opened in order to copy data.

- The Organizer function is used for renaming and deleting most items such as **Tables, Views and Calendars**.

- The two tab titles above that are self explanatory are:
  - ➢ **Maps** – These are predefined tables for exporting data, and
  - ➢ **Modules** – These are Visual Basic Macros.

23 WHAT IS NEW IN MICROSOFT PROJECT

There were very few changes made in functionality of Microsoft Project 2003 and for the benefit of users upgrading from Microsoft Project 2000 I have kept the new features from 2002 to 2003 in a separate section.

Earlier versions on Microsoft Project 2003 did not function correctly and it was not possible to outdent some tasks. A Hotfix Package (software patch) is available from the Microsoft website to correct this problem.

23.1 What is New in Microsoft Project 2003 Standard

23.1.1 Copy Picture to Office Wizard

There is a new function available on the **Analysis** toolbar that runs a wizard to copy a picture to PowerPoint, Word or Visio.

23.1.2 Print a view as a report

There is a new wizard available for displaying views and printings. Display the **Project Guide** toolbar and click on the Reports tab to run this function.

23.1.3 Options

In Microsoft Project 2000 there was an Option Titled **Workgroup**, this was replaced with **Collaborate** in 2002 and then removed in 2003 Standard.

Microsoft Project 2003 had a new option added titled **Security** allowing:

- The properties of Author, Manager, Company and Last Saved by are removed from a file when it is saved, and

- There are security options that may be set to nominate which Macros may be used or not used. This is aimed at preventing Macros with a virus being activated.

23.2 *What Was New in Microsoft Project 2002 Standard*

There were many features added or amended in the release of Microsoft Project Standard 2002. The following is a list of important features added that are considered to be useful for planning and scheduling projects. The additional enterprise functions of Microsoft Project Professional 2002 and Microsoft Project Server will not be discussed in this book.

Topic	Notes
• **Timescale**	The timescale, such as in Gantt Chart, may be displayed with one, two or three tiers with each tier displaying a different unit of time. By default, the timescale is shown in two tiers. The timescale may be adjusted by double-clicking the timescale or selecting **Format, Timescale…..**
• **Smart Tags**	This feature provides information about your scheduling results as well as some ease of use features to change your results. Microsoft Project 2003 does not allow user to create and customize the **Smart Tags**.
• **Multiple Baselines**	Microsoft Project 2003 can save 11 Baselines over the course of a project. To save a baseline, select **Tools, Tracking**, and then **Save Baseline….**
• **Status Date Calculation Options**	The Calculation Options form has additional options that allow user to automatically adjust where actual and remaining work of new in-progress activities are placed with respect to the **Status Date**. These options are found under **Tools, Option…, Calculation** tab.
• **Earned Value**	There is an additional field titled **Physical % Complete** which may be used for calculating the **Earned Value** of the Project based on any of the Baselines. Select **Tools, Option…**, select the **Calculation** tab and click on the Earned Value… button.
• **Project Guide**	The Project Guide allows user to define project parameters such as tasks, tracks, project calendar, resource, and report, etc. using a guide steps wizard. The Project Guide is activated by default and you may disable this features under **Tools, Option…, Interface** tab.
• **Summary Task Baseline Recalculation**	The baseline of Summary Tasks may not be valid when tasks are added, deleted or moved to another Summary Task. There are options found under **Tools, Tracking, Save Baseline…** to recalculate baseline data for the associated summary tasks.

23.2.1 Timescale

The timescale, such as in Gantt Chart, may be displayed with one, two or three tiers with each tier displaying a different unit of time. By default, the timescale is shown in two tiers. The timescale may be adjusted by double-clicking the timescale or selecting **Format, Timescale.....** You may choose to display:

- One tier, the Middle,

- Two tiers, the Middle and Bottom, or

- All three tiers, as displayed below.

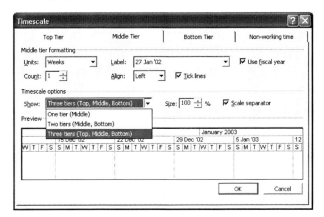

You may define and adjust the timeline (such as day, week, month and year) at each tier, depending on the level of detail you wish to present.

23.2.2 Graphical Indicators - Smart Tags

Microsoft Project 2003 uses smart tags to explain scheduling calculations and advise users of alternative options that may be more desirable. A green triangle in the edited cell indicates that the edit just performed has made a change to the task that has scheduling ramifications. The indicator only appears in the view types of Gantt, Sheet and Usage. A notice of a scheduling change hovers over the indicator, and clicking on the indicator displays alternate choices. The indicator in most cases displays as long as the edit may be undone; once a new edit is made the indicator disappears. Edits for which Feedback indicators display are:

- Additional resource assignment,

- Edits to Start and Finish,

- Edits to Work, Units or Duration, and

- Deletion in the Name column.

The example to the right has had a description highlighted and deleted.

Select **Tools, Options...**, **Interface** tab to select which indications are displayed.

23.2.3 Multiple Baselines

This feature allows you to save all baseline fields up to a total of 11 times for one project. The **Tools**, **Tracking**, **Save Baseline…** dialog now has a dropdown list for each of the 11 baselines. Likewise, the Clear Baseline dialog has the same dropdown list. When a baseline is saved, the last date saved is stored with the baseline as well and is displayed in the dialog for future reference.

To accomplish this, 10 additional Baseline Start, Baseline Finish, Baseline Work, Baseline Duration, and Baseline Cost have been added.

The **Save interim plan** fields allow you to copy one baseline to another. You can now choose which baseline you would like to use in Earned Value calculations

23.2.4 Status Date Calculation Options

New functions have been introduced in Microsoft Project 2003 intended to assist schedulers to place the new tasks as they are added in a logical position with respect to the **Status Date**. If the **Status Date** has not been set the **Current Date** is used.

Full details of this function are available in the **TRACKING PROGRESS** chapter, page 15-19.

23.2.5 Earned Value and Physical % Complete

There is an additional field titled **Physical % Complete**, which may be used for calculating the **Earned Value** of the Project based on any of the Baselines. Select the **Tools**, **Option…**, **Calculation** tab and click on the [Earned Value…] button to open the **Earned Value** form. You may now select:

- The **Default task Earned Value method:**
  - ➤ **% Complete** or
  - ➤ **Physical % Complete**, which may be edited in a column.

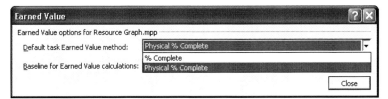

- The **Baseline for Earned Value Calculations:** and then select one of the 11 Baselines.

23.2.6 Project Guide

The Project Guide is accessed via a new toolbar titled **Project Guide**. The Project Guide includes options for **Tasks, Resources, Track, Report**, and **Next Steps** and **Related Activities**. The Project Guide will not be covered in detail as it is self-explanatory.

- When an option is selected from the Project Guide toolbar, a side-pane is displayed with a list of Help topics on the left of your screen.

- The Hide/Show option simply closes or opens the side-pane for the selected option. **Next Steps** and **Related Activities** display all the default Project Guide-based help available.

- The remaining options offer detailed information on each topic and include wizards to walk you through some specific goals.

- The View to the right of the side-pane updates to correspond with the action selected. Likewise the side-pane updates to display pertinent information as new data is entered into the project plan.

The picture below is an example of Project Guide in Microsoft Project 2003.

23.2.7 Summary Task Baseline Recalculation

By default, after the initial baseline is saved, a summary task's baseline is not updated when a subtask is modified, added or deleted. There are now two new options in the Save Baseline dialog that allow you to choose when summary task baseline information gets refreshed when saving a baseline for selected tasks. The options are:

- Roll up baseline to all summary tasks, and

- Roll up baseline from subtasks into selected summary task(s).

The first option allows baseline data from the immediate summary task to roll up into its ancestor summary tasks. The second option forces Microsoft Project to roll up the baseline details from its own subtasks. Details of this function are found in the **TRACKING PROGRESS** chapter. See page 15-4.

24 ITEMS NOT COVERED IN THIS BOOK

The following subjects are not covered in this book. This list is not exhaustive but is intended to give a guide to the other functions available in Microsoft Project 2003.

- **File**, **Save As Web Page…** – Saves the data in HTML format.

- **File**, **Save As Workspace…** – Saves and opens more than one file at a time.

- **File**, **Send To** – Emails your data to other people.

- **Format**, **Drawing** – Formats your drawings.

- **Edit**, **Paste Special…** – Allows options for pasting data or graphics into the schedule.

- **Edit**, **Paste as a Hyperlink** – Pastes data as a Hyperlink, the hyperlink is pasted into the Hyperlink columns.

- **Edit** and **Insert Objects** – Incorporates pieces of information from another application that may be displayed on the bar chart using OLE, Object Linking and Embedding.

- **Insert**, **Hyperlink…** – Allows you to save a Hyperlink to another file. The link need not be to another Microsoft Project file. You may click on the hyperlink icon in the **Task Information** column, and the function will take you to the file by opening the associated application to view the data. You may right-click on the Hyperlink to access the Hyperlink menu to edit, copy, etc.

- **Insert**, **Drawing** – Used to draw lines and other common geometrical objects (commonly found in graphics drawing software packages) on a Gantt Chart.

- **Tools**, **AutoCorrect Options…** – Specifies how the Spelling AutoCorrect function operates.

- **Tools**, **Import Outlook Tasks…** – Imports a list of tasks from Outlook.

- **Tools**, **Level Resources…** – This function delays tasks until resources become available and prevents overloading of resources.

- **Tools**, **Resource Sharing** – Shares resources with other projects.

- **Tools**, **Link Between Projects…** – Creates a link between two different projects.

- **Tools**, **Macro** – This function allows you to store a number of keystrokes and invoke them in one action. This is useful when executing repetitious keystroke operations. You may need to understand the Visual Basic programming language to fully implement this feature.

- **Collaborate** – These options are mainly used in conjunction with Project Server which is beyond the scope of this book

- **Help**, **Detect and Repair…** – Fixes problems with Microsoft Project 2003.

- **Compare Project Versions** – This function is found on the **Compare Project Versions** toolbar and allows the comparison of two project files to determine which data items have been changed.

- The **Analysis** toolbar has three options:
  - ➤ **Adjust Dates** – To change the start date of the project and associated task constraint dates.
  - ➤ **Analyze Timescale Data in Excel…** – Allows you to export time-phased data to Excel, this function is covered in this book.
  - ➤ **PERT Analysis** –Functions like a Monte-Carlo Simulation. **PERT Analysis** also has its own toolbar.

Details of all these topics may be found in the User Manual and Help.

25 APPENDIX 1 – SCREENS USED TO CREATE VIEWS

Microsoft Project 2003 has a complex method of accessing the data on screen.

- The screen may be split with an **Upper** and **Lower Pane**.
  - ➢ The **Upper Pane** displays all project information, except when a filter is applied.
  - ➢ The **Lower Pane** displays information about the task or tasks that are highlighted in the upper pane.
- A **View** may be created and edited. A **View** is based on a **Screen**.
  - ➢ A **Combination View** sets the view for both the Upper and Lower Pane.
  - ➢ A **Single View** may be applied to either the **Upper** or **Lower Pane** as long as the **Screen** may be displayed in that **Pane**.
- There are 14 **Screens**, most of which may be applied to the **Upper** or **Lower Panes** through **Views**.
  - ➢ There are some restrictions. For example, the **Calendar** screen may not be applied to the bottom pane.
  - ➢ Some **Screens** are not useful when displayed in the incorrect pane. It is better to display the **Task** form in the bottom **Pane** and leave a **Gantt Chart** in the **Upper Pane**.
  - ➢ Some **Screens** are very similar to each other, such as the **Task** screen and the **Task Details** screen.
- Some **Screens** have **Details** forms where the content of a **View** may be changed. An example of this is a **Task Usage** view, which may be formatted to show **Work** or **Costs** and **Cumulative** or **Period**.
- Some Screens are split vertically and have a left-hand side and a right-hand side such as the **Gantt Screen**. Other **Screens** do not split vertically, like the **Task Screen** and the **Task Details Screen**, which are used in the **Task Form** view and the **Task Details Form** view.

Upper Pane

Lower Pane

Gantt Screen, this is split vertically here.

RHS of Gantt Screen

LHS of Gantt Screen

Task Form Screen that has many Details forms but not split vertically.

The following table summarizes the **Screen**, **View** and **Details** options:

	Screen Name	Panes	Split Vertically	Details Form Options	Format Column Options
1	Calendar	Upper Only	No	None	Right-click Format Options Task List… Go To… Timescale… Gridlines… Text Styles… Bar Styles… Zoom… Layout… Layout Now Remove Split
2	Gantt Chart	Best in Upper	Yes	Bars and Columns may be formatted	Yes
3	Network Diagram	Best in Upper	No	Task Boxes may be edited	No
4	Relationship Diagram	Either	No	None	No
5	Resource Form	Best in Lower	No	Hide Form View ✓ Schedule Cost Work Notes Objects	No
6	Resource Graph	Best in Lower	No	Gridlines… Bar Styles… Remove Split ✓ Peak Units Work Cumulative Work Overallocation Percent Allocation Remaining Availability Cost Cumulative Cost Work Availability Unit Availability	No
7	Resource Name Form	Best in Lower	No	Hide Form View ✓ Schedule Cost Work Notes Objects	No
8	Resource Sheet	Either	No	None	Yes

	Screen Name	Panes	Split Verti-cally	Details Form Options	Format Column Options
9	Resource Usage	Either	Yes	Detail Styles... / ✓ Work / Actual Work / Cumulative Work / Baseline Work / Cost / Actual Cost	No
10	Task Details Form	Best in Lower	Yes	Hide Form View / ✓ Resources & Predecessors / Resources & Successors / Predecessors & Successors / Resource Schedule / Resource Work / Resource Cost / Notes / Objects	No
11	Task Form	Best in Lower	No	Hide Form View / Resources & Predecessors / Resources & Successors / ✓ Predecessors & Successors / Resource Schedule / Resource Work / Resource Cost / Notes / Objects	No
12	Task Name Form	Best in Lower	No	Hide Form View / Resources & Predecessors / Resources & Successors / Predecessors & Successors / Resource Schedule / ✓ Resource Work / Resource Cost / Notes / Objects	No
13	Task Sheet	Best In Upper	No	None	Yes
14	Task Usage	Best in Lower	Yes	Detail Styles... / ✓ Work / Actual Work / Cumulative Work / Baseline Work / Cost / Actual Cost	Yes

The following table displays the Screens and provides some background on each:

Screen Name	Note and/or Screen Dumps
1. Calendar	May be displayed in top pane only. 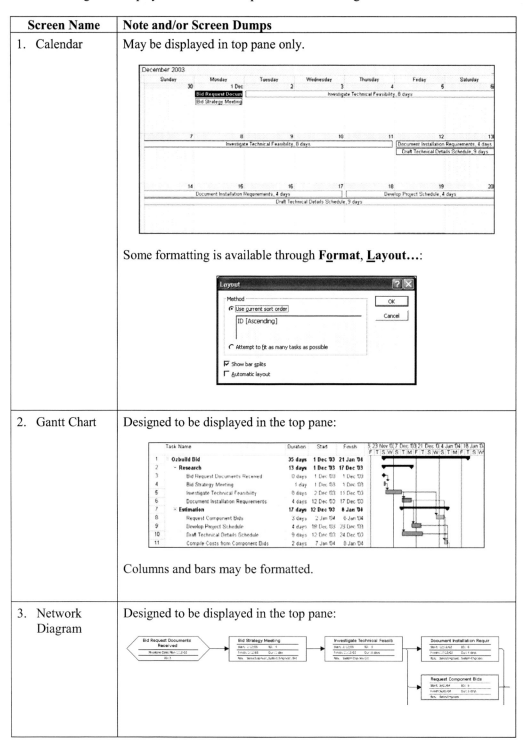 Some formatting is available through F**o**rmat, **L**ayout…:
2. Gantt Chart	Designed to be displayed in the top pane: Columns and bars may be formatted.
3. Network Diagram	Designed to be displayed in the top pane:

Screen Name	Note and/or Screen Dumps
4. Relationship Diagram	This displays relationships between tasks and may not be printed or edited. 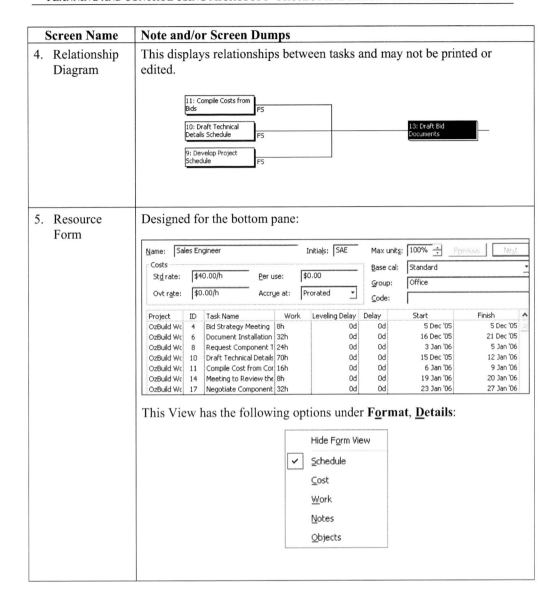
5. Resource Form	Designed for the bottom pane: This View has the following options under **F**o**rmat**, **Details**:

Screen Name	Note and/or Screen Dumps
6. Resource Graph	This View is designed to be displayed in the bottom pane: 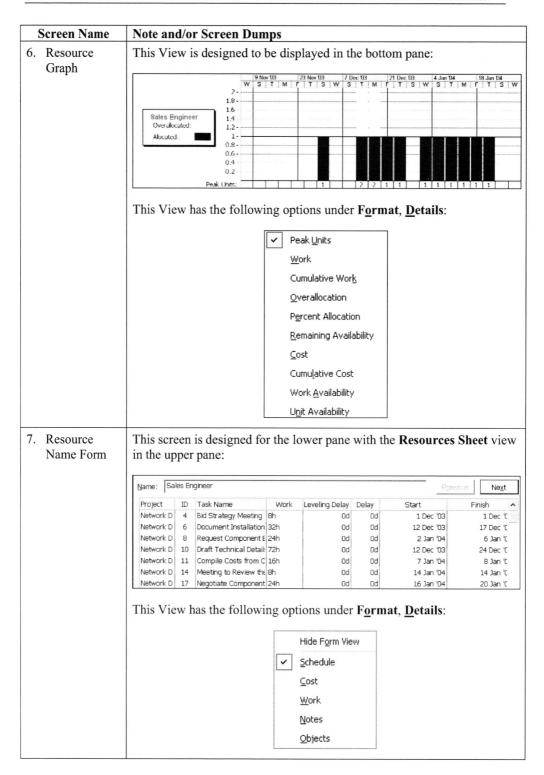 This View has the following options under **Format**, **Details**: ✓ Peak Units Work Cumulative Work Overallocation Percent Allocation Remaining Availability Cost Cumulative Cost Work Availability Unit Availability
7. Resource Name Form	This screen is designed for the lower pane with the **Resources Sheet** view in the upper pane: Name: Sales Engineer [Previous] [Next] | Project	ID	Task Name	Work	Leveling Delay	Delay	Start	Finish
---	---	---	---	---	---	---	---
Network D	4	Bid Strategy Meeting	8h	0d	0d	1 Dec '03	1 Dec 'C
Network D	6	Document Installation	32h	0d	0d	12 Dec '03	17 Dec 'C
Network D	8	Request Component E	24h	0d	0d	2 Jan '04	6 Jan 'C
Network D	10	Draft Technical Detail	72h	0d	0d	12 Dec '03	24 Dec 'C
Network D	11	Compile Costs from C	16h	0d	0d	7 Jan '04	8 Jan 'C
Network D	14	Meeting to Review the	8h	0d	0d	14 Jan '04	14 Jan 'C
Network D	17	Negotiate Component	24h	0d	0d	16 Jan '04	20 Jan 'C	 This View has the following options under **Format**, **Details**: Hide Form View ✓ Schedule Cost Work Notes Objects

Screen Name	Note and/or Screen Dumps
8. Resource Sheet	This screen may be used in the top or bottom pane and the columns may be formatted with the **Table and Columns** functions: 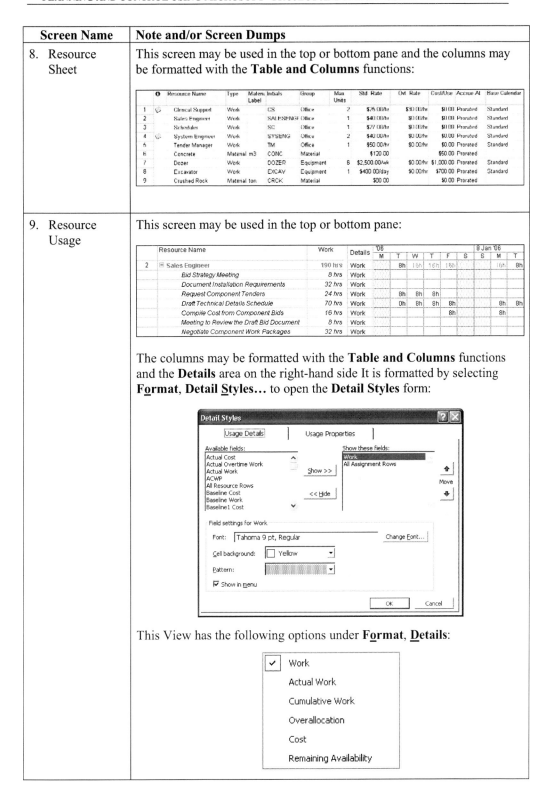
9. Resource Usage	This screen may be used in the top or bottom pane: The columns may be formatted with the **Table and Columns** functions and the **Details** area on the right-hand side It is formatted by selecting **Format, Detail Styles…** to open the **Detail Styles** form: This View has the following options under **Format, Details**:

Screen Name	Note and/or Screen Dumps
10. Task Details Form	This form is best displayed in the bottom pane and displays information about the task highlighted in the top pane: This View has the following options under **Format**, **Details**: Hide Form View ✓ Resources & Predecessors Resources & Successors Predecessors & Successors Resource Schedule Resource Work Resource Cost Notes Objects
11. Task Form	This form is best displayed in the bottom pane. This View has the following options under **Format**, **Details**: Hide Form View ✓ Resources & Predecessors Resources & Successors Predecessors & Successors Resource Schedule Resource Work Resource Cost Notes Objects

Screen Name	Note and/or Screen Dumps
12. Task Name Form	This form is best displayed in the bottom pane. This View has the following options under **Format**, **Details**:
13. Task Sheet	This View is similar to the Gantt but without displaying the bars. The columns may be formatted using the **Table** and **Columns** functions.

Screen Name	Note and/or Screen Dumps
14. Task Usage	This view displays the tasks in the columns and the resources and work on the right-hand side:

	Task Name	Assignment Units	Work	Details	M	T	W	T	F	S	S	M	T	W	T	F
7	⊟ **Estimation**		**232 hrs**	Work		8h	32h	32h	32h			32h	16h	16h	10h	8h
8	⊟ Request Component Tender		24 hrs	Work		8h	8h	8h								
	Sales Engineer	*100%*	*24 hrs*	Work		8h	8h	8h								
9	⊟ Develop Project Schedule		32 hrs	Work		0h	8h	8h	8h			8h				
	Scheduler	*100%*	*32 hrs*	Work		0h	8h	8h	8h			8h				
10	⊟ Draft Technical Details Sch		160 hrs	Work		0h	16h	16h	16h			16h	16h	16h	10h	8h
	Sales Engineer	*100%*	*70 hrs*	Work		0h	8h	8h	8h			8h	8h	8h	2h	
	Systems Engineer	*100%*	*90 hrs*	Work		0h	8h	8h	8h			8h	8h	8h	8h	8h
11	⊟ Compile Cost from Compon		16 hrs	Work					8h			8h				
	Sales Engineer	*100%*	*16 hrs*	Work					8h			8h				

The columns may be formatted using the **Table** and **Columns** functions.

The information displayed on the right-hand side of the screen may be set by selecting **Format**, **Details**:

Detail Styles...

✓ Work

Actual Work

Cumulative Work

Baseline Work

Cost

Actual Cost

The formatting of the right-hand side of the screen may be changed by selecting **Format**, **Detail Styles...** to open the **Detail Styles** form:

26 INDEX

PROJECT CONSORT

Project Consort is a software tool designed to assist project managers using either the PMBOK® Guide "Project Scope Management" process or the "Product-based planning" technique defined as part of the PRINCE2™ Project Management Method. Project data may be simply exported and exported to Microsoft® Project.

BACKGROUND

The *PMBOK® Guide* "Project Scope Management" process has been learned by over 120,000 PMP qualified project managers and the PRINCE2 approach to project management is used by about 30,000 qualified project managers in the UK, but up until now there has been a desperate shortage of easy-to-use software tools to help those managers using the vitally important techniques.

PROJECT CONSORT addresses the need to support project managers by automating the key elements of the "Project Scope Management" process and the "Product Based Planning" technique

FEATURES

Project Consort has an intuitive "click, drag and type" graphical user interface, which project managers can use to easily create and maintain all the important diagrams and text required in the Planning (PL) process within PRINCE2.

☐ **Work Breakdown Structure** (WBS) and/or the **Product Breakdown Structure** diagram (PBS);

Note:

This software product supports PRINCE2™ Product Based Planning and PMBOK® Guide Project Scope Management

☐ **Product Descriptions** for each work product on the WBS/PBS;

PROJECT CONSORT

- **Product Flow Diagram** for all the products identified on the WBS/PBS;
- **Project Activities** to structure the work needed;
- Project **Daily Log**;
- **Product Description** reports and **Project Activity** reports;
- **Stage PBSs** and **PFDs** as the project progresses;
- Create **Resources**, **Teams** and enter **Assignments**; and
- Create an **OBS** chart.

Many potential errors are automatically prevented because these are all consistently merged into a single "PBP container".

Documents can be exported in various formats, including DHTML, PDF, Excel, Word.

Most importantly, Project Consort will create project plans for instant import and export to Microsoft® Project!

BENEFITS OF PROJECT CONSORT

- **Reduces the amount of project manager time** needed to create and maintain consistent Product Based Plans.
- Provides **interactive tracking** of all these project elements and the relationships between them, thus reducing time to find information within the plan.
- Includes **help files and integrated tutorials** to show how to use the toolset.
- Provides **example projects** to demonstrate an integrated view of a Product Based Plan.
- Provides valuable support in **learning and applying the underlying PRINCE2™ AND *PMBOK® Guide* methods.**
- Eases the creation of plans for Microsoft Project.
- Provides a **Visual Status** mechanism to highlight incomplete products in ongoing projects.
- The **Reader Version is free of charge**, so any one may access the data without a licence.

PRODUCT ENVIRONMENT

Project Consort can be installed on windows based PCs running Windows 98 or later, as a standalone application or as a Microsoft Project Add-in.

AVAILABILITY

Project Consort is available through Eastwood Harris Pty Ltd at www.eh.com.au, download your trial version now.

Eastwood Harris Pty Ltd Web: www.eh.com.au Email: harrispe @eh.com.au Tel: +61 (0)4 1118 7701 Fax: +61 (0)3 9856 7700

DecisionEdge Suite for Microsoft Project
Complete Set of Project Graphics and Reports for Better Business Decisions

The DecisionEdge Suite for Microsoft Project gives managers the enhanced graphics and tabular reports they need to better understand and communicate key project information. Bundled with over 70 new charts and reports, DecisionCharts helps you better manage resources, keep stakeholders informed, understand project status, and measure project performance using earned value.

✓ **Understand** – Choose from over 70 new and improved reports and charts to best suit your needs

✓ **Communicate** – Share project snapshots with full support for common graphic file formats and a wide range of printers and plotters

✓ **Control** – Filter, scroll, and drill-down to see trends and make earlier decisions

✓ **Interact** – Not just pretty pictures, the DecisionEdge Suite is an interactive portal into live business data

✓ **Customize** – Change colors and styles to make charts and reports look just the way you want them

✓ **Create** – With *DecisionEdge Designer,* developers can create and share completely new charts and reports with all DecisionEdge users

The DecisionEdge Suite for Microsoft Project Includes Both DecisionCharts and DecisionReports
It comes with more than 70 new and improved charts and reports that help managers better understand key information about their tasks, resources, costs, and overall project performance. They can view and customize any of these charts by filtering data, changing colors, adding and moving logos, and making other changes. They can also keep the whole team informed by sharing project snapshots in standard file formats such as bitmap (.BMP), JPEG (.JPG), Acrobat (.PDF)*, and TIFF, or by sending them directly to a printer or plotter.

Companies with specific requirements will want *DecisionEdge Designer*. Developers and technical consultants can use this sophisticated toolkit to create completely new graphics and reports that can be shared with all DecisionEdge users. DecisionEdge Designer provides unlimited possibilities for showing and formatting data with different chart and report types, computed elements, and interactive dashboards.

The DecisionEdge Advantage:
- Get started quickly with new charts and reports designed specifically for Microsoft Project
- Quickly understand and communicate key information with interactive graphics and reports
- Keep the whole team informed of project status more effectively with pictures
- Generate the custom graphics and reports you need to run your business
- Stop using spreadsheets and other manual workarounds
- Deploy a complete business intelligence solution for better business decisions

*Adobe Acrobat or similar PDF writer required to generate PDF files.

DecisionCharts Graphic Types

Bar/Line Chart
Great for showing trends over time.

Head Count By Resource

Dashboard Chart
This chart combines up to four different charts into one interactive portal, giving stakeholders the ability to understand key project information in just one glance.

Task Dashboard

Gantt Chart
Classic plot of time-based activities.

Critical Path Gantt

Pie Chart
Shows the percentage composition of a data element.

Resource Usage - Actual

Bubble/Matrix Chart
Allows for comparison across data elements by adding the dimension of bubble size.

Task Matrix

Map/Diagram Chart
This special custom chart helps managers better understand how data fits into the overall project.

Lot 12 - Map Chart Sample

DecisionReports Features

Task Earned Value Report

Add custom colors for greater impact →

Use **DecisionEdge Designer** to create custom reports for specific needs

Show details about any project element →

← Create calculated fields with VBScript to show the right information

← Enhance understanding with numbers that change color based on custom

Requirements
Software: - O/S: Windows 2000 or Windows XP; *Microsoft Office Project:* Microsoft Project 2002 or higher (Standard, Professional, or Server).
Hardware: 30MB hard drive for each client; at least 256MB RAM

Download a Free Demo Copy Today
http://www.decisionedge.com

DECISIONEDGE™
SOFTWARE FOR BETTER BUSINESS DECISIONS